ALLIANCE SECURITY

DATE DUE			

Studies in Defense Policy

TITLES IN PRINT

Support Costs in the Defense Budget: The Submerged One-Third
Martin Binkin

The Changing Soviet Navy
Barry M. Blechman

Strategic Forces: Issues for the Mid-Seventies
Alton H. Quanbeck and Barry M. Blechman

U.S. Reserve Forces: The Problem of the Weekend Warrior
Martin Binkin

U.S. Force Structure in NATO: An Alternative
Richard D. Lawrence and Jeffrey Record

U.S. Tactical Air Power: Missions, Forces, and Costs
William D. White

U.S. Nuclear Weapons in Europe: Issues and Alternatives
Jeffrey Record with the assistance of Thomas I. Anderson

The Control of Naval Armaments: Prospects and Possibilities
Barry M. Blechman

Stresses in U.S.-Japanese Security Relations
Fred Greene

The Military Pay Muddle
Martin Binkin

Sizing Up the Soviet Army
Jeffrey Record

Where Does the Marine Corps Go from Here?
Martin Binkin and Jeffrey Record

Deterrence and Defense in Korea: The Role of U.S. Forces
Ralph N. Clough

Women and the Military
Martin Binkin and Shirley J. Bach

The Soviet Military Buildup and U.S. Defense Spending
Barry M. Blechman and others

Soviet Air Power in Transition
Robert P. Berman

Shaping the Defense Civilian Work Force: Economics, Politics, and National Security
Martin Binkin with Herschel Kanter and Rolf H. Clark

The Military Equation in Northeast Asia
Stuart E. Johnson with Joseph A. Yager

Youth or Experience? Manning the Modern Military
Martin Binkin and Irene Kyriakopoulos

Paying the Modern Military
Martin Binkin and Irene Kyriakopoulos

Defense in the 1980s
William W. Kaufmann

The FX Decision: "Another Crucial Moment" in U.S.-China-Taiwan Relations
A. Doak Barnett

Planning Conventional Forces, 1950–80
William W. Kaufmann

Blacks and the Military
Martin Binkin and Mark J. Eitelberg with Alvin J. Schexnider and Martin M. Smith

U.S. Arms Sales: The China-Taiwan Tangle
A. Doak Barnett

Soviet Strategic Forces: Requirements and Responses
Robert P. Berman and John C. Baker

U.S. Ground Forces and the Defense of Central Europe
William P. Mako

Alliance Security: NATO and the No-First-Use Question
John D. Steinbruner and Leon V. Sigal, Editors

ALLIANCE SECURITY:
NATO AND THE NO-FIRST-USE QUESTION

John D. Steinbruner and Leon V. Sigal
EDITORS

Jonathan Alford
Johan Jørgen Holst
William W. Kaufmann
Gert Krell
Thomas Risse-Kappen
Hans-Joachim Schmidt
David N. Schwartz
Leon V. Sigal
John D. Steinbruner

THE BROOKINGS INSTITUTION
Washington, D.C.

Copyright © 1983 by
THE BROOKINGS INSTITUTION
1775 Massachusetts Avenue, N.W., Washington, D.C. 20036

Library of Congress Catalog Card Number 83-72566

ISBN 0-8157-8118-0
ISBN 0-8157-8117-2 (pbk.)

9 8 7 6 5 4 3 2 1

FOREWORD

ARRANGEMENTS for the defense of Western Europe have become the object of intensified public anxiety in recent years. That anxiety was heightened by NATO's decision in 1979 to proceed with the deployment of new intermediate-range nuclear missiles and at the same time to seek an arms control agreement between the United States and the Soviet Union that might impose mutual restraints on nuclear weapons in Europe. Political debate over these initiatives has renewed longstanding questions about the appropriate role of nuclear weapons in providing for the security of Europe and about the feasibility of defense by nonnuclear means alone. The debate was sharpened considerably in 1982 when a group of prominent Americans forcefully raised the issue of renunciation of first use of nuclear weapons. As a means of reducing NATO's reliance on nuclear weapons, they argued for a formal declaration of no first use similar to one that the Soviet Union had long advocated and shortly thereafter unilaterally announced as a prominent part of its own security policy. Following the American suggestion and the Soviet announcement, four prominent Germans equally forcefully objected to the idea, arguing that it would undermine deterrence in Western Europe.

In this volume, American and European scholars examine the underlying security issues involved in this debate. They seek to identify the principal arguments and set forth the evidence for the benefit of those—voting citizens and public officials alike—whose political judgments will ultimately determine how the debate is resolved.

The study was organized jointly by the Brookings Institution and the International Institute for Strategic Studies. Colonel Jonathan Alford is the institute's deputy director. Johan Jørgen Holst is director of the Norwegian Institute of International Affairs. William W. Kaufmann, a consultant to the Brookings Foreign Policy Studies program, is a member of the faculty of the Massachusetts Institute of Technology. Gert Krell is an assistant director at the International Institute for Strategic Studies; his collaborators Thomas Risse-Kappen and Hans-Joachim Schmidt are with the Hessian Foundation for Research on Peace and Conflict in Frankfurt. David N. Schwartz is a research associate in the Brookings Foreign Policy Studies program. Leon V. Sigal, a visiting scholar in the same program, teaches government at Wesleyan University. John D. Steinbruner is director of the Brookings Foreign Policy Studies program.

The contributors are grateful to Jan R. Liss and Patricia A. O'Brien for providing administrative support; to Nancy A. Ameen for research assistance; to Lawrence Freedman, Kenneth Hunt, and Michael Kugler for comments on the manuscript; to James D. Farrell for editing it; and to Alan G. Hoden for verifying its factual content. Virginia R. Black, Antoinette G. Buena, Susan E. Nichols, Thomas T. Somuah, and Ann M. Ziegler provided the secretarial support; Nancy Snyder did the proofreading; and Ward & Silvan prepared the index.

The study was financed in part by a grant from the Ford Foundation, whose assistance the Brookings Institution and the International Institute for Strategic Studies gratefully acknowledge. The views expressed are those of the authors and should not be ascribed to the International Institute for Strategic Studies or the Ford Foundation, to those who commented on the manuscript, or to the trustees, officers, or other staff members of the Brookings Institution.

BRUCE K. MACLAURY
President

August 1983
Washington D.C.

CONTENTS

Tables

Figure

Abbreviations and Acronyms

ADM	Atomic demolition munition
ALCM	Air-launched cruise missile
ASW	Antisubmarine warfare
ERW	Enhanced radiation weapon
GLCM	Ground-launched cruise missile
GSFG	Group of Soviet Forces in Germany
ICBM	Intercontinental ballistic missile
INF	Intermediate-range nuclear forces
LTDP	Long-term defense plan
MBFR	Mutual and balanced force reductions
MIRV	Multiple independently targetable reentry vehicle
MLF	Multilateral nuclear force
MRV	Multiple reentry vehicle
NFU	No first use
NSWP	Non-Soviet Warsaw Pact
QRA	Quick reaction alert
SACEUR	Supreme Allied Commander, Europe
SALT	Strategic arms limitation talks
SHAPE	Supreme Headquarters, Allied Powers Europe
SIOP	Single integrated operations plan
SLCM	Submarine-launched cruise missile
START	Strategic arms reduction talks

CHAPTER ONE

INTRODUCTION

John D. Steinbruner

WHEN Martin Luther nailed his ninety-five theses to the door of a church in Wittenberg, he did far more than publicize issues of theological doctrine. From the perspective of nearly five centuries, we can appreciate that what at first appeared to be a highly specialized conceptual matter struck at the foundations of Europe and had eminently practical consequences.

In this century orthodoxy has a more secular character. It seems quite fanciful to suppose that a contemporary conceptual dissent, in an age when dissent is common, could trigger consequences on the scale of the Protestant Reformation. Without minimizing these differences, it is worthwhile to contemplate the historical power of conception in assessing prevailing ideas about nuclear weapons. Conceptions of nuclear strategy are now accepted as fundamental to the international order; they are the ruling dogmas of our time. Prominent departures from doctrine are resisted with a seriousness that testifies to their practical importance, and not unreasonably so. Though it would have required superhuman prescience to understand in 1517 that Luther's concept of faith would alter the course of human history, it is all too apparent that the destructive power of existing nuclear arsenals could do so if that power were mismanaged. Prevailing strategic conceptions are principal tools of management.

It was a significant event, therefore, when in the spring 1982 issue of *Foreign Affairs* a central doctrine of strategic security was sharply disputed by four authors—McGeorge Bundy, George F. Kennan, Robert S. McNamara, and Gerard Smith—who have been among the most prominent figures in the development of American foreign policy in the age of nuclear weapons.[1] The title of their article was bordered in orange on the dignified cover of the journal—not quite the door of the church but nonetheless a symbol of something unusual. The message they conveyed entered instantly into the main channels of political debate. The incumbent American secretary of state, Alexander Haig, issued a flamboyantly worded attack even before its formal publication. The West German defense minister, Hans Apel, was more circumspect in his reaction but nonetheless firm in his disapproval, a position widely shared in the defense ministries of Europe. In international professional circles the authors were quickly accorded the rare tribute of a spontaneous colloquial label—the ''Gang of Four''—wryly acknowledging that ruling conceptions were indeed at issue and that a modern heresy of considerable practical significance had been pronounced.[2]

The article evolved from an underlying judgment shared among the authors. From their individual experience, each had separately concluded that no American president could responsibly authorize the initial use of nuclear weapons in defense of Western Europe. If accepted as an axiom, as they believed it must be, that judgment would vitiate the officially established doctrine of NATO defense and require substantial changes in Alliance security arrangements. In their published text the authors conveyed their judgment with diplomatic indirection and discussed its implications with deferential tentativeness, suggesting for further study and debate a formal declaration of policy that NATO would not be the first to use nuclear weapons. Their purposes were not obscured, however, by the judicious language they adopted. No first use, or NFU, was advanced as the conceptual spearhead for a program of fundamental change.

The thrust of this particular spear was not, as a casual observer might suppose, directed toward the Soviet Union, the planned target of NATO's nuclear weapons. Though Soviet leaders had long proposed mutual no-first-use declarations as a means of easing tension, and though Soviet Foreign Minister Andrei Gromyko dramatically announced a unilateral Soviet no-first-use policy before the United Nations in June, shortly after the *Foreign Affairs* article appeared, such declarations are of limited material consequence for the opponent. Modern nuclear arsenals provide both the inherent capacity to use nuclear weapons first and a strong incentive to do so if they are used at all. A declaration of intent can be reversed or simply violated at the brink of war, and suspicious defense planners are virtually certain to assume that their opponent would do so. With all that conceded, the deeper purpose of the no-first-use idea is to induce internal structural changes in NATO's defense preparations.

Three underlying conditions have long attracted concern. The first is the state of conventional defense in Western Europe—the ability of ground armies and tactical air units to repel an attempted Soviet invasion. Throughout the history of the Alliance, decisive Soviet superiority in these conventional means of war has been assumed and the conclusion drawn that NATO's conventional forces are too weak in relative terms to deter an attack. No first use challenges both the premise and the conclusion. Its proponents assert in principle the feasibility of a conventional defense of NATO robust enough to prevent war from breaking out. They argue for resource allocations and operational doctrines designed to achieve that objective.

The second concern is the relationship between conventional forces and nuclear weapon deployments. As NATO forces have evolved, the capability to use nuclear weapons has been closely associated with conventional forces. Artillery and tactical air units that provide supporting firepower for the ground armies responsible for holding NATO territory can use both conventional and nuclear ordnance and are trained to do so. The elaborate management procedures necessarily associated with nuclear weapons inhibit flexibility in conventional operations and pose hard choices for NATO commanders. In net effect the presence of nuclear delivery systems in forward units introduces a strong bias toward their use in combat, if not actually first then certainly very early. The no-first-use idea argues for a sharp separation between conventional and nuclear operations and for a clear disengagement of nuclear delivery systems from forward positions.

Finally, advocates of change contend that a higher standard of protection should be afforded the NATO nuclear posture. At the moment many of the nuclear weapons deployed under NATO auspices, particularly those based on land in Western Europe, are highly vulnerable to preemptive attack, not only from Soviet nuclear weapons but also from conventional explosives or chemical weapons delivered by Soviet tactical air units. That condition creates strong pressures for both sides to attempt preemption at the outset of any serious engagement. Given the sluggish decisionmaking procedures that encumber the Alliance, it is believed that the Soviets would enjoy a clear advantage in this particular race. The no-first-use idea requires that nuclear forces maintained under

NATO be able to support the retaliatory operations upon which the overall Western doctrine of deterrence rests, and that the present incentive for preemption be diminished as a threat to the safe management of crises.

These issues of Alliance security and their implications are examined in the following chapters by European and American scholars who have participated in the analytic development of NATO defense policy. Unlike the "Gang of Four," they have not assumed the advocate's burden of forcing the issues to the center of attention, nor have they attempted to resolve them decisively. Their purpose is simply to articulate the major considerations involved in judging the arguments for change, including the political factors that are inevitably associated with any proposed change in the established policies and engrained habits of human institutions. Whereas the stated aim of the *Foreign Affairs* article was to "start a discussion, not to end it," the aim of this study is to advance that discussion by identifying its terms and making its intricacies accessible to those who have not explored the tortuous paths that have brought the issues to their current state. This is a necessary step toward any resolution. The issues require broad collective judgment, and consensus extending far beyond the precincts of specialists.

Notes

1. McGeorge Bundy and others, "Nuclear Weapons and the Atlantic Alliance," *Foreign Affairs,* vol. 60 (Spring 1982).

2. As is noted in chapters 2 and 9, the four authors of the *Foreign Affairs* article did not originate the no-first-use idea, which had been discussed in the professional literature for more than a decade. Their endorsement gave the idea a prominence it had not previously achieved, in effect lifting it from professional discussion into active political debate.

CHAPTER TWO

A HISTORICAL PERSPECTIVE

David N. Schwartz

THE CALL for NATO to adopt a nuclear no-first-use policy evokes issues that have arisen periodically during the Alliance's thirty-year history.[1] What is the proper relationship between the conventional and nuclear components of NATO's deterrent? How effective would nuclear weapons be in reversing an impending conventional defeat? Is a reliable conventional defense feasible against the threat posed by the Warsaw Pact? Is the threat to use nuclear weapons first if need be to prevent conventional defeat a necessary or desirable element of NATO's flexible response strategy?

The convoluted history of NATO's handling of these issues is difficult for the outside observer to interpret. Yet an understanding of how NATO arrived at its current posture is essential to an appreciation of the options for, and constraints upon, future change.

The 1950s: Massive Retaliation

The founders of the North Atlantic Alliance had no coherent vision of the form it would eventually take when the North Atlantic Treaty was ratified in 1949.[2] All could agree that in an increasingly hostile postwar world, a credible U.S. commitment to the defense of Western Europe was probably necessary to forestall a recurrence of the violence that had devastated Europe in the earlier half of the decade. There was less agreement on how to effect this commitment: would the solemn pledge contained in the North Atlantic Treaty be sufficient, or would a more formal military organization, involving U.S. and Western European troops integrated into a formal NATO command structure, be required to give teeth to the political commitment of the Treaty? With the onset of the Korean conflict in 1950, the transatlantic consensus on this issue favored the latter course, and plans began to be drawn up for a NATO military organization.

In those early years, U.S. nuclear supremacy over the Soviet Union was widely thought to be the most important element of NATO's deterrent posture. To some at least, President Harry S. Truman's winning of congressional approval for the stationing of U.S. troops in Europe in peacetime was important only insofar as it guaranteed that American soldiers would be killed in any Soviet aggression against the West, thus involving the United States directly and invoking the U.S. threat to use its nuclear arsenal against the Soviet Union if its allies were attacked.

For the Truman administration, however, the troops were more than hostages. The Berlin blockade of 1948 had demonstrated the willingness of Soviet leaders to confront the West over vital interests in Europe despite the American nuclear monopoly. President Truman and his foreign policy advisers, particularly Secretary of State Dean Acheson, were persuaded that NATO required a more balanced military capability, including a robust nonnuclear component, to deter the broad spectrum of politico-military pressures the Soviet bloc might bring to bear against the West. They made this argument in their testimony before Congress on the troop issue; indeed, they envisioned the deployment of troops to Europe in peacetime as part of a broader Western European program to develop strong conventional forces capable of repelling a Soviet invasion.

American officials shared the view of many Europeans that the requirements for effective conventional defense were formidable. Working with fragmentary intelligence of uncertain reliability, Western analysts estimated that the Soviet Union had 175 divisions against which NATO would have to plan its defense. Western military planners concluded that NATO would require some 96 active and reserve divisions to meet this threat. Thus were born the so-called Lisbon force goals, agreed to by the NATO ministers at their February 1952 meeting. It was the first but by no means the last time that the threat was overstated, or that the resulting NATO goals remained unmet.

These goals seem imposing even today, after three decades of relative peace and prosperity. For the Western European nations at that time, struggling to recover from a war that had destroyed a significant part of their capital and labor, the goals seemed too high to be worth attempting. Conventional forces were improved, to be sure, but failure to meet the goals set in 1952 led NATO to rely increasingly on the threat of nuclear retaliation to deter virtually any kind of aggression, whatever the level. This was the era of "massive retaliation."

The shift in emphasis came to be reflected in the military forces NATO deployed in Europe and in the policy pronouncements of NATO leaders. The United States began gradually to introduce so-called tactical nuclear weapons into its troop deployments in Europe. Designed for use on the battlefield or in direct support of battlefield operations, these weapons made their first appearance in Europe in 1954, with the introduction of the 280mm nuclear cannon into the European theater. Soon added to them were nuclear gravity bombs, nuclear mortar and artillery shells, nuclear land mines, nuclear air defense missiles, and even a jeep-mounted nuclear recoilless gun, whimsically named the Davy Crockett. At first these weapons were deployed only with American troops, but as the decade passed arrangements were made by which other NATO armies could share tactical nuclear weapons with the United States. A typical arrangement called for the allied military force to operate the delivery system—for example, a fighter-bomber—while the United States retained custody of the nuclear weapon until the president authorized its release to the allied contingent. Arrangements such as these came to be known as "dual key."

It is significant that these weapons were introduced into forces-in-being, with no serious attempt made to separate nuclear units from conventional units. For example, artillery units were expected to perform both nuclear and conventional missions as the occasion required. The same was true for tactical air forces. While this duality resulted from a complex set of factors—among them the difficulty of radically revising force structures and the theory that nuclear weapons could be used to supplement conventional firepower—it had the consequence of tying nuclear and conventional forces together in ways that could impair conventional defense.

Introduction of these weapons into Europe was encouraged in part by the technical feasibility of the weapons themselves, in part by overly optimistic assumptions that they could be used without disastrous consequences for NATO, in part by arguments that they could be used to compensate for deficiencies in NATO's conventional forces. Budgetary considerations were also a key factor in virtually every NATO capital, including Washington. The "New Look" policies of President Dwight D. Eisenhower and Secretary of State John Foster Dulles made explicit the budgetary rationale for increased reliance on nuclear weapons for Alliance deterrence and defense. Dulles's own articulation of the doctrine of massive retaliation in January 1954 was entirely clear:

> The total cost of our security efforts [in the recent past] at home and abroad, was over $50 billion per annum, and involved, for 1953, a projected budgetary deficit of $9 billion, and $11 billion for 1954. This was on top of taxes comparable to wartime taxes; and the dollar was depreciating in effective value. Our allies were similarly weighed down. This could not be continued for long without grave budgetary, economic, and social consequences.
>
> But before military planning could be changed, the President and his advisers, as represented by the National Security Council, had to take some basic policy decisions. This has been done. The basic decision was to depend primarily upon a great capacity to retaliate, instantly, by means and at places of our own choosing. . . . As a result, it is now possible to get, and share, more basic security at less cost.[3]

NATO's planners were quick to follow the American lead. If budgetary constraints undermined U.S. determination to meet the Lisbon force goals while heightening reliance on the early use of relatively cheap tactical nuclear weapons, those constraints were even more compelling to the European members of NATO, still struggling to regain prosperity in the postwar world. Deputy Supreme Allied Commander, Europe (SACEUR) Bernard L. Montgomery spoke candidly in support of the massive retaliation policy when he addressed the Royal United Services Institute in London in late 1954:

> I want to make it absolutely clear that we at SHAPE are basing all our planning on using atomic and thermonuclear weapons in our own defense. With us it is no longer: "They may possibly be used." It is very definitely: "They will be used, if we are attacked." In fact, we have reached the point of no return as regards the use of atomic and thermonuclear weapons in a hot war.[4]

By 1957, then, the Lisbon force goals had been revised downward through the adoption of a plan called MC-70, which projected a five-year program to build up to thirty active divisions for the central front. Even the revised plan, modest as it was compared to the Lisbon goals, seemed unattainable despite sustained American efforts and the growing German rearmament program. During the same period, as if to undercut the conventional effort, NATO adopted a strategic concept called MC-14/2 that envisioned the early and massive use of tactical and strategic nuclear weapons in response to Warsaw Pact aggression.

Ample evidence suggests that the American policymakers responsible for this shift toward placing greater reliance on nuclear deterrence were aware of its potential shortcomings.[5] That they did not disclose their misgivings probably reflected a political judgment that persuading the public on both sides of the Atlantic of the efficacy of the New Look must take precedence over a more nuanced official articulation of the policy. This judgment was not shared by a growing number of nongovernmental observers of U.S. and NATO defense plans, who viewed the shift toward reliance on the early use of nuclear weapons with increasing concern. The debate stimulated by these observers was at times passionate and inarticulate, at times coldly rational. It is possible here only to summarize the major lines of criticism:

Credibility. Most critics of the New Look argued that while the threat of nuclear retaliation might be credible—and hence a strong deterrent—against a limited but important range of devastating, all-out conventional attacks, the nuclear deterrent possessed only limited credibility against a wide range of more likely, less intense conventional threats. They observed that a U.S. nuclear monopoly had not prevented the Soviet Union from exerting strong pressure against West Berlin in 1948; had not forestalled the aggressive consolidation of Soviet power in Eastern Europe; had not deterred war in Korea; and had not deterred probing by communist governments throughout the world. They noted that when Western interests were directly threatened by conventional aggression, the United States had shown great reluctance to use the nuclear threat even in the face of imminent military failure (for example, when Chinese forces almost succeeded in pushing the UN forces out of the Korean peninsula). While such reluctance was prudent, it undercut the future utility of the nuclear threat as a deterrent. The growing nuclear power of the Soviet Union, and the inevitable vulnerability of the U.S. homeland to Soviet nuclear attack, would only hasten the erosion of credibility over time.

The utility of tactical nuclear defense. Proponents of NATO's tactical nuclear posture argued that these weapons would favor the defense in actual military operations. Critics challenged this assumption. Numerous war games and analyses suggested that the massive increase in firepower inherent in these weapons would, if matched by the Soviets, chew up NATO's manpower much faster than would conventional operations. The massive destruction and confusion their use would cause on the battlefield would impose unprecedented strains on orderly command, control, and communications, making the achievement of military objectives doubtful. Once the agonizingly difficult decision to use tactical nuclear weapons had been made, the size and scope of the requirements for their use to make a military difference would engender strong pressures toward escalation to greater levels of violence, quite possibly leading to an all-out intercontinental nuclear exchange. Hence this use of nuclear weapons in NATO's defense would not only fail to offset conventional deficiencies, it could also lead to a global nuclear conflict. Meanwhile the territory being defended would probably be reduced to rubble. In the densely populated regions of central Europe in which a tactical nuclear engagement would take place, the number of civilian casualties would certainly erase any meaningful distinction between a "tactical" war and a "strategic" war.

Implications of the U.S. nuclear monopoly within NATO. Finally, some analysts observed that the virtual U.S. monopoly of nuclear weapons within NATO imposed an inherent strain on any NATO policy that relied on the threat of nuclear retaliation in all circumstances. The credibility of NATO's deterrent depended on the perception that the United States would have the political will to authorize the use of those weapons when U.S. territory was not under direct attack. That perception would become increasingly open to doubt as the Soviet Union developed the ability to hold U.S. territory a nuclear hostage while prosecuting a war in Europe. If the Soviets could assume that the United States would remain paralyzed, the risk of aggression against Western Europe would increase dramatically. This line of argument was to become a rationale—though not the only one and perhaps not even the decisive one—for the pursuit of independent nuclear deterrents by the United Kingdom and France. But if one accepted the argument, then the British and French forces would become equally unable to extend a deterrent umbrella over the nonnuclear European allies. The logical consequence of this dilemma—a proliferation of national nuclear arsenals among other NATO countries, particularly the Federal Republic of Germany—was too dangerous to ignore.

It would be a mistake to conclude that these critiques—argued within governments and in public, through confidential memoranda, journal articles, and books—fell upon deaf ears. Certain officials were receptive. At least one high-ranking NATO official, SACEUR General Lauris Norstad, made an explicit attempt to reorient the by then heavily nuclear NATO posture toward a closer balance between conventional and nuclear resources. In his vigorous pursuit of the MC-70 force goals and his articulation of a more demanding role for conventional forces—to force a "pause" upon an aggressor before he committed further aggression that would inevitably engage NATO's nuclear "sword"—Norstad demonstrated some sensitivity to critics of the New Look. Yet he and others, U.S. Army Chief of Staff General Maxwell Taylor among them, met with stiff opposition from military planners, particularly in the Strategic Air Command, who argued that the Soviet conventional threat required planning for an early nuclear response, and from politicians throughout the Alliance who contended that to deemphasize the nuclear threat would erode the deterrent or be politically and financially unacceptable to Western societies.

The 1960s: Flexible Response

The last years of the Eisenhower presidency saw the debate take shape in private and in public. Eisenhower's last secretary of defense, Thomas Gates, was apparently sensitive to concerns about the New Look and massive retaliation, for he took several important steps to introduce a degree of flexibility and centralized control into U.S. military planning, particularly at the strategic nuclear level. Dulles was also moving in this direction, and reportedly instructed the Joint Chiefs of Staff to take the requirements of conventional defense more seriously. But it fell to the Kennedy administration to begin a serious effort to move NATO away from its nuclear addiction.[6] President Kennedy himself was sympathetic to the views of the critics; indeed, he had made a thoughtful critique of Eisenhower's defense policies a central part of his campaign platform. The men he brought to power with him, such as Robert McNamara, Paul Nitze, Maxwell Taylor, and McGeorge Bundy, shared many of his concerns.

Within weeks of taking office, Secretary of Defense McNamara prodded the Pentagon bureaucracy into making a thorough review of U.S. and Alliance defense policies and programs. Over the next two years, the findings resulted in a number of major changes in U.S. defense policies and programs. The strategic force buildup that had begun in the last years of the Eisenhower administration was given renewed momentum, with a particular eye toward increasing the flexibility, redundancy, and survivability of strategic systems. A major investment was made in U.S. conventional forces, found dangerously inadequate for contingencies such as the 1961 Berlin crisis. Indeed, there is some evidence that the administration abandoned plans for adopting a no-first-use policy in the wake of that crisis.[7] At the same time, the buildup of tactical nuclear weapons in Europe begun in the mid-1950s continued until the stockpile exceeded 7,000 warheads.

The relationship between strategy, doctrine, and military programs is never a clear one, and it would be an oversimplification to assert that all this activity was guided by a single comprehensive strategy. But McNamara and his staff were convinced of a few basic postulates that shaped defense decisionmaking. Taken together, they came to be known as the strategy of flexible response. Central to that strategy was the need to build a military posture that would give decisionmakers considerable flexibility in responding to aggression at all levels. The "search for options" was held to be essential for the credibility and effectiveness of a deterrent that would have to operate against a wide spectrum of possible contingencies, ranging from minor border incidents to major politico-military crises, from actions to block the Berlin corridor to an all-out nonnuclear offensive against Western Europe to a full-scale intercontinental nuclear war.

At the strategic nuclear level, a flexible response called for options other than a massive strike against all Soviet military and industrial targets. To the extent possible, the United States would introduce flexibility into its strategic planning, tying target packages to politico-military objectives. In particular the United States would retain the option to avoid striking Soviet population centers, giving the Soviets a marginal but important incentive to do the same—the "no cities" doctrine. Aside from giving the president alternatives other than surrender or nuclear suicide—in fact, by virtue of giving the president such options—it was hoped that doubts about America's willingness to use its nuclear arsenal in defense of its allies could be managed, if not laid to rest, thus reducing the pressures for proliferation inherent in NATO's New Look.[8]

At the conventional level, flexibility required a force capable of mounting a serious nonnuclear defense in Europe without necessarily resorting to nuclear weapons. While such use would never be explicitly ruled out, an effective conventional capability would put the onus of nuclear escalation squarely on the aggressor.

For those who remained skeptical, McNamara had some surprising answers. One product of the thorough review he had ordered was a revised assessment of the Soviet conventional threat. Proceeding from a review of basic aggregate data, Pentagon analysts found that NATO's manpower and gross national product were comparable to, if not greater than, those of the Warsaw Pact. If a gap existed in conventional forces, the problem lay not in the amount of basic resources but in their allocation. The analysts then took a detailed look at actual Soviet capabilities and found that of the 175 so-called divisions in the Soviet order of battle, many were at extremely low levels of readiness in both manpower and matériel. More precise analyses conducted over the next several years all pointed in the same direction: assessments of the magnitude of the Warsaw Pact's conventional superiority, for more than a decade the basis of the contention that NATO had no choice but to rely on early use of nuclear weapons against a conventional attack, had been vastly exaggerated. As two of the key analysts later wrote,

Eliminating paper divisions, using cost and firepower indexes, counts of combat personnel in available divisions, and numbers of artillery pieces, trucks, tanks, and the like, we ended up with the same conclusion: NATO and the Warsaw Pact had approximate equality on the ground. Where four years earlier it had appeared that a conventional option was impossible, it now began to appear that perhaps NATO could have had one all along.[9]

It was one thing for the U.S. government to convince itself that greater flexibility was needed in strategic nuclear planning and that renewed emphasis on the conventional option was both desirable and feasible. It was another thing entirely to gain a consensus for this approach in European capitals, where the U.S. strategic nuclear planning process was a mystery, where the assumption of Warsaw Pact conventional superiority had become the conventional wisdom, and where a domestic political price would be exacted for any change in NATO strategy.

In bits and pieces, the strategy of flexible response had leaked to European audiences through McNamara's congressional testimony and through speeches by administration officials such as Paul Nitze and Roswell Gilpatric. European governments were understandably nervous. Major decisions were being made in Washington that had a direct bearing on Alliance security. Yet the full rationale for these decisions had never been clearly articulated, much less debated within an Alliance forum. Kept in the dark, many European governments began to suspect that the United States was underestimating the sacrifices that a strong conventional defense would impose on the allies; that Washington was changing the basis of Alliance security without adequate consultation;

and, perhaps most distressing, that the United States had decided to withdraw the strategic nuclear umbrella that had made deterrence possible.

Recognizing that such suspicions, if unchecked, would have damaging political consequences and compound the difficulty of persuading European governments that the conventional option was feasible if appropriate steps were taken, McNamara laid out the new American strategy in some detail at a meeting of NATO ministers in Athens in May 1962.[10] He presented the main lines of the new approach, stressing the credibility of the U.S. strategic nuclear guarantee, given the global nature of any nuclear conflict between NATO and the Warsaw Pact; the requirement for flexible options and centralized command and control at the strategic nuclear level; the strategic damage that could be done to Alliance objectives by the proliferation of independent national nuclear deterrents; the escalatory dangers inherent in the use of tactical nuclear weapons; the substantial contribution to deterrence that could be made by a strong nonnuclear posture; and the feasibility of achieving such a posture.

That McNamara chose to stress the inherent dangers of using tactical nuclear weapons, particularly as a substitute for a conventional response, reflected his strong belief that the burden of escalation to the nuclear level should be placed where it belonged—on the aggressor. In this sense, flexible response was conceived as a no-first-use strategy. That McNamara did not deny the utility of tactical nuclear weapons for deterrent purposes is not inconsistent with this interpretation. He was arguing, rather, that NATO's excessive reliance on those weapons would be particularly irresponsible in time of crisis or war, especially when safer alternatives were available. In his own words,

I would be less than candid if I pretended to you that the United States . . . believes that the Alliance should depend solely on our nuclear power to deter the Soviet Union from actions not involving a massive commitment of Soviet force. Surely an Alliance with the wealth, talent, and experience that we possess can find a better way than this to meet our common threat.[11]

There was, of course, a certain irony in this position. Under McNamara and his successor, Clark Clifford, the authorized number of U.S. tactical nuclear weapons in Europe increased from about 2,500 to about 7,200.[12] Yet it is clear that McNamara's policy preferences lay in the direction of deemphasizing reliance on nuclear weapons.

The strategy McNamara articulated and pressed on the allies in numerous ways over the next five years met with stiff resistance. The French rejected his arguments against independent nuclear forces and moved ahead with plans to develop their own, outside the control of NATO. Others also saw in McNamara's presentation an ill-disguised attempt to remove the U.S. nuclear guarantee from Europe, but argued that only an explicit U.S. commitment to a nuclear strategy for NATO would enable the West to mount an effective deterrent. Some contended that reemphasis of the conventional option made war more thinkable, hence more likely, and thus undermined the deterrent.

A smaller group rejected McNamara's assertion that the escalatory pressures arising from the use of tactical nuclear weapons would hasten NATO's defeat, arguing instead that the weapons could be used effectively in limited ways as a force multiplier for conventional operations. This position found favor in the United States, where academic debate had produced a limited nuclear war strategy incorporating the weapons as a central element of the force posture. Others, still accepting past threat assessments, remained convinced that conventional defense, while desirable in principle, was infeasible in fact, and that flexible response meant "flexible backwardness" in that the doctrine would enable the United States to trade European space for U.S. decision time, thus conceding NATO territory to Warsaw Pact aggression. Rarely expressed but never far from the surface was a belief that the escalatory potential inherent in the tactical nuclear arsenal was beneficial to Europe, in that its use would quickly lead to an intercontinental nuclear exchange involving the territory of the United States.

The debate engendered by these positions was intense and in fact persists in various forms to this day. Nevertheless, a historic compromise was reached through a long and difficult process that culminated in 1967 in the Alliance's adoption of a new strategic concept that embodied flexible response.

In a document known as MC-14/3, successor to MC-14/2, the Alliance formally acknowledged the importance of having the ability to respond directly to aggression at whatever level it is initiated. Termed "direct defense," this concept implied a degree of seriousness regarding conventional requirements that had been lacking in the earlier strategic concept. Also envisioned in the new strategy was the notion of "deliberate escalation"—that NATO would retain the option of deliberately escalating the conflict, to the nuclear level if necessary, if efforts at direct defense failed to make the enemy cease hostilities and withdraw. The

Alliance would still rely on the threat of general nuclear war, carried on by the American and British strategic forces, if all else failed.

In exchange for the allies' acceptance of McNamara's demand that conventional requirements be taken seriously, the United States accepted a certain ambiguity in the relationship between direct defense and deliberate escalation. The circumstances in which NATO would resort to escalation, in particular in which the Alliance would deliberately bring the conflict to the nuclear level, were not spelled out. Ambiguity allowed those to whom early first use of nuclear weapons seemed essential to argue that NATO strategy agreed with them, and that the retention of a large tactical nuclear arsenal was justified. It also permitted critics of a tactical nuclear defense to argue that NATO strategy and the requirements of direct defense implied a greater commitment to strengthening conventional forces. Yet, by accepting the notion of deliberate escalation without clarifying the circumstances in which it would take place, the Alliance implicitly shelved the suggestion inherent in McNamara's 1962 Athens speech that the burden of escalation should be placed on the aggressor. The compromise thus rejected the implicit no-first-use strategy broached by the U.S. secretary of defense in his advocacy of flexible response. By the same token, the fight within NATO over requirements and force levels would persist.

The 1970s: Force Posture Adjustments

Throughout the 1970s adjustments in the force posture, both conventional and nuclear, increasingly reflected the new strategy of flexible response and its inherent ambiguities.

The tactical nuclear forces came under close scrutiny early in the decade, largely as the result of U.S. congressional concern about the aging, obsolescent, and increasingly vulnerable arsenal in Western Europe. Responding to congressional pressure, Secretary of Defense James R. Schlesinger initiated a series of modifications in these forces within the authorized ceiling of 7,000 weapons. For example, old surface-to-surface missiles such as the Sergeant were replaced by the modern 70-km-range Lance missile. Schlesinger also authorized increased research on ways to "clean up" the stockpile by redesigning weapons so as to minimize their fallout and other unintentional damage to civilian populations. Not until some years later, in 1977, did these efforts attract much attention, when U.S. plans to produce "clean" weapons (the so-called neutron bomb) were made public. In the controversy that followed, most thoughtful proponents of qualitative modernization admitted that such changes would have only a marginal effect on the "usability" of the weapons for relatively limited objectives. Opponents contended that just this additional usability would erode deterrence and make a nuclear war more likely, though not appreciably less destructive.[13] As it happened, in 1978 the United States unilaterally abandoned its plans to produce these weapons—after successfully bringing pressure to bear on its allies to accept them—prompting a minor political crisis within the Alliance.

In broad terms, then, the 1970s brought marginal improvements in the reliability, accuracy, and peacetime security of U.S. tactical nuclear weapons in Europe. However, while recognizing their limited military value and even after making these qualitative improvements, the Alliance never made a basic change in the role of these weapons in Alliance planning. Their function was taken largely as a given, both by those who believed that flexible response required the ability to conduct flexible nuclear operations in Europe, and by those who believed that their use would rapidly escalate out of control and lead the superpowers into a strategic confrontation that would somehow be settled over Europe's head.

Skeptics of the importance of these systems, particularly as compared to conventional forces, remained vocal during the decade. If they failed to bring about a substantial reduction in NATO's tactical nuclear forces, they were more successful in making the case for conventional force improvements.[14] By the mid-1970s, several congressional attempts to cut the number of U.S. troops in Europe having been defeated, the United States turned to improvements in its own conventional forces. Between 1975 and 1982,

—Three divisions and two brigades were added to the U.S. Army force structure, and the brigades deployed in Europe. Support units were reallocated to combat roles, thereby increasing the combat-to-support manpower ratio. Some have argued that this shift enables NATO better to withstand a Soviet conventional attack; others have questioned whether the reallocation was wise, noting the importance of support units in sustaining military operations.

—Active army units were "heavied up" through the introduction of mechanized units and the conversion of infantry units into mechanized units.

—Sets of equipment for four additional reinforcement divisions were pre-positioned in West Germany.[15]

Concurrently the United States sought to assure that the conventional improvements required by the evolving Soviet threat would be adopted throughout the Alliance. To this end, Washington initiated a long-term defense plan (LTDP) "to address selected deficiencies in forces, equipment and procedures." The LTDP, which NATO formally adopted in 1978, calls for several kinds of improvement in conventional forces:

Enhanced readiness

Rapid reinforcement

Strengthened European reserve forces

Improvements in maritime capabilities

Integrated air defenses

More effective command, control, and communications (C^3)

Rationalized procedures for joint development and procurement of weapons

Measures to promote logistics coordination and to increase war reserves.[16]

By 1981, work on this rather lengthy "laundry list" was far from complete. In his final annual report, Secretary of Defense Harold Brown pointed to readiness, maritime posture, logistics, and C^3 as areas in which NATO had made real progress. In other key areas—electronic warfare, reserve training and equipment, war reserve stocks of ammunition and fuel, provision of additional European reserve brigades, and the like—the Alliance would have to "renew its efforts."[17] Faced with such requirements and buttressed by its substantial though dwindling advantage in tactical nuclear weapons, NATO ended the 1970s with much left to do on the conventional side, and amid heated bickering over the ability of individual members to achieve the 3 percent growth in real defense spending that was agreed to when the LTDP was adopted.

Conclusion

This glance at NATO's past suggests several insights of relevance to today's debate.

NATO's reliance on nuclear weapons for the purposes of deterrence, or to compensate for conventional weaknesses, has deep historical and political roots. The fact that MC-14/3 embodies a political compromise reached only after critical struggles within the Alliance endows this document with a political weight far greater than most such planning guidance has had in the past. It represents not only a military strategy but also a bulwark against reopening divisive issues of nuclear strategy that many believed—and still believe—have the potential to fragment the Alliance.

Meeting stiff resistance over the past twenty years, efforts to reduce NATO's nuclear dependence and bolster the conventional option have been succeeded by efforts to do the latter without doing the former. Nevertheless, attempts have been made. In one important sense, McNamara's argument in the early 1960s had an implicit no-first-use theme. In the final compromise over flexible response, that theme was rejected. The compromise did, however, legitimate and pave the way for recognition that the conventional option had been too long neglected and needed to be revitalized if NATO's overall deterrent posture was to be credible. This has led to significant improvements in conventional forces, although they have fallen short of what NATO could do to build a fully reliable conventional defense.

Because NATO has been unable to reduce significantly its reliance on tactical nuclear weapons, the size of the force has remained relatively constant. (One thousand warheads were withdrawn in 1980 pursuant to the December 1979 decision on intermediate-range nuclear forces, leaving about 6,000 warheads in place.) Some qualitative changes have been made in the existing stockpile, but in broad posture and function it remains configured much as it was from the late 1950s to the early 1960s—a force designed to deter, in part by compensating for conventional inadequacies.

By the same token, the strategy adopted in 1967 has not changed the way nuclear forces have been integrated into conventional forces for planning purposes. Indeed, flexible response and the requirements of deliberate escalation have given renewed emphasis to integration in the name of multiplying the commander's options.

It is these considerations, shaped by events and decisions over a thirty-year period, with which today's leaders will have to contend. While NATO's past need not be construed as a straitjacket into which all future actions must fit, it can and should serve as a valuable reminder of why certain choices were not made. It should also stimulate constructive consideration of the alternatives before us.

Notes

1. Indeed, it is difficult to identify a subject related to NATO about which more has been written. Perhaps the best general bibliography remains Morton H. Halperin, *Limited War in the Nuclear Age* (John Wiley and Sons, 1963), pp. 133–84. In the 1950s two excellent edited volumes covered much of the debate: William W. Kaufmann, ed., *Military Policy and National Security* (Princeton University Press, 1956); and Klaus Knorr, ed., *NATO and American Security* (Princeton University Press, 1959). Halperin also made a special study of the no-first-use issue: M. H. Halperin, "A Proposal for a Ban on the Use of Nuclear Weapons," Institute for Defense Analyses, Special Studies Group, Study Memorandum no. 4 (Washington, D.C.: IDA, 1961). See also Richard H. Ullman, "No First Use of Nuclear Weapons," *Foreign Affairs*, vol. 50 (July 1972), pp. 669–83; Fred Charles Iklé, "NATO's 'First Nuclear Use': A Deepening Trap?" *Strategic Review*, vol. 8 (Winter 1980), pp. 18–23; and Laurence D. Weiler, "No First Use: A History," *Bulletin of the Atomic Scientists*, vol. 39 (February 1983), pp. 28–34, which contains interesting material on Soviet attitudes toward the issue.

2. The themes in this section are treated in detail in Robert Endicott Osgood, *NATO: The Entangling Alliance* (University of Chicago Press, 1962). A more detailed account of NATO's first year can be found in Lawrence S. Kaplan, *A Community of Interests: NATO and the Military Assistance Program, 1948–1951* (Government Printing Office, 1980).

3. John Foster Dulles, "The Evolution of Foreign Policy," *Department of State Bulletin*, vol. 30 (January 25, 1954), p. 108.

4. Cited in Osgood, *NATO: The Entangling Alliance*, p. 110.

5. See the major planning document of the New Look, NSC 162/2, now declassified and available in *The Pentagon Papers: The Defense Department History of United States Decisionmaking on Vietnam*, vol. 1, Senator Gravel edition (Boston: Beacon Press, 1971), pp. 412–29.

6. This account is based on William W. Kaufmann, *The McNamara Strategy* (Harper and Row, 1964); Desmond Ball, *Politics and Force Levels: The Strategic Missile Program of the Kennedy Administration* (University of California Press, 1980); and Alain C. Enthoven and K. Wayne Smith, *How Much Is Enough? Shaping the Defense Program, 1961–1969* (Harper and Row, 1971).

7. See Lawrence Freedman, *The Evolution of Nuclear Strategy*, Studies in International Security, 20 (Macmillan Press, 1981), p. 242.

8. The introduction of flexibility into U.S. targeting strategy in the early 1960s is well documented. However, the public record makes clear that the degree of flexibility introduced was not as great as some at the time would have liked. See Henry S. Rowen, "Formulating Strategic Doctrine," *Commission on the Organization of the Government for the Conduct of Foreign Policy* (Murphy Commission), pt. 3 of vol. 4 appendixes (GPO, 1976), pp. 219–34.

9. Enthoven and Smith, *How Much Is Enough?* pp. 140–41.

10. David N. Schwartz, *NATO's Nuclear Dilemmas* (Brookings Institution, 1983), pp. 156–65.

11. Ibid., pp. 160–61.

12. Stockholm International Peace Research Institute (SIPRI), *Tactical Nuclear Weapons: European Perspectives* (New York: Crane, Russak, 1978), p. 16.

13. By increasing radiation and minimizing blast at very low yields, it was argued, "clean" weapons would be ideal for stopping armored assaults without producing the high levels of collateral damage associated with earlier weaponry. This characteristic would, according to proponents, enhance deterrence. This argument struck opponents as displaying excessive enthusiasm for nuclear "war-fighting," thus undermining deterrence.

14. See, for example, William P. Mako, *U.S. Ground Forces and the Defense of Central Europe* (Brookings Institution, 1983), pp. 27–30.

15. Ibid., pp. 23–27.

16. *Department of Defense Annual Report, Fiscal Year 1982*, p. 207.

17. Ibid., p. 78.

CHAPTER THREE

NUCLEAR DETERRENCE
IN CENTRAL EUROPE

William W. Kaufmann

WEAKNESSES in the current NATO military posture have disturbed allied policymakers for many years and have stimulated a number of attempted remedies. As early as 1962 the United States, despite its quantitative nuclear superiority, was advocating an allied conventional buildup and a deemphasis of nuclear deterrence. By 1967 new strategic guidance for allied commanders, MC-14/3, envisioned a deterrent posture based on the forces and the plans to execute, as necessary, a sequence of three distinct types of military operations: direct defense of NATO territory with conventional forces; escalation, if required, to the local use of nuclear weapons; and finally, if all else failed, resort to general nuclear war.[1]

MC-14/3 did not meet the American objective of having the allies endorse the acquisition of a nonnuclear deterrent fully capable of halting an all-out conventional attack by the Warsaw Pact. But its intent certainly was to encourage greater increases in and reliance on allied nonnuclear capabilities. Nuclear weapons were to be considered for use only after a period of conventional operations, and only after those operations had begun to fail. This policy was reemphasized as late as May 1977, when the Alliance affirmed that "while modern collective security would require a spectrum of nuclear and non-nuclear capabilities, the strengthening of NATO's conventional forces must be given first priority."[2]

Whatever the intentions and the rhetoric, MC-14/3 and its later manifestations have failed to revolutionize either allied attitudes or the military posture of the Alliance. That they did not do so, and that nuclear deterrence continues to be seen as the main function and salvation of NATO, should hardly come as a surprise. Crises have come and gone in Europe, but war has not broken out for thirty-eight years. How much this result has been due to the particulars of the NATO deterrent cannot be stated with any confidence. Nonetheless, any proposal for major change in the strategy and posture of the Alliance not only must take account of this history; it must also deal with a number of propositions about deterrence that argue strongly against change, especially change as seemingly radical as no first use (NFU).[3]

The Case for the Status Quo

What are the most important of these propositions? Perhaps the first is that, after the devastation of World War II, Europe cannot survive another major conflict on its soil. Instead it must stake everything on deterrence, to the extent that détente and arms control cannot substitute for it. If deterrence fails, Europe is lost.

Deterrence of a potential opponent armed with nuclear weapons obviously requires a nuclear component. But a second proposition in the allied lexicon is that NATO must rely on nuclear weapons for more than the deterrence of nuclear attack. This is said to be so for several reasons. The Alliance is currently inferior to the Warsaw Pact in conventional power, and inferior by a wide margin. Furthermore, it cannot overcome that inferiority at a cost acceptable to its members. Even if it could, the risk of a failure in deterrence would exist, since political and military leaders are much more willing to gamble on the outcome of a conventional war than they are on the results of a nuclear exchange.

The nuclear deterrent, on the other hand, is seen as virtually immune to failure: witness the postwar history of Europe. The note of success of the deterrent has been so great not only because of the dangers inherent to everyone in a nuclear war, but also because nuclear weapons used tactically favor the defense over the offense. As a consequence, they compensate on the cheap for weaknesses in allied conventional forces. Furthermore, nuclear weapons in Europe provide the powder train to light the intercontinental nuclear fires, thus assuring that neither the United States nor the Soviet Union could escape the consequences of a conflict in Europe. Independent nuclear deterrents in Great Britain and France presumably help to promote this escalatory effect, as does the deployment of U.S. delivery systems in Europe that can reach targets in the USSR. In the circumstances, neither superpower has an incentive to upset the status quo.

These basic propositions have several corollaries. Not only are conventional weaknesses in the NATO posture quite tolerable; their removal could actually lessen the need for and the will to use nuclear weapons. As matters now stand, a first use of nuclear weapons by NATO is seen as necessary—and required early in the war—to preserve the porous allied front. In light of that necessity, who can doubt the ability and willingness of the Alliance to decide rapidly on and authorize first use in response to a large nonnuclear attack? And who can doubt that NFU, by contrast, is simply a first step on the slippery slope toward no use of nuclear weapons at all, no matter how desperate the military circumstances? Indeed, confidence in American willingness to use nuclear weapons has eroded substantially during the past twenty years as Soviet nuclear capabilities have grown. Adoption of NFU would result in a total collapse of that confidence. Rather than stimulate a signficant improvement in the allied conventional posture, it would simply revive old efforts to establish a European nuclear deterrent independent of the United States. Alternatively, some form of neutralism might be its fruit.

In light of these arguments, it is quite conceivable that the principal allies will prefer to retain the status quo. But other choices are clearly possible. NFU could be adopted in the expectation that it would give NATO a greater incentive to build up its conventional capabilities. Another option is to soldier on as before—to maintain current declaratory policy and strategic guidance, but continue the long-standing effort led by the United States to improve both the nuclear and the conventional components of the deterrent.

Before the option of change is dismissed, several questions deserve to be answered. To begin with, how can propositions about the effectiveness and credibility of a particular deterrent be tested? How well does the existing deterrent score according to these tests? With or without NFU as a policy, what changes, if any, could be made, and at what cost, in order to increase its credibility?

Conditions of Deterrence

While deterrence is almost certainly the principal function of NATO, what constitutes a deterrent that is effective, credible, and conducive to stability in a crisis is not an issue that excites much systematic discussion within the Alliance. Constructing a deterrent is frequently thought to require programs that are somehow different from those needed to deal with a failure of deterrence (or war-fighting, to use the awkward but more evocative term), even though the two are bound to overlap. A serious deterrent, after all, must consist not only of a threat, or a declaration about the dire results that will follow from an unacceptable act; it must also consist of the physical capabilities, the plans, the deployments, and the level of performance needed to carry out the threat. Otherwise the threat may be taken as a bluff.

So far, only one modestly satisfactory way has been found to design a deterrent and test its effectiveness. The method consists of five major steps. The first develops a specific capability to take one or more military actions thought appropriate to deterrence. The second assumes that deterrence nonetheless has failed and that the opponent has committed some form of transgression. The third commits the deterrent capability on its intended course and measures its ability to carry out the deterrent threat. The fourth, and perhaps the most critical of the steps, tests the sensitivity of the deterrent's performance to changes in a variety of factors, including the military capabilities of the opponent and the way in which he uses them.

The last step consists of adjusting the deterrent capability to the desired level of effectiveness. Mutual deterrence and stability are presumably achieved when each party to a dispute is able, through deterrence, to prevent the other from upsetting the status quo by military means, and when none of the parties is tempted by opposing vulnerabilities or driven by suspicion and fear to attack the other before he himself is attacked.

Several key assumptions underlie most uses of this methodology. One is that any penalty sufficient for the purposes of deterrence—the cost, as it were, to be inflicted on the enemy—can be readily calculated and incorporated into the deterrent. Another is that measuring the power of the deterrent to impose the prescribed penalty is a relatively straightforward task. Still another is that if, under adverse conditions—conditions favorable to the opponent—the penalty has a high probability of being inflicted, the capability will serve as an effective deterrent. Finally, it tends to be assumed that effectiveness and credibility are essentially synonymous.

How valid are these four assumptions, particularly when it comes to evaluating the complex NATO deterrent? It is difficult to quarrel with the proposition that if the capability works well under hypothetical combat conditions, its performance can be considered a measure of its deterrent power, although arguments inevitably arise about the validity of the tests to which the capability has been subjected. What constitutes an effective deterrent, that is, one with enough power to prevent war, is a somewhat different matter.

Thinking on this subject has been conditioned by the emphasis of the past thirty-eight years on the strategic nuclear problem. Effectiveness in that realm has been measured by the ability of the strategic offensive forces to inflict some level of damage on the enemy, frequently specified as a percentage of the civilian population and industrial economy destroyed. But the effectiveness of conventional forces is usually considered to be a function of their ability to defend territory, destroy enemy forces, or seize and occupy enemy assets. Although conventional forces can also inflict great damage on enemy urban and industrial targets, they cannot do it as massively and rapidly as nuclear forces. Moreover, it is often considered to be illegal or immoral to attack such targets in conventional warfare, at least when it comes to deliberately killing civilians. It is also the case that even nuclear capabilities can be used against specific military and war production targets as well as against cities. In fact, the so-called tactical nuclear forces of NATO are supposed to be able to conduct quite traditional land, sea, and air campaigns with their remarkably increased firepower. To what extent they actually can, and what roles and missions the nuclear forces more generally can be counted on to perform, particularly as compared with the conventional forces, is not a question that can be ignored or arbitrarily answered in any assessment of the NATO deterrent.

Issues also arise in setting the conditions under which effectiveness is to be measured. Where the strategic nuclear forces are concerned, it has become de rigueur to assume that the enemy will attempt to remove or reduce the deterrent by means of a surprise attack. Hence the correct test of deterrent effectiveness is seen as the ability of the strategic forces to survive even an attack coming as a bolt out of the blue, and to do so in sufficient numbers and operating capability to launch, penetrate enemy defenses, and destroy their designated targets. Recently it has become almost as customary to apply equally demanding tests to the conventional forces. Thus the enemy is allowed to launch an attack with very little political or technical warning. A critical test of the nonnuclear deterrent is whether it can respond with sufficient speed and power to halt the enemy's initial assault. To the extent that the nuclear forces in a theater are given analytical consideration (which is not very often), it is usually assumed that the United States and its allies will initiate their use, so that surprise attacks by the enemy need not be taken into account for planning or operational purposes.

Finally there is the assumption that effectiveness, however defined and tested, automatically equates with credibility, which can be defined as the probability that the deterrent threat would, if challenged, be implemented. But is there a significant probability that the United States would promptly retaliate against 200 cities in the event of a Russian nuclear attack confined to U.S. strategic targets that is likely to cause 10 million, but not 150 million, American fatalities? Would this or some less indiscriminate form of retaliation be more probable in the event of a Soviet nuclear attack limited to Western Europe or Japan? What is the probability that NATO would be able and willing promptly to authorize the tactical use of one or more nuclear weapons in response to imperfect information about an impending conventional collapse in central Europe? Uncertainty about the answers is bound to exist in this difficult realm, in part because no formal tests of credibility have been devised. But agreement could almost surely be reached that the probability of implementing such threats in these circumstances falls well below 50 percent. Of course, where the stakes are high the deterrent may still be fairly credible to all concerned (particularly if some flexibility is built into it), even though the probability of implementing it may appear quite low.

Unfortunately, however, the problem does not end there. What might seem credible to friend and foe under noncrisis conditions could become so frightening to the citizens and leaders of the deterring power in the event of a crisis that its credibility would rapidly and publicly drain away. Furthermore, the opponent could accelerate the drain by heightening the tension of the confrontation through oblique maneuvers designed to test the other side's nerve. In other words, what must finally be in question about NATO's capabilities is not only the effectiveness of the deterrent under plausibly adverse conditions, but also the probability that some or all of its components would be used in the event that deterrence should fail.

When the conditions of deterrence are spelled out, how well current NATO capabilities can meet them is an open question. The members of the Alliance deploy all the elements of modern deterrence in their nuclear and nonnuclear forces. But are they so proportioned as to provide adequate insurance against future dangers? Do they provide the right kinds and levels of effectiveness no matter how malevolently the opponent may behave? Will their threats be credible to all relevant audiences when policymakers come under the stress of confrontation and crisis? If not, what measures could be taken to improve the effectiveness and credibility of the deterrent? To answer these questions, each component of the deterrent requires a measure of review.

Despite recurrent doubts about the reliability of the United States, the Alliance still depends for its strategy of deterrence upon the "NATO triad"—strategic nuclear forces, tactical nuclear capabilities, and conventional forces—of which the two nuclear components are primarily but not exclusively American. NATO guidance continues to assume as a basis for planning that an attack on Western Europe could lead to a general war involving all three components of the deterrent. The guidance also assumes that NATO would be the one to initiate the tactical and strategic use of nuclear weapons. As a first step in evaluating the deterrent, it is therefore appropriate to consider the ability of the strategic nuclear forces of the United States (and possibly of Great Britain and France as well) to participate in a general nuclear war and to execute their strategic mission.

Strategic Deterrence and Its Limits

The strategic mission consists in attacking a number of targets located primarily in the Soviet Union. Strategic nuclear war, however, is usually described as a separate and decisive process to which no capabilities other than intercontinental ballistic missiles (ICBMs), submarine-launched ballistic missiles (SLBMs), and long-range bombers armed with air-launched cruise missiles (ALCMs) make any significant contribution. While such a description may indeed be accurate, for more than twenty years the mission of the U.S. strategic nuclear forces has also been related to and has complemented the missions of the tactical forces in Europe and elsewhere. Just as in World War II, today's long-range missiles and bombers are supposed to destroy targets deep in the enemy's rear that permit him both to interfere with the strategic mission and to operate, support, and reconstitute his own strategic and tactical forces.

In contrast to the World War II bombers based in England and Italy, modern U.S. strategic weapons are designed explicitly as second-strike forces, even though no president has formally abjured using them in a first strike. It should also be noted that all of them are given their targets and coordinated strike plans by a central organization, the Joint Strategic Targeting Plans Staff (JSTPS) in Omaha, Nebraska. Out of the total, several hundred SLBM warheads are allocated in response to the concerns of the Supreme Allied Commander, Europe (SACEUR).[4] SACEUR's deputy for nuclear planning in fact has had the right for some years to inspect that portion of the single integrated operations plan (SIOP) dedicated to covering the nuclear threat to Europe based in the USSR, a threat consisting primarily of SS-20, SS-4, and SS-5 intermediate- and medium-range ballistic missiles and the Backfire, Blinder, and Badger medium-range bombers.

Despite recent hand-wringing, these forces remain formidable in their destructive power. But how credible would they be in deterring conflict? Whatever NATO's military guidance may say, it is highly improbable that the U.S. strategic forces would ever be ordered to launch a first strike against targets in the Soviet Union in response to a conventional invasion of Western Europe. Indeed, this probability has been close to zero for at least twenty-five years. Reluctance even to consider this contingency may have been heightened by the growth of Soviet strategic nuclear power, but the enormity of the decision is such that this reluctance preceded by some years what has come to be known as strategic nuclear parity. From the standpoint of the United States, there was never a golden age of strategic nuclear superiority that has since been misplaced or recklessly thrown away.

It is generally understood, however, that a nuclear attack on the U.S. strategic forces or on other targets in North America would result in prompt retaliation. And despite loose statements to the contrary, there is a high probability that the retaliating forces would have enough surviving warheads to eliminate a large number of military and economic targets in the Soviet Union and to destroy several hundred urban-industrial targets as well, if that should be deemed desirable. This capability would exist even if the Soviet Union struck without warning and destroyed most of the U.S. ICBMs, all the SLBMs in port, and all the long-range bombers that were not on alert. If the attack came during a crisis and the U.S. strategic forces had gone on a very high alert— which they would almost certainly do in the event of a major confrontation in Europe—the retaliation would be even more assured and devastating. While attacks that avoided population centers might kill at least 100 million fewer people in each country than would direct attacks on cities, the fatalities could still be in the tens of millions. Surgical nuclear wars are a most unlikely event.

In light of these awesome numbers an obvious point must be made: there is at least some probability that the main U.S. strategic forces would attack targets in the USSR in response to a nuclear bombardment of selected targets in Western Europe by launchers based in the Soviet Union. That NATO-committed SLBMs, Pershing IIs, or ground-launched cruise missiles (GLCMs) would preempt such a bombardment is much less plausible. That the Soviet Union would risk such an attack in the first place, thereby giving the United States the opportunity (however unlikely to be seized) to strike first with its strategic forces, must be classified as most doubtful. Nonetheless, the existence of such a possibility, and the understandable reluctance of U.S. decisionmakers (along with their British and French counterparts) to unleash a general nuclear war in response to it, does not mean that the contingency is all that worrisome or that credible deterrents to it are lacking.

Much of the debate about nuclear exchanges and their deterrence takes place apart from the real world. Hypothetical attacks are prompted by mechanistic fears that the other side is about to strike, or are completely unmotivated even when they are not simply engineering tests of how the opposing forces might perform. Whether the contingency of a limited nuclear attack on Europe rests on a stronger foundation is difficult to say. Soviet leaders conceivably might become so paranoid as to wish to devastate all of Europe, although the United States would make a more plausible target for such madness. Somewhat more likely is that the Kremlin might wish to seize, occupy, and exploit Europe's resources and skills. But since long-range nuclear forces can only destroy targets—they cannot seize anything—the Russian plan would be aborted if the allies could disrupt a follow-up invasion. It is precisely the forces and logistics for such an invasion, located as they would be in Eastern Europe, that could be attacked without necessarily triggering the central nuclear exchange.

There is at least as much reason to believe that the United States (or Britain and France) would respond in this way to a limited Russian attack as there is to believe that the Soviet Union would launch such an attack in the first place. However awkward it may be to equate Eastern Europe with Western Europe, or to suggest that the Soviet Union and the United

States might conceivably escape direct damage from such a catastrophe, the objective presumably is deterrence rather than an equitable distribution of destruction. Western Europe may be hostage to prudent behavior by the United States, but the Soviet Union has hostages to fortune as well.

Strategic Prospects

The nuclear status quo may afford only cold comfort to those among the NATO allies who do not have nuclear capabilities of their own. But outright nuclear sharing with the nonnuclear states seems out of the question for the foreseeable future, even though the United States has provided those who wanted them with short-range delivery systems for nuclear weapons held nearby in U.S. custody. It is doubtful that other solutions in the form of land-based and U.S.-controlled intermediate-range launchers, such as Pershing IIs and GLCMs, or expanded and modernized British and French strategic capabilities, will suddenly transform the strategic component of the NATO posture into a deterrent to more than a first strike by their counterparts in the USSR. An attenuated form of nuclear sharing akin to the old multilateral nuclear force or tied to a voting formula on the model of the International Monetary Fund probably has at least as dubious a future. Efforts to give the strategic forces a more comprehensive role in deterrence by changing their mission from a limited number of strategic bombing options to the conduct of some complicated and extended form of war-fighting are almost certainly doomed to the same failure that awaits all abstractions of this kind. For better or for worse, a major component of the current NATO posture, whoever controls it, has been and almost certainly will remain immobilized except as a deterrent to nuclear attacks by the Soviet Union.

This does not mean that a second-strike posture, joined with a sensible choice of targets, somehow degrades the credibility of a deterrent, whatever the declaratory policy that goes with it. Quite the contrary is to be expected, whether strategic or tactical forces are at issue. A deterrent designed for a second strike does not preclude a first strike. What it does preclude is the ability of the Soviet Union to gain an exploitable advantage by striking first. That said, the onus of being the first to use nuclear weapons has grown steadily heavier since 1945, especially as uncertainty about the eventual results of such an act has deepened. The decision to respond to a nuclear attack is more manageable, particularly if realistic options for response are available to the launchers and their commanders. Someone else, however adventurous or mad, has already made the basic choice, and a demonstration of the ability to respond in a controlled fashion may help to bring the madness to an end—provided the communications for that purpose are still available. A decision not to respond, on the other hand, might simply encourage a continuation of the madness.

No doubt the option of general nuclear war will remain on the NATO books. But serious planning requires recognition that the United States, or for that matter Great Britain and France, would be most unlikely to undertake the strategic mission against targets in the USSR except in retaliation for direct nuclear attacks on their home territories. Nor is it likely that any NATO-assigned nuclear forces, wherever they might be based, would attack targets in Eastern Europe except in retaliation for attacks on Western Europe. For all practical purposes, then, the longer-range nuclear forces of the Alliance cannot be considered available as an instrument of NATO policy except for second-strike purposes. Consequently they cannot substitute for other and more usable capabilities as a deterrent to most military actions by the Pact. Even though they can carry out their mission of strategic bombing, their role for many years has been to rule out a first strike by their Soviet counterparts. No tinkering with the strategic forces will significantly change this limited but essential function. Realism on that score is essential.

Tactical Nuclear Deterrence

Where does this analysis leave NATO's tactical nuclear capabilities? An interesting anomaly of the allied military posture is that sauce for the strategic goose has not been sauce for the tactical gander. Unlike strategic nuclear forces, what are described as the tactical or theater nuclear forces do not constitute a separate and distinct entity. Rather, they have been treated as a kind of firepower—whether in the form of atomic demolition munitions (ADMs), artillery shells, bombs, anti-aircraft, missile, or torpedo warheads, or depth charges—to be delivered in some cases by specialized systems, but primarily by dual-purpose launchers such as howitzers and tactical aircraft. As the U.S. Army might put it, nuclear firepower is organic to NATO's conventional forces. Admittedly the warheads, with the exception of those aboard the quick-reaction alert (QRA) land-based aircraft and a number of naval vessels, are kept in a relatively small number of storage sites under normal, nonalert conditions, guarded by 25,000 to 30,000 custodians. But the launchers themselves are integral parts of divisions, corps, armies, and air wings, while both weapons and launchers are aboard submarines and other warships. Consequently both the deployed warheads, of which about 6,000 are now in and around Europe, and their delivery systems are no better prepared to absorb a nuclear attack than are the conventional forces to which they are wedded. To put it bluntly, these nuclear capabilities have not been well designed to withstand either a nuclear strike or a concentrated conventional attack.

Whether this configuration should or even can be changed depends in part on the validity of the assumptions that justify and have supported the posture for thirty years. When the idea of using nuclear weapons tactically was first put forward, the United States was expected to possess a monopoly in this realm for some years to come; and it was thought that, even after the Soviet Union had broken the monopoly, U.S. stockpiles of warheads would remain both more numerous and more advanced than anything the USSR could acquire. It was also assumed that, given a traditional military engagement on land and in the air, any use of nuclear weapons would favor the defense, or NATO, since the Warsaw Pact was bound to be the attacker.

The latter assumption seemed entirely logical at the time. So long as NATO could provide a screen of ground forces along its front amounting to thirty divisions, the attacker would have to concentrate his forces in one or more sectors of the front in order to break through the screen. The enemy concentration in turn would provide lucrative tactical targets for allied nuclear weapons, which would break up the attack. Thus, while strategic forces were bombarding the enemy rear and destroying the sinews of war, tactical nuclear weapons would not only be used first by NATO in the field but would also make up for the presumed allied inferiority in conventional forces, since one low-yield weapon could incapacitate at least one enemy company armed with conventional weapons.

The original nuclear weapons were less than ideal for this purpose. They were bulky, heavy, and expensive in the use of fissionable materials. Because their yields were quite high, they were likely to endanger allied troops if detonated very close to the front and cause substantial civil damage through blast, fire, and fallout. Indeed, during a tactical air exercise (known as Carte Blanche) conducted in four Western countries and run on a north-south axis between Hamburg and Munich in June 1955, the dropping of some 335 hypothetical nuclear weapons resulted in the calculation that 1.7 million Germans would have been killed and another 3.5 million injured.[5] To avoid such an outcome and enhance troop safety while preserving the alleged benefits of nuclear weapons, a move was begun toward lower-yield weapons ranging down even to sub-kiloton munitions. This trend culminated in the development of enhanced radiation weapons, otherwise known as neutron bombs.

Despite these technological advances and the growth in the NATO nuclear stockpile, the Soviet Union's acquisition of roughly comparable nuclear capabilities has undermined the original assumptions. The existence of these Soviet capabilities, now frequently described as superior to those of NATO (however little foundation there may be to the description), has made clear that any plans and operations based on the premise of a continuing NATO nuclear monopoly are quite absurd. Even the idea that the Alliance would assuredly have the advantage of a first use of nuclear weapons is open to doubt, quite apart from whether anything is to be gained from such a move against an allegedly superior opponent. Most alarming of all, in light of the way NATO's nuclear capabilities are maintained in peacetime and would be deployed if the Alliance ever embarked on an alert, are the questions that arise about the survivability of these capabilities in the event of an attack on them by the Soviet Union with nuclear or even conventional weapons. NATO may insist on continuing to have first use as its policy, but the time has long since passed when it could count on being able to exercise that option.

The growth of Soviet nuclear capabilities has cast additional doubt on the old assumptions about the benefits to be derived from the tactical use of nuclear weapons. It may be true that nuclear shells and bombs can destroy an enemy concentration of force. But they can be equally useful for tearing holes in a defensive position, especially if the attacker is not too scrupulous about the safety of his own troops and is willing to employ airburst weapons of high yields. While allied nuclear weapons may be able to destroy enemy formations at a rapid rate, there is every reason to believe that Soviet nuclear weapons can eliminate allied units with equal dispatch. If the many analyses of hypothetical tactical nuclear exchanges have any merit, they strongly suggest that nuclear weapons do not compensate for manpower deficiencies, and that the side with the larger conventional forces simply "wins" more rapidly if the campaign becomes nuclear than if it remains purely conventional. The more probable result, however, is that the nuclearized theater would quickly become a shambles, with enormous military and civilian casualties on both sides of the front. Nonnuclear forces are resilient in the face of conventional fire that inflicts casualties of several percent during a fighting day. They are likely to collapse very quickly when hit by nuclear weapons that can inflict casualties at a rate of perhaps 25 percent a day.

Europeans may believe that nothing could be worse than a reenactment of World War II and that nuclear deterrence, even with its risks of failure, remains a better bet than a heavy reliance on nonnuclear deterrence. But there should be no illusion about the consequences of a nuclear exchange in Europe. At one extreme, a careful targeting of nuclear weapons combined with airbursts and low yields could hold civilian fatalities in Western Europe to a few million. But less controlled exchanges, with groundburst weapons of moderate to high yields, could increase the fatalities to 100 million or more.[6] Such a prospect is likely to deter the defender as much as the attacker. The result is certain to be a deterrent of low credibility that invites challenges, nibbles, and tests—with the danger that bluffs will be made and bluffs will be called.

Panaceas

A dawning and reluctant recognition of these realities has had some peculiar effects. One has been an aversion to putting allied forces on alert—whether over Berlin, Czechoslovakia, or Poland—for fear of the impact on the behavior of the Soviet Union. Another has been a search for ways of harvesting the advantages of nuclear weapons without having to incur their risks.

Enhanced radiation weapons (ERWs) represent one of these panaceas. ERWs are small thermonuclear weapons that have an atomic trigger and produce all the outputs of a standard fission weapon, but in different proportions. A one-kiloton ERW, for example, has the potential for doing greater military damage and less civilian damage, if accurately delivered, than a one-kiloton fission weapon. But it is not at all clear that these properties make ERWs any easier to use than standard atomic weapons or add to the credibility of NATO's nuclear deterrent.[7] The existence of ERWs will neither reduce the vulnerability of their launchers to preemptive attack, nor make a nuclear exchange less calamitous should the Soviet Union respond to their use either with ERWs of its own or with standard fission weapons. The probability that NATO could use ERWs without engendering a nuclear response, simply because the other side has no ERWs in its stockpile, does not seem high enough to warrant measurement. To paraphrase Gertrude Stein, a nuclear weapon is a nuclear weapon is a nuclear weapon.

Another panacea, the demonstrative use of one or more nuclear weapons, gives the superficial appearance of greater effectiveness and credibility. It has therefore had a substantial run as a way out of NATO's nuclear dilemma. The theory is quite simple. The Warsaw Pact is assumed, as usual, to be on the verge of breaking through the thin crust of NATO's conventional defenses. SACEUR informs the political leaders of the Alliance that the collapse is about to occur. NATO quickly signals its ultimate intention to go to a large-scale nuclear response by firing a nuclear-armed surface-to-air missile or exploding one or more nuclear weapons over a military target. The Pact, recognizing the folly of its ways, halts the attack and returns to East Germany.

The theory begs for acceptance. It also begs more questions than it seems to answer. Like many other theories in the nuclear realm, it, too, assumes that the Soviet Union—in the great tradition of Fontenoy—will gracefully concede the first nuclear volley to NATO. Whatever the nature of the demonstration (and the firing of a surface-to-air missile could be interpreted as a loss of nerve rather than a demonstration of escalatory intent), there is always a certain vagueness about the demands that are to accompany it. Is the Pact supposed simply to stop, even if its forces have already gained some German territory, or is it to retreat and pay damages? How much time does the Kremlin have to decide? What is to happen if the demonstration is ignored by Moscow but duly noticed by the population of Western Europe? And what if the Soviet Union responds with a major nuclear attack?

One must also ask how to prepare for the demonstration and hedge against its failure. Do the leaders of NATO warn the Kremlin that a demonstration is about to take place, or does it come as a surprise? Do they allow SACEUR to disperse his forces, release nuclear weapons to his control, and authorize him to prepare his full nuclear capability for the possibility that the Soviet Union will either respond in kind or launch a large-scale nuclear response for which it has been handed the initiative? What if SACEUR disperses his forces to get ready for a Soviet nuclear retaliation and the Pact chooses instead to continue its conventional operations (against an even more porous defense), meanwhile pointing out to the world that it, unlike NATO, has refrained from the barbarity of nuclear warfare? In short, as is always the question when the use of nuclear weapons arises, should you attack the king unless you intend to kill him?

These questions have no certain answers, but two points seem clear. First, nuclear demonstrations raise as many issues as any other use of nuclear weapons. Second, as experience within the United States and the Alliance has borne out, time will be needed to arrive at any nuclear decision and communicate it to the proper military authorities. Assuming the Soviet Union does not preempt them with a nuclear attack of its own, the heads of allied governments will face agonizing choices as they approach the nuclear threshold. The military situation will have to be assessed, and some heads of government may refuse to accept without question the judgment of the military authorities that nuclear action is required. Western leaders next must choose the nuclear option, specify the weapons to be released, and agree upon any declaration that is to accompany the release. They must also consider plans for future contingencies, the amount of latitude to be delegated to the military authorities—including not only SACEUR but also CINCSAC, CINCLANT, and CINCPAC[8]—and procedures for the release of additional weapons. Conceivably all these judgments, made in the fog of war, could be reached, communicated, and implemented in a few hours. The more likely eventuality is that they would take not hours but days.

Suppose in these circumstances that the Warsaw Pact makes a conventional attack and that, as is often assumed by the NATO military authorities, the allied defenses begin to sag under the weight of the attack after three days. Suppose further that either the president of the United States alone or the NATO heads of government in consultation (personally? by telephone?) take four days to decide to cross the nuclear threshold. By that time, again according to the current wisdom, the forces of the Pact may have advanced to or crossed the Rhine. It is by no means clear what the targets for the NATO nuclear strike would be, what delivery systems would be available, or whether any kind of local nuclear action would be feasible. Many of the most urgent targets would be on NATO territory. Moreover, since attacks on NATO's nuclear assets with conventional ordnance are believed to be the priority mission of Soviet Frontal Aviation, one must assume that a Soviet campaign successful enough to seize NATO territory would also seriously degrade those nuclear weapons stationed on the Continent. It is primarily for these reasons that NATO's military commanders periodically recommend that the decision to use nuclear weapons be predelegated to them to facilitate a prompt delivery of those weapons.

Nuclear decisions might be made with great speed by the allied heads of government in the event of a conflict. For planning purposes, however, it seems unwise to take an optimistic view of the prospects. If the Alliance intends to be serious about deterrence, it must assume that it cannot count on obtaining the first use of nuclear weapons; that its nuclear capabilities—the strategic component aside—are vulnerable to attack by the Soviet Union, possibly even with conventional weapons; and that the first use of nuclear weapons will not necessarily confer a military or psychological advantage on NATO. Furthermore, unless the allies can maintain a forward defense with conventional forces for at least a week, the opportunities for a nuclear demonstration or some other acceptably limited use of nuclear weapons may simply vanish. Yet ironic though it may seem, if enough time has been bought to agree on a release of nuclear weapons, actual first use may prove unnecessary and undesirable after all.

Possibilities for Change

If these conclusions are correct, it would seem that NATO does not have and may never have had a particularly credible nuclear deterrent—however comforting it may appear in noncrisis conditions—and that, independently of NFU, changes in the posture are in order. The main weakness of the tactical nuclear capability is clear. Too much of it takes the form of vulnerable short-range artillery (to which perhaps more than a third of the stockpile may be assigned), land-based aircraft (assigned another third), and unusable atomic demolition munitions (about 5 percent of the stockpile), as can be seen in table 3-1. Artillery and aircraft are precisely the systems that would be most needed to buttress NATO's conventional defenses. By contrast, only about 10 percent of the stockpile is allocated to surface-to-surface missiles. This percentage could rise if 572 Pershing IIs and GLCMs are deployed, depending on whether

Table 3-1. Nuclear Weapons in Europe, 1982

Type	Number
Atomic demolition munitions	300
Artillery shells (155mm and 203mm)	2,250
Surface-to-surface missiles (Honest John, Lance, Pershing I)	500[b]
Gravity bombs	1,850[a,b]
Surface-to-air missiles (Nike Hercules)	700
Maritime weapons	400[a]
Total	6,000[c]

Source: Jonathan Alford, "Tactical Nuclear Weapons in Europe," *NATO's Fifteen Nations*, special issue, no. 2 (1981), p. 80.

a. About 150 of the total (bombs and depth charges) are British.
b. French warheads (100 or more for the Pluton missile and aircraft) are not included.
c. Reduction from 7,000 to 6,000 owing to the withdrawal of obsolete artillery rounds and bombs.

they are added to the capability or substituted for existing delivery systems.

All of NATO's land-based missiles are or will be deployed to known and targetable locations in peacetime and are to be dispersed to secret wartime positions when NATO goes on an alert. Whether the Soviet Union will be able to locate and target those emergency sites is not certain. Perhaps the longer-range systems such as Lance, Pershing, and GLCM will be more difficult to destroy with a preemptive Soviet attack than aircraft on bases and artillery concentrated near a known front. What is certain is that a relatively small and crowded area such as Western Europe is a poor location for peacetime mobility or hardened silos, which in any event are rapidly losing their value as a way of minimizing missile vulnerability.

Submarine-based missiles are more survivable, as both the British and French have recognized, but they suffer from several handicaps. Communication with them can be less certain than with land-based systems; they are more costly for a given number of warheads (but probably not for a given number of survivable warheads); and, unless controlled by a multinational mechanism, they seem to lack the symbolism and reassurance to some allies that is associated with nuclear capabilities based on the European continent.

Another problem concerns the targets for these tactical systems. The alleged merit of the shorter-range systems, particularly of the dual-purpose artillery, is that they can attack with low-yield weapons precisely those elements of the enemy offensive that most directly threaten to collapse the NATO front: armored formations and other ground units.

Similarly, the vulnerable QRA aircraft, with higher-yield weapons, are supposed to be so flexible that they can attack targets of opportunity farther behind the enemy's lines, including his reserves, and thereby contribute directly to the disruption of his offensive power. By contrast, longer-range missiles will be able for some time to attack only fixed, known targets such as air bases, supply depots, and parts of the enemy's line of communication. Thus there appears to be a rather awkward trade-off between the survivability of these tactical systems and the comprehensiveness of the target sets they can cover. The present posture with its mix of systems combines high vulnerability with a wide range of targets (including mobile targets) and a fair number of targeting options for decisionmakers. Furthermore, though this is frequently overlooked in discussions of the European nuclear balance, the current posture is reinforced by the survivable Poseidon warheads, which could be used to attack interdiction and other targets in Eastern Europe. By contrast, a less vulnerable posture relying solely on longer-range land-based or submarine-based missiles would be limited to a smaller range of fixed targets.

If the current posture is modified, the choice along this spectrum of possibilities no doubt will depend on more than military considerations. From the standpoint of force planning, however, the choice will be a function not only of survivability but also of the objectives being sought. Plans for extended tactical nuclear campaigns and controlled escalation almost certainly will remain figments of the imagination. At most, tactical nuclear forces (like the strategic forces) will be capable of only a few barrages; it is entirely conceivable that both sides would collapse into chaos after only one exchange. In these circumstances it is difficult to believe that a very large target set must be covered for force planning purposes. As is suggested in table 3-2, perhaps a total of 1,610 targets would be generous, of which no more than 700 would be mobile troop targets. The remainder would consist of airfields, shorter-range missiles, division bases in Eastern Europe, and key choke points on the line of communication between the Soviet Union and the intra-German border.

If the objective is solely a demonstration, the number of targets can be small—perhaps no more than a dozen—and the posture can consist of a few of the more survivable long-range systems, which would permit the removal of all warheads for ADMs, surface-to-air missiles, artillery, and tactical aircraft. If, on the other hand, the goal is to maintain a number of targeting choices, including the ability on a one-time basis to

Table 3-2. Tactical Nuclear Targets and Proposed Weapons Allocation, Central Region of Europe

Item	Airfields in Eastern Europe	Short-range missile sites in Eastern Europe	Company-sized troop units at the front	Division bases in Eastern Europe	Total
Number of targets	170	650	700	90	1,610
Weapons required	213	813	875	113	2,014
Poseidon	213	72	. . .	113	398
Pershing II	. . .	108	. . .	. . .	108
Ground-launched cruise missile	. . .	464	. . .	. . .	464
Pershing I	. . .	72	. . .	. . .	72
Lance	. . .	97	. . .	. . .	97
Hypothetical helicopter force	. . .	. . .	875	. . .	875

Sources: Author's estimates; and International Institute for Strategic Studies, *The Military Balance, 1981–1982* (London: IISS, 1981), pp. 128–29.

cover all 1,610 targets on the list, the posture will probably have to include short-range as well as long-range delivery systems, and the number of weapons (depending on their basing mode and expectations about second-strike survivability) might run as high as 2,014, assuming only one sortie per launcher and no reloads. Even this more ambitious capability would require only about one-third of the current stockpile.

Although this larger force would be more difficult to protect, it should permit the substitution of missiles for QRA aircraft and could be designed so as to replace all the short-range launchers that are now organic to the ground forces. As an illustration, special helicopter units could be formed with the capability to deliver low-yield nuclear weapons by rocket. These units could substitute for dual-purpose artillery but could be held well to the rear of the combat zone and dispersed in the same way as missiles in the event of warning. From their dispersal areas they could be ordered to attack enemy troop targets once the decision to use nuclear weapons had been made. No more than 220 helicopters would be needed for this specialized force. To cover all fixed targets in Eastern Europe, the allied Lance and Pershing I forces, the Pershing IIs and GLCMs (if deployed), and the Poseidon warheads already committed to SACEUR should suffice. Thus the incremental cost of a separate tactical nuclear capability would entail little more than the investment in the helicopters, their weapons, and their support. Some of that cost could be offset by savings from reductions in custodial personnel and cancellation of current programs for the production of new nuclear warheads for artillery and the Lance missile.

An additional advantage of this separate force would be that, if the allies so desired, a separate nuclear command could be established directly under SACEUR. Such a command would probably facilitate the implementation of NATO decisions about the use of nuclear weapons. It would also relieve current commanders of the need to plan and prepare for both conventional and nuclear operations. Separate alerting procedures for the conventional and nuclear components would become feasible as well. Above all, the new command would release dual-purpose launchers from their nuclear role and ensure their availability for the strengthening of NATO's nonnuclear defenses.

Notes

1. Robert W. Komer, "Maritime Strategy vs. Coalition Defense," *Foreign Affairs*, vol. 60 (Summer 1982), p. 1125.

2. *Department of Defense Annual Report, Fiscal Year 1979*, p. 73.

3. Karl Kaiser and others, "Nuclear Weapons and the Preservation of Peace: A German Response," *Foreign Affairs*, vol. 60 (Summer 1982), pp. 1157–70.

4. John D. Steinbruner, *The Cybernetic Theory of Decision: New Dimensions of Political Analysis* (Princeton University Press, 1974), pp. 206–13.

5. Robert Endicott Osgood, *NATO: The Entangling Alliance* (University of Chicago Press, 1962), pp. 126–27.

6. Alain C. Enthoven and K. Wayne Smith, *How Much Is Enough? Shaping the Defense Program, 1961–1969* (Harper and Row, 1971), p. 128.

7. Fred M. Kaplan, "Enhanced-Radiation Weapons," *Scientific American*, vol. 238 (May 1978), pp. 44–51.

8. The acronyms stand, respectively, for Supreme Allied Commander, Europe; Commander-in-Chief, Strategic Air Command; Commander-in-Chief, Atlantic; Commander-in-Chief, Pacific. All four have nuclear forces under their commands, including SACEUR in his capacity as CINCEUR (Commander-in-Chief, Europe).

CHAPTER FOUR

NONNUCLEAR DETERRENCE

William W. Kaufmann

MOST current assessments of the military situation in central Europe raise a daunting question: if it is true that NATO's conventional forces are vastly inferior to those of the Warsaw Pact, that its tactical nuclear capabilities are vulnerable and in any event difficult to use, and that the strategic nuclear capabilities at the disposal of the Alliance are strictly retaliatory forces with a very limited role, what has kept the Soviet Union from invading Western Europe?

One possible answer is that the Kremlin, at least since the death of Stalin, has harbored no serious intention of attacking NATO. Another is that since NATO has a much greater stake in defending Western Europe than the Soviet Union has in seizing it, even the low probability of a quick allied nuclear response is a sufficient deterrent. Still a third possibility is that the standard assessment of NATO's conventional weaknesses has been and remains wrong.

Interestingly enough, five U.S. secretaries of defense have in various degrees supported this third possibility during the last eight years. In 1975, Secretary of Defense James R. Schlesinger, Jr., said that "in an age of essential nuclear parity, few of us would be happy with a concept for the defense of Western Europe that was heavily dependent on an early recourse to nuclear weapons. Most of us would agree, once having looked at the facts, that a nonnuclear defense of Western Europe is feasible. It also is desirable, from the standpoint of deterrence, that such a defense should be backed up and reinforced at all times by theater nuclear forces." Schlesinger went on to say, "As matters now stand, NATO has the capability and the resources to attain a more equal balance with the Pact even though it deploys a smaller number of divisions and has certain serious vulnerabilities that we are working to correct."[1]

Two years later, Secretary of Defense Donald H. Rumsfeld noted that "any assessment of the current balance of conventional power in Central Europe must evaluate NATO's ability to contain an attack with little or no warning as well as a major mobilization and deployment by the Warsaw Pact." He concluded, "At present, the United States and its allies in NATO have sufficient active forces to maintain an acceptable ratio of defense-to-offense against either type of attack. However, it would be a mistake to conclude that, because of an acceptable ratio, we have high confidence of conducting a successful forward defense in all instances."[2]

As recently as 1980, Secretary of Defense Harold Brown noted somewhat more pessimistically that "in Eastern Europe, the Soviets have improved their ability to launch heavy attacks with relatively little advance preparation and warning." But, he continued, "NATO can buy the capabilities necessary to deal with these attacks" and the members of the Alliance "have already gone a long way, in fact, toward acquiring the forces and weapons that should give them high confidence in their defenses."[3]

Even in 1982, the more apprehensive Caspar W. Weinberger, current secretary of defense, said of NATO's conventional defenses, "Although substantial progress has been made in strengthening NATO's forces, the Alliance's posture today has numerous weaknesses that erode its capability. . . . As a result, the quality of NATO's deterrent posture has weakened in recent years, and an accelerated U.S. and allied force improvement effort is needed if NATO is to retain a viable initial defense capability during the 1980s."[4] Perhaps Secretary Weinberger did not realize that he was endorsing the idea that as recently as 1982 NATO still had in its conventional forces "a viable initial defense capability." But that possibility aside, grounds other than secretarial authority exist for questioning the prevailing wisdom that the Warsaw Pact enjoys great nonnuclear superiority.

Trends in Soviet Capabilities

The impression of superiority has been shaped largely by two factors. The first is the widely proclaimed growth of Soviet conventional (as well as nuclear) forces during the last two decades or so. The second is the sense of overwhelming numbers resulting from that growth, a sense assiduously fostered by American and Russian commentators alike.

Since the mid-1960s, the Soviet Union has increased the manpower in its ground and tactical air forces from 1.4 million to about 2.1 million men (not counting 450,000 border guards and internal security units of an essentially military character). As a consequence of this increase, the number of Soviet divisions has risen from 148 to more than 180, and of fighter-attack aircraft, including those used for reconnaissance and electronic countermeasures, from 3,200 to around 4,600. Although the total size of the Soviet general purpose navy has actually declined during this period, its tonnage has increased by nearly 50 percent as the oceangoing part of the fleet—surface combatants, submarines, amphibious warfare ships, and auxiliary vessels—has been modernized with higher-quality ships. Of this blue-water fleet, 294 ships are said to be surface combatants, 259 general purpose submarines (of which 99 are nuclear powered), and 84 amphibious warfare ships, for a total of nearly 640.[5]

These numbers are indeed overwhelming when compared with their American counterparts: roughly a million men and women in the U.S. Army and Marine Corps; 19 active-duty Army and Marine divisions; fewer than 2,600 Air Force tactical fighters; and only 450 or so major naval combatants, amphibious warfare ships, and auxiliary vessels. When NATO forces in place are compared with the in-place forces of the Warsaw Pact, as shown in table 4-1, the tactical air and naval discrepancies look less shocking. But the Pact's ground forces dwarf those of NATO in the number of divisions, tanks, armored fighting vehicles, and artillery pieces.

If these numbers are approximately correct, what reasons exist for questioning the ability of the Pact to conquer NATO in a conventional war and to do so with great dispatch? One reason, quite simply, is that what are known as static comparisons, while not irrelevant to a military analysis, are only one factor among the many that must be taken into account when projecting the outcome of a conventional engagement in a particular theater of war—and hence when evaluating the effectiveness and credibility of a deterrent.

Defense of the Sea Lanes

The current naval situation illustrates most clearly why the prevailing wisdom about Soviet conventional superiority must be treated with caution. Should a nonnuclear war break out in central Europe, and

Table 4-1. NATO and Warsaw Pact Nonnuclear Forces in Place in Europe, 1982[a]

Category	NATO	Warsaw Pact
Military manpower (millions)	2.6	4.0
Ground forces		
Divisions	84	173
Main battle tanks	13,000	42,500
Antitank guided weapon launchers (crew served and/or mounted)	8,100	24,300
Artillery/mortars (tubes 100 mm and above, including rocket launchers)	10,750	31,500
Armored personnel carriers and infantry fighting vehicles	30,000	78,800
Helicopters		
Attack	400	700
Transport/support	1,400	300
Combat aircraft		
Fighter-bomber/ground attack	1,950	1,920
Interceptors	740	4,370
Bombers	. . .	350
Reconnaissance	285	600
Naval forces		
Aircraft carriers	7	. . .
Kiev-class ships	. . .	2
Helicopter carriers	2	2
Cruisers	15	21
Destroyers and frigates	274	182
Amphibious ships (ocean-going)	41	16
Mine warfare ships	257	360
Long-range attack submarines	60	149
Sea-based tactical and support aircraft (including helicopters)	712	146
Land-based and tactical support aircraft	180	719
Land-based antisubmarine warfare aircraft and helicopters	450	179

Source: North Atlantic Treaty Organization, *NATO and the Warsaw Pact: Force Comparisons* (Brussels: NATO Information Service, 1982), pp. 8, 11, 15–16.

a. According to the editorial note in the source, "France is a member of the North Atlantic Alliance but does not participate in its military structure. No account of French forces is taken in this comparison."

should the fighting last more than a few weeks, NATO would depend heavily for resupply on its sea lines of communication—in the Atlantic between North America and Western Europe and, to a lesser extent, in the Mediterranean, and from the head of the Persian Gulf around the Cape of Good Hope to ports in the Netherlands, Belgium, and possibly France. The Soviet Union would no doubt wish to disrupt these lines of communication. However, of the four Soviet fleets, the second largest is based on Vladivostok in the Far East, and it can be kept from threatening the Persian Gulf routes by being bottled up in the Sea of Okhotsk. Another fleet in the Baltic Sea can be prevented quite easily from moving into the North Sea. The Black Sea Fleet might in the short run deny NATO the use of the eastern Mediterranean, but its life expectancy in those waters would be quite short. Furthermore, it can be cut off from its home base if it lingers in the Mediterranean, and it has virtually no prospect of getting through the Strait of Gibraltar and into the Atlantic.

This leaves the Northern Fleet, based near Murmansk, as the main threat to the critical line of communication between the United States and its European allies. It consists of approximately 82 surface combatants, 135 general purpose submarines (of which approximately 57 are nuclear powered), and 80 long-range naval aircraft, as can be seen in table 4-2.

Although the primary mission of the Northern Fleet probably is to protect the Soviet ballistic missile submarines stationed in the Barents Sea, its surface combatants, general purpose submarines, and long-range bombers could also attack the Atlantic line of communication over which the United States would ship the bulk of its reinforcements, replacements, and supplies for central Europe. Thus, in assessing NATO's ability to strengthen and sustain its combat forces in Germany, the Northern Fleet rather than the entire Soviet Navy is what must be taken into account.

In attempting to counter the Northern Fleet, NATO must choose between two basic strategies. The first, hallowed by British and American naval tradition, is to attempt to destroy the Northern Fleet in or near its bases. Even with the projected expansion of the U.S. Navy, this strategy looks less than promising for the foreseeable future. U.S. and allied ships would have to come within easy range of Soviet land-based aircraft, surface combatants, and submarines in order to close with the Northern Fleet, and would be highly vulnerable to attack. They would have little prospect of crippling the Soviet submarine fleet, however well they might perform against the surface combatants and long-range aircraft.

The second choice is to practice what has been called a strategy of long-range blockade and attrition. Geography, a factor ignored in static comparisons, greatly strengthens the ability of the NATO navies to execute this strategy. In order to reach the main Atlantic shipping routes, Soviet surface combatants and submarines would have to traverse the

Table 4-2. Distribution of the Soviet Navy by Fleet

Components	Fleet and fleet headquarters				
	Northern Severomorsk	Baltic Baltiysk	Black Sea[a] Sevastopol	Pacific Vladivostok	Total
Fleet ballistic missile submarines	45	...	...	24	69
Attack submarines	135	22	22	80	259
Major surface combatants	82	42	84	86	294
Minor surface combatants	120	294	210	210	834
Amphibious warfare ships	12	50	53	54	169
Principal auxiliary support ships	72	19	36	73	200
Total	466	427	405	527	1825
Bombers	80	120	80	100	380

Source: International Institute for Strategic Studies, *The Military Balance, 1981–1982* (London: IISS, 1981), p. 13.
a. The Caspian Flotilla and the Mediterranean Squadron are included in the Black Sea Fleet.

relatively narrow waters between Greenland, Iceland, and the United Kingdom—the so-called GIUK barrier. These passages can be mined and patrolled by submarines, surface combatants, and aircraft. Even the long-range Soviet Backfire and Bear naval aircraft would have to penetrate NATO land- and sea-based warning systems and air defenses to attack allied warships and merchant convoys. Hence, whether NATO can protect its most vital sea line of communication depends less on how its navies compare numerically with the combined Russian fleets, category by category, than on how it can exploit favorable geography with the right kinds of platforms and weapons to prevent the Soviet Northern Fleet from destroying an excessive amount of allied shipping in a war of attrition at sea.

Still other factors enter into a serious analysis of NATO's prospects at sea. For example, once Soviet surface combatants move outside the range of their land-based aircraft, they must rely primarily on their shipboard radars, air defenses, sonars, and offensive weapons to warn and protect them from attacks by allied aircraft and submarines. The probability that they would suffer severe losses is rather high.

To take another example, Soviet submarines are fast but noisy. They also appear to be difficult to maintain, their weapon loads are small, and their time on station is limited unless they can be resupplied at sea or from overseas bases. Consequently not many of them could be sent out at any one time, they would be vulnerable to attack while running NATO's multiple defense barriers to and from their home port, and a majority of them probably would be sunk within about three months. (See table 4-3.) Indeed, standard analyses of the war at sea suggest that while the allies would suffer serious shipping losses during the early stages of a war in Europe, essential tonnage for NATO would get through and the threat to the sea lines of communication would be contained. This in turn would permit NATO to shift some of its naval forces to other important but less vital oceans and seas.[6]

Whether such an outcome can be defined as NATO naval superiority must be left to individual observers and offices of net assessment. Insofar as military outcomes can be measured, however, it does seem to be the case that, whatever the static comparisons may show, NATO has a rather high probability of achieving its essential objectives at sea. While the Soviet Union has a numerical advantage in surface combatants and submarines, their tonnage is relatively low and they are widely dispersed because of the politico-military problems Russian leaders think they

Table 4-3. Battle of the Atlantic: A Ninety-Day Campaign

Submarine schedule[a]	Submarines sent on station[b]	Ships at risk	Ships sunk with a torpedo lethality of:				Submarines returned from station	Submarine losses	Percent of submarine force
			0.5	0.4	0.3	0.2			
D day to D + 30	30	210	89	71	53	35	10	20	0.333
D + 15 to D + 45	15	420	44	35	27	18	5	10	0.166
D + 30 to D + 60	15	420	44	35	27	18	5	10	0.166
D + 45 to D + 75	10	420	30	24	18	12	3	7	0.116
D + 60 to D + 90	5	420	15	12	9	6	2	3	0.050
Total	...	...	222	177	134	89	...	50	0.833
Addenda									
Percent of ship sailings lost	...	...	11.70	9.40	7.10	4.70	...	...	...
Ratio of ships sunk to submarines sunk	...	...	4.44	3.54	2.68	1.78	...	...	...

Source: Author's estimates based on Charles DiBona and William O'Keefe, "Quantifying the Sealane Defense Problem," in Paul H. Nitze and others, *Securing the Seas: The Soviet Naval Challenge and Western Alliance Options* (Boulder, Colo.: Westview Press, 1979), pp. 337–82.
a. D stands for the day of attack.
b. Each submarine is assumed to be armed with ten torpedoes.

face in several parts of the world. NATO, and the United States in particular, must disperse their assets to some degree as well. But wherever the Soviet fleets are located, the Alliance enjoys major technical and geographic advantages. They give it better than median confidence that with existing naval forces it can support essential land and tactical air operations in Europe.

Warsaw Pact Ground Forces

Does the accepted wisdom stand up any better when a close look is taken at what NATO's ground forces can accomplish in central Europe? Although the answer must be more cautious than in the case of the allied navies, it nevertheless challenges the view that NATO is vastly inferior to the Warsaw Pact in conventional capability or that it is far from having a credible nonnuclear deterrent in central Europe.

For a number of reasons the situation may be less precarious than is generally supposed, even after the Soviet buildup of recent years. To begin with, all of NATO's ground forces would not engage all of the Pact's ground forces somewhere on an infinite flat plain. The United States, for its part, has major treaty commitments in addition to NATO that could tie down some of its forces in the Persian Gulf and in northeast Asia. But the Soviet Union, with its extended land frontiers and its sense of encirclement by hostile neighbors, has an even larger number of commitments, mostly self-imposed. Of its more than 180 divisions, at least 46 are stationed in the Far East in the vicinity of China and Japan. Another 5 or 6 are occupied in Afghanistan and 20 are deployed in proximity to Iran and eastern Turkey, while approximately 28 more are thought to be oriented toward southern Europe and northern Norway. Thus, in the short run, as table 4-4 suggests, the Soviet forces most likely to be used in any attack on central Europe (shown in figure 4-1) are the 26 divisions located in East Germany, Poland, and Czechoslovakia, the 33 divisions said to be in the three western military districts of the USSR, and possibly as many as 20 divisions that could be drawn from the general staff reserve. The number of divisions could be increased still further by mobilizing the large pool of Russian reservists trained during the previous five years and by equipping new units with stocks of older equipment (which the Russians seem never to throw away). But an additional buildup of this character would take several months and severely strain an economy already short of manpower.

Table 4-4. The Ground Forces of the Warsaw Pact

Location	Orientation	Type of division				
		Tank	Motorized rifle	Airborne	Other	Total
Soviet ground forces						
East Germany	Central Europe	9	10	...	...	19
Poland	Central Europe	2	...	...	...	2
Czechoslovakia	Central Europe	2	3	...	...	5
Hungary	Southern Europe	2	2	...	...	4
Military districts of the USSR						
Baltic	Central Europe	3	5	2	...	10
Belorussian	Central Europe	9	2	1	...	12
Carpathian	Central Europe	2	9	...	...	11
Leningrad	Norway	...	8	1	...	9
Kiev	Southern Europe	7	4	...	...	11
Moscow	General reserve	2	6	1	...	9
Odessa	Southern Europe	...	6	1	...	7
Ural	General reserve	1	5	...	...	6
Volga	General reserve	...	5	...	...	5

North Caucasus	Turkey and Iran	1	5	...	6
Trans-Caucasus	Iran	...	11	1	12
Turkestan	Afghanistan	...	5	1	6
Central Asia	China	1	6	...	7
Siberia	Japan and China	...	5	...	5
Transbykal	China	3	7	...	10
Far East	China	1	20	...	21
Mongolia	China	1	2	...	3
Total	...	46	126	8	180
East European ground forces					
East Germany	Central Europe	2	4	...	6
Czechoslovakia	Central Europe	5	5	...	10
Poland	Central Europe	5	8	1	15
Bulgaria	Southern Europe	...	8	...	8
Hungary	Southern Europe	1	5	...	6
Romania	Southern Europe	2	8	...	10
Total	...	15	38	1	55

Sources: IISS, *The Military Balance, 1981–1982*, pp. 10–21; and *Department of Defense Annual Report to the Congress, Fiscal Year 1983*, app.: "Soviet Military Power."

Figure 4-1. Corps Sectors and Likely Avenues of Attack in the Central Region of NATO

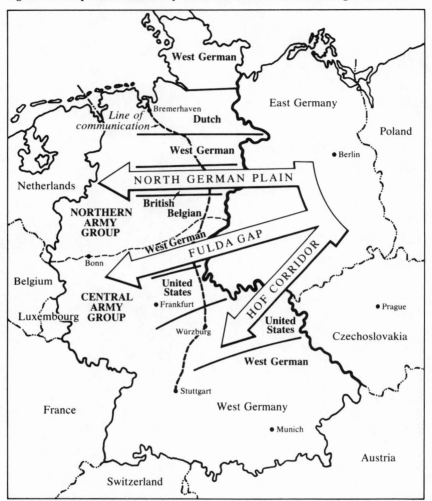

Sources: Richard D. Lawrence and Jeffrey Record, *U.S. Force Structure in NATO: An Alternative* (Brookings Institution, 1974), p. 31; and Congressional Budget Office, *U.S. Ground Forces: Design and Cost Alternatives for NATO and Non-NATO Contingencies,* prepared by Pat Hillier and Nora Slatkin (CBO, 1980), p. 11.

In addition to as many as 79 divisions of its own, the Soviet Union could supposedly count on another 31 divisions drawn from the armies of East Germany, Czechoslovakia, and Poland for an invasion of NATO's central region. It is frequently argued in this connection that NATO and SACEUR cannot depend on forces that are not actually committed to them in peacetime. Thus, French and other divisions are often excluded from the immediate allied order of battle. The Pact's order of battle is usually exempt from similar doubts, even though more questions arise about the availability and effectiveness of the 31 Eastern European divisions than about the uncommitted units of France, the United States, and other allied nations. Conceivably the Soviet general staff could be certain of the participation and full performance of these NSWP (non-Soviet Warsaw Pact) divisions in an unprovoked attack on central Europe, launched with little or no warning. A more likely contingency is that the NSWP forces could be relied on fully only if they were persuaded that a threat to their countries was developing within NATO. Under some conditions, Russian forces might even have to neutralize them to protect the lines of communication between East Germany and the USSR. Thus, while it may prove desirable for planning purposes to assume that the Pact threat to central Europe consists of as many as 110 divisions (79 Soviet and 31 NSWP), the performance of nearly 30 percent of them remains problematical.

There are also grounds for doubting whether these 110 divisions should be treated as equivalent to an equal number of NATO divisions. Various methods exist within the defense planning community (Soviet as well as American) for measuring the performance of the complex organism known as a division. For the most part, they relate to the firepower of the unit combined with its effectiveness and mobility. By these measures, the best of the Soviet divisions are now rated nearly on a par with the best of the NATO divisions. Yet if U.S. and Soviet divisions are compared, an average U.S. division is nearly 40 percent larger in manpower; the division slice (or the division with a prorated share of corps, army, and support forces) is probably more than twice as large; and—if both were acquired in the U.S. economy—the U.S. division slice is from 1.4 to 3 times more costly. (See table 4-5.)

Exactly why the U.S. Army can obtain only 20 percent more combat power in a division slice that is at least twice as large and perhaps three times as costly (in dollar terms) as its Soviet counterpart is a question that was raised and not fully resolved twenty years ago.[7] It has been largely ignored in the more recent rush to emphasize the growth of the Soviet threat. Several possible explanations for this apparent U.S. inefficiency may put that growth into perspective.

First, Soviet firepower per division may appear to be so high simply because the Russians, being short of maintenance capability and spare parts, deploy a large number of weapons (including replacement weap-

Table 4-5. The Cost of U.S. and Soviet Divisions in the U.S. Economy, Fiscal Year 1981
Billions of dollars unless otherwise specified

Item	U.S.	Soviet
Estimated defense outlays (retired pay excluded)	143.80	215.70
Share of outlays allocated to ground forces (excluding Marines)	25.30	47.50
Number of active and reserve division-equivalents	32	180
Average cost per division	0.79	0.26
Cost ratio	3:1	
Alternative calculation 1		
Number of active and reserve division-equivalents	32	173
Average cost per division	0.79	0.27
Cost ratio	2.9:1	
Alternative calculation 2		
Number of active-duty division-equivalents	18	46
Average cost per division	1.40	1.00
Cost ratio	1.4:1	

Sources: *Department of Defense Annual Report, Fiscal Year 1983*, p. A-2; and Central Intelligence Agency, National Foreign Assessment Center, *Estimated Soviet Defense Spending: Trends and Prospects*, SR78-10121 (CIA, 1978), p. 3.

ons), in contrast to the U.S. policy of providing fewer weapons along with the capability to maintain them.

Second, while the firepower measure is intended to reflect not only the number and mix of weapons in a particular unit but also the rate at which they are fired, the indications are that the Russian army with its smaller support establishment cannot sustain the high rates of fire from its weapons that are characteristic of the U.S. Army. If all this is true, then Soviet firepower is being overstated and is likely to decay rapidly in combat. This would explain the observed Russian practice of committing divisions to battle in two or more echelons rather than all at once. Thus, if 90 divisions were in the attacking force, perhaps no more than 45 might be put on the combat line at any one time.

Third, the U.S. Army invests much more heavily than does the Red Army in nonfirepower assets related to the acquisition of targets, command and control, and tactical mobility. Either this greater investment is wasteful, or it should be reflected in greater effectiveness for the American units. If the latter is the case, U.S. divisions—and those of West Germany—probably should be considered substantially more lethal than their Soviet counterparts.

It is also worth recalling that the Soviet Union puts more than 180 divisions into the field in an army that is said to comprise no more than 1,825,000 men. If the usual allowances are made for various kinds of organizational overhead (central headquarters personnel, training, tran-

Table 4-6. Warsaw Pact Divisions Oriented toward Central Europe, by Origin and Category

	Category[a]			
Origin	*1*	*2*	*3*	*Total*
Soviet Union	26	7	26	59
East Germany	6	. . .	. . .	6
Czechoslovakia	7	. . .	3	10
Poland	10	3	2	15
Subtotal	49	10	31	90
Soviet Union (by D + 120)	. . .	. . .	20	20
Total	49	10	51	110

Sources: *Department of Defense Annual Report, Fiscal Year 1983*, app.: "Soviet Military Power," p. 6; and IISS, *The Military Balance, 1981–1982*, pp. 10–20.

a. Definition of categories:
  1 is combat-ready: 75–100 percent of authorized wartime strength;
  2 is reduced strength: 50–75 percent of authorized wartime strength;
  3 is cadre strength: below 50 percent of authorized wartime strength.

sients, individuals on leave, and prisoners), this total amounts to a field force of roughly 1.2 million men, or an average of 6,600 per division slice. Apparently, however, there is no such "average" Soviet division. Rather, there are three categories of divisions, most of which depend on the mobilization of reservists (few of whom receive refresher training after they leave active duty) to bring them to their authorized strengths.

Category 1 divisions, of which there are only 46, located primarily in Eastern Europe and the Far East, come closest to what the U.S. Army would rate as fully combat ready. But most of these category 1 divisions lack the support units needed to sustain them in combat for more than a few days. Moreover, they spend a good portion of their time absorbing raw recruits, many of whom now come from Soviet Asia, and they train with their older equipment, keeping newer equipment in storage. Category 2 divisions, 38 in all, are even shorter of manpower and may not have full complements of equipment. The nearly 100 category 3 divisions for the most part consist of cadres rather than combat units. As such, they probably rate well below U.S. National Guard and Reserve divisions in peacetime combat power and effectiveness.

The ground forces of East Germany, Czechoslovakia, and Poland follow the Soviet model. (See table 4-6.) All six East German divisions are classified as category 1 and combat ready. But the Czechs have three category 3 divisions, while the Poles maintain three category 2 and two category 3 divisions. Like their Soviet tutors, the Eastern Europeans must rely on reservists both for additional divisional personnel and for support forces. The entire Warsaw Pact depends on trucks and other assets drawn from the civilian economy for its logistic operations. Some army equipment is also used in peacetime to support the civilian economy.

It has been suggested that the emphasis on blitzkrieg tactics in the Soviet military literature may reflect a combination of experience against the Germans in World War II, an aggressive intent on the part of postwar Soviet leaders, and a determination to disrupt NATO's strategy of nuclear defense. But it could also be the necessary product of the limitations under which the Pact's ground forces are obliged to operate. Because units are short of logistic support, may not have large stocks of ammunition and other combat consumables, and lack much in the way of organic maintenance, Soviet strategists—whatever their preferences—may have little choice but to seek quick results through blitzkrieg tactics. Certainly the ground forces as presently constituted are not well suited to extended campaigns of offense or defense.

Warsaw Pact Attack Options

Despite data supporting these hypotheses, the tests most frequently used by military analysts to assess the capabilities of current NATO forces and to decide what additional allied capabilities may be needed place great emphasis on the speed with which the Warsaw Pact forces prepare for an invasion of central Europe and on the breakneck nature of their attacks. These tests involve three levels of hypothetical attack (see table 4-7):

—A "smash and grab" attack with limited territorial objectives carried out by the 19 Soviet divisions in East Germany (known as the Group of Soviet Forces, Germany, composed of category 1 units), all 6 of the East German divisions, and perhaps 5 Czech divisions (all of which are also in category 1), for a total of 30 divisions ready to roll after only four days of preparation.

—A more ambitious attack, perhaps with the seizure of all of West Germany, the Netherlands, and Belgium as its objective, conducted by the Soviet and NSWP ground forces in East Germany, Poland, and Czechoslovakia, for a total of 57 divisions (including 3 in category 2 and 5 in category 3) deployed for action after approximately nine days of mobilization.

—What might be termed the expected threat to all of Western Europe from the Pyrenees to the North Sea, which would involve as many as 90 divisions (the 57 in Eastern Europe plus the 33 from the three western military districts of the Soviet Union), all of them fully ready for an attack after only fourteen days of mobilization and deployment.

Several characteristics of these hypothetical attacks are particularly noteworthy. Preparations for them are assumed to occur with remarkable speed and efficiency; all Pact forces reach full combat power and effectiveness even though, in the two most serious cases, divisions in categories 2 and 3 participate in the attack. Moreover, unless NATO takes herculean measures to respond to these rapid preparations, with the heaviest burden falling on the most distant member (the United States), the attack occurs before all available allied forces have deployed to their wartime positions. Finally, the third case—involving 90 fully combat-ready Pact divisions—is both too massive and too fast in preparation for the allies to handle, even after a large investment in expensive airlift and equipment pre-positioned in Germany for reinforcing U.S. divisions. The Alliance also is likely to crumble before the Pact's 57 divisions if U.S. ground forces and airlift happen to be caught fighting in another theater of war such as the Persian Gulf. Indeed, it is frequently assumed that an attack on Europe follows almost immediately on the heels of U.S. involvement elsewhere.

How valid are these tests and the inferences to be drawn from them? No one doubts that the Pact can put together an invasion force of some kind in a very short time. But how well organized it would be, and whether the units would have the combat power and effectiveness generally attributed to them, is quite another matter. In general, high mobilization rates entail a substantial loss of performance; full performance is likely to be achieved only with relatively gradual preparations. Configured as they are, the forces of the Warsaw Pact cannot escape the trade-off between speed and effectiveness.

While it is unlikely that the Pact could prepare for war without providing warning to NATO, it must be conceded that NATO could be caught short-handed by a Pact mobilization and deployment. It is important to understand why. NATO would probably receive strong indications of large-scale Pact military activities within hours of their initiation. In that sense, but only in that sense, the probability of surprise would be low.[8] Unfortunately, NATO is unlikely to exploit the warning

Table 4-7. Warsaw Pact Ground Forces and Their Availability for the Central Region of Europe

| | Warsaw Pact ground forces mobilize, deploy, and attack at: | | | | | | | | | |
| | M + 4[a] | | M + 9[a] | | M + 14[a] | | M + 90[a] | | M + 120[a] | |
Origin	Divisions	Combat power[b]	Divisions	Combat power[b]	Divisions	Combat power[b]	Divisions	Combat power[b]	Divisions	Combat power[b]
Soviet forces in										
East Germany	19	760,000	19	760,000	19	760,000	19	760,000	19	760,000
Czechoslovakia	...	...	5	194,000	5	194,000	5	194,000	5	194,000
Poland	...	...	2	72,000	2	72,000	2	72,000	2	72,000
USSR	...	...	...	...	33	1,201,200	33	1,201,200	53	1,929,200
East Germany	6	218,400	6	218,400	6	218,400	6	218,400	6	218,400
Czechoslovakia	5	200,000	10	400,000	10	400,000	10	400,000	10	400,000
Poland	...	...	15	462,000	15	462,000	15	462,000	15	462,000
Total	30	1,178,400	57	2,106,400	90	3,307,600	90	3,307,600	110	4,035,600

Sources: *Department of Defense Annual Report, Fiscal Year 1981*, p. 112; U.S. Department of the Army, *Field Manual: Maneuver Control*, FM105-5 (Dept. of the Army, 1973), apps. E, F, G; and author's estimates.
a. M stands for mobilization day.
b. Combat power is the fighting value of the force based primarily on firepower scores.

time it receives, particularly given the commingling of nuclear weapons with allied nonnuclear capabilities. NATO is reluctant to start alerting its forces except when the threat is immediate and evident, and is firmly opposed to delegating alerting authority to its senior military commanders. It has also rejected other measures to minimize this lag in response.

NATO's decisionmaking difficulties provide one explanation for the widespread impression of allied nonnuclear vulnerability. But what about the conventional capabilities themselves? Are they not the principal source of vulnerability? The answer depends in part on the method used to measure the outcome of hypothetical conflicts between NATO and the Pact. Static comparisons obviously are not very helpful for this purpose. They produce no outcomes, nor do they suggest remedial actions other than impractical proposals for more or less symmetrical forces—if the Pact has 110 divisions and 22,000 tanks, then NATO must have approximately equal numbers in order to prevent defeat.

Military analysts have developed more systematic methods of assessing the interaction of opposing forces. Though these methods do not represent the full complexity of a military engagement, they do allow a number of variables that affect the outcome of a battle to be taken into account: the firepower, effectiveness, mobility, and sustainability of the opposing forces; differences in terrain and the extent of man-made or natural obstacles; the characteristics of lines of communication and their vulnerability to ground and air attack; whether forces are on the offensive or defensive; the element of surprise, both strategic and tactical;[9] tactics such as concentrating offensive forces against particular sectors of the defense; and the manning of units, the degree of their training, and the state of their morale. Numerical values can be assigned to all of these factors, which can then be introduced into standard equations to yield calculations of the course and possible outcome of a conflict. How changes in any variable will affect a given outcome can also be calculated.

These methods have an interesting virtue: they are extensively discussed in the Soviet military literature, in a way suggesting that Soviet military planners take them seriously. They thus offer a means of assessing the performance of NATO forces using roughly the same means employed by the Soviets. Since deterrence is NATO's central purpose, it is not irrelevant that the two sides have this methodology in common.

Table 4-8. **NATO Ground Forces and Their Availability for the Central Region of Europe**

| | NATO ground forces mobilize, deploy, and defend at: | | | | | | | | | |
| Origin | M + 4 | | M + 9 | | M + 14 | | M + 90 | | M + 120 | |
	Divisions	Combat power	Divisions	Combat power	Divisions	Combat power	Divisions	Combat power	Divisions	Combat power
Belgium	2	50,000	2⅔	67,000	2⅔	67,000	2⅔	67,000	2⅔	67,000
Britain	4	104,000	5	130,000	5	130,000	5	130,000	5	130,000
Canada	⅓	13,000	⅔	25,000	⅔	25,000	⅔	25,000	⅔	25,000
Denmark	1	24,000	1⅔	40,000	1⅔	40,000	1⅔	40,000	1⅔	40,000
France	3	78,000	7	182,000	7	182,000	7	182,000	7	182,000
Netherlands	2⅓	70,000	3	90,000	3	90,000	3	90,000	3	90,000
United States										
In United States	...	...	3⅓	160,000	6⅓	304,000	9⅓	448,000	9⅓	448,000
In West Germany	5⅔	272,000	5⅔	272,000	5⅔	272,000	5⅔	272,000	5⅔	272,000
West Germany	12	420,000	14	490,000	14	490,000	14	490,000	14	490,000
Total	30⅓	1,031,000	43	1,456,000	46	1,600,000	49	1,744,000	49	1,744,000

Sources: IISS, *The Military Balance, 1981–1982*, pp. 4–10, 27–37; U.S. Dept. of the Army, *Field Manual: Maneuver Control*, apps., E, F, G; and author's estimates.

NATO Ground Forces

Central to any such analysis are NATO's ground forces. (See table 4-8.) If French and Danish ground forces are included in the order of battle for the central region—and it is at least as reasonable to include them as it is to count Polish and Czech forces on the Pact side—the NATO peacetime deployment amounts to around $30\frac{1}{3}$ divisions, of which 12 are West German and nearly 6 American. Within about three days of a NATO decision, these divisions could man their forward defensive positions in Germany. Within approximately nine days, the deployed force could be increased to about 43 divisions. This total could rise to 46 divisions in fifteen days (if U.S. plans for rapid reinforcement can be completed and implemented as intended) and thereafter to as many as 62 divisions, depending on the time available for deployment, the extent to which U.S. forces might be committed elsewhere, and whether NATO had gone forward with programs to organize, equip, and exercise the reserve formations it already carries on its books.

These are not unimpressive numbers. Furthermore, since German and American divisions are larger and more powerful than their equivalents in the Pact, simply counting divisions understates NATO's relative strength. The issue, however, is whether they would be powerful, effective, agile, and sustainable enough to stop the most challenging Pact attacks. In order to evaluate the effects of such variables and focus on outcomes rather than inputs, it is essential to go beyond the static balancing of forces. Again, though no such approach can yield certain answers, it makes sense to evaluate the performance of NATO forces using models that both U.S. and Soviet military planners tend to use.

These models require explicit statements about the firepower and effectiveness of opposing forces. Methods exist for computing both inputs, albeit in a highly aggregated form. The firepower potential of both the NATO and Warsaw Pact forces (and, more important, the firepower ratios) can be readily estimated from public sources. The effectiveness of firepower is not often treated as a separate variable and is sensitive to a variety of factors. Table 4-9 lists several of these factors and illustrates the rates of effectiveness that might be assigned to attacking and defending forces.

Once these statements about firepower and effectiveness are available, one can measure the expected results of the three standard Pact

Table 4-9. Basis for Effectiveness of Ground Forces

Mode	Probability of:				Overall probability of damage per day
	Acquiring targets	Firing weapons	Weapon reliability	Hitting targets	
Defense of					
Position	.45	.20	.90	.50	.040
Fortified zone	.45	.20	.90	.50	.040
Offense against					
Position	.45	.20	.90	.25	.020
Fortified zone	.45	.20	.90	.15	.012
Degraded offense against					
Position	.45	.16	.90	.25	.016
Fortified zone	.45	.16	.90	.15	.010

Source: U.S. Dept. of the Army, *Staff Officers' Field Manual: Organizational, Technical, and Logistical Data,* FM-101-10-1 (Dept. of the Army, 1971), pp. 4-6, 4-7.

attacks on NATO—those occurring at M + 4 (that is, after four days of mobilization), at M + 9, and at M + 14.[10] In addition, Pact attacks at M + 90 and M + 120 are analyzed, not only because they raise interesting problems but also because they are given so little attention.

Despite NATO's fear of surprise attacks, no doubt engendered in part by the view that they favor the Pact, the probability that the Soviet Union could put together an attacking force of 30 divisions in four days and would bet on catching NATO by surprise—all for the purpose of making a limited territorial gain and demonstrating a lack of allied will—is rather low. The worldwide consequences of such an action, even if it were successful and could be controlled, would be out of all proportion to the gains. Furthermore, NATO with its currently deployed ground forces can either stop such an attack in its tracks or pinch it off should it make some initial territorial gains. The key uncertainties are whether the allies would respond promptly to warning that preparations for the attack were under way, and whether they would be able and willing to concentrate the necessary forces on the correct axis of attack. These uncertainties give rise to more than an 80 percent probability of a Pact breakthrough sufficient to make substantial territorial gains in Germany, assuming the conflict were halted after seven days. (See table 4-10, case A-2.) The attack might also cut the peacetime U.S. line of communication to Bremerhaven, which runs dangerously close to allied forward defenses, as shown in figure 4-1.

The United States has proposed to minimize these and other uncertainties by moving the peacetime location of the U.S. divisions in

Germany much closer to their emergency war positions, at an estimated cost of about a billion dollars. Another way for the allies to achieve the same ends is to build permanent barriers along the border between East and West Germany.[11] It is estimated that a belt of quite effective obstacles to an attack could be created at a cost of about a million dollars a kilometer, or between $700 million and $800 million for the entire frontier. Standard military data indicate that such barriers would decrease the relative effectiveness of a given offensive force by as much as 40 percent. Thus they would provide a major hedge against a slow allied response to warning of both small and massive attacks. They would also reduce to essentially zero the probability that the enemy could achieve even a temporary advance with a smash and grab attack. Indeed, using 17 allied divisions supplemented by barriers, NATO should be able to halt even a concentrated attack by 30 Pact divisions, as shown in table 4-10 (case A-4).[12]

NATO's problems would be more complex and serious in the event of the hypothetical Pact attack with 57 divisions following nine days of preparation. As tables 4-5 and 4-6 indicate, an attack of this magnitude would involve all 26 category 1 Soviet divisions, while Eastern Europe would contribute 23 category 1, 3 category 2, and 5 category 3 divisions. More than 50 percent of the attacking force would be Eastern European. In the unlikely event that all these divisions could be brought to their estimated combat power and effectiveness (both of which are probably exaggerated), they would have better than a 70 percent chance of defeating the $30\frac{1}{3}$ deployed NATO divisions in a frontal attack (case B-1). This assumes that they face no special obstacles but that NATO's forces are still twice as effective as those of the Pact as a result of being initially on the defensive. Even if the presence of major barriers reduced the effectiveness of the attacker to 30 percent rather than 50 percent of the defender's effectiveness, the attacker would still have better than a 40 percent chance of driving back the allied forces, gaining increasing amounts of territory, and eventually destroying NATO (case B-2). According to these calculations, the main Pact ground forces would have advanced about 42 kilometers after seven days of war.

However, the combination of barriers and three more NATO divisions (for a total of 33) would give the Alliance near certainty of stalemating the Pact with at best minor territorial gains (case B-3). Without barriers, a NATO force of 44 divisions would be required at the assumed levels of effectiveness to achieve the same result (case B-4). Thus some

Table 4-10. **Hypothetical Conflicts between NATO and the Warsaw Pact in the Central Region of Europe**

Case	Time of attack	Warsaw Pact			NATO				NATO			Probability of Pact success	Advance through D + 7 (kilometers)
		Divisions	Combat power[a]	Effectiveness	Divisions	Combat power[a]	Effectiveness	Type of attack	Strategic delay	Tactical error	Barriers		
A-1	M + 4	30	1,178.4	.020	30⅓	1,031.0	.04	Frontal	No	No	No	..	..
A-2	M + 4	30	1,178.4	.020	30⅓	1,031.0	.04	Concentrated	No	Yes	No	.80	122
A-3	M + 4	30	1,178.4	.020	30⅓	1,031.0	.04	Concentrated	No	No	No	..	..
A-4	M + 4	30	1,178.4	.012	16⅔	657.0	.04	Concentrated	Yes	No	Yes	..	..
A-5	M + 4	30	1,178.4	.012	30⅓	1,031.0	.04	Concentrated	No	Yes	Yes	..	..
B-1	M + 9	57	2,106.4	.020	30⅓	1,031.0	.04	Frontal	No	No	No	.70	51
B-2	M + 9	57	2,106.4	.012	30⅓	1,031.0	.04	Frontal	Yes	No	Yes	.45	42
B-3	M + 9	57	2,106.4	.012	33	1,159.0	.04	Frontal	Yes	No	Yes	..	..
B-4	M + 9	57	2,106.4	.020	44	1,489.5	.04	Frontal	No	No	No	..	..
B-5	M + 9	57	1,685.1	.010	31	1,054.0	.04	Frontal	Yes	No	Yes	..	..
B-6	M + 9	57	1,685.1	.016	31⅓	1,066.0	.04	Frontal	Yes	No	No	..	..
B-7	M + 9	57	2,106.4	.012	30⅓	1,031.0	.04	Concentrated	Yes	No	Yes	.60	66
B-8	M + 9	57	2,106.4	.012	42	1,418.5	.04	Concentrated	No	Yes	Yes	..	..
B-9	M + 9	57	2,106.4	.012	36⅓	1,271.0	.04	Concentrated	Yes	Yes	Yes	.50	50

B-10	M + 9	57	1,896.0	.016	43	1,456.0	.04	Concentrated	No	No	No	.50	27
B-11	M + 9	57	1,896.0	.010	43	1,456.0	.04	Concentrated	No	Yes	Yes	..	..
C-1	M + 14	90	3,307.6	.012	36⅓	1,271.0	.04	Frontal	Yes	No	No	.70	105
C-2	M + 14	90	2,646.1	.010	36⅓	1,271.0	.04	Frontal	Yes	No	No	.30	48
C-3	M + 14	90	2,646.1	.010	43	1,456.0	.04	Concentrated	No	No	No	..	..
D-1	M + 90	90	3,307.6	.020	46	1,600.0	.04	Concentrated	No	No	No	.90	173
D-2	M + 90	90	3,307.6	.012	46	1,600.0	.04	Concentrated	No	No	Yes	.55	60
D-3	M + 90	90	2,977.0	.016	46	1,600.0	.04	Concentrated	Yes	No	No	.85	134
D-4	M + 90	90	2,977.0	.010	46	1,600.0	.04	Concentrated	Yes	Yes	Yes	..	..
D-5	M + 90	90	3,307.6	.020	49	1,744.0	.04	Concentrated	No	No	No	.85	136
D-6	M + 90	90	3,307.6	.012	49	1,744.0	.04	Concentrated	No	No	Yes	.35	34
D-7	M + 90	90	3,307.6	.012	52	1,820.0	.04	Concentrated	No	No	Yes	..	..
E-1	M + 120	110	4,035.6	.020	46	1,600.0	.04	Concentrated	No	No	No	.95	207
E-2	M + 120	110	4,035.6	.012	46	1,600.0	.04	Concentrated	No	No	Yes	.75	126
E-3	M + 120	110	4,035.6	.020	49	1,744.0	.04	Concentrated	No	No	No	.95	184
E-4	M + 120	110	4,035.6	.012	49	1,744.0	.04	Concentrated	No	No	Yes	.70	90
E-5	M + 120	110	4,035.6	.012	52	1,820.0	.04	Concentrated	No	No	Yes	.65	76
E-6	M + 120	110	4,035.6	.012	62	2,220.0	.04	Concentrated	No	No	Yes	..	..
E-7	M + 120	110	4,035.6	.012	70	2,552.0	.04	Concentrated	No	Yes	Yes	..	..

Source: Author's estimates based on data in tables 4-4, 4-6, 4-7, 4-8, 4-9, and on equations in the appendix.

a. In thousands.

combination of barriers and a relatively small number of additional divisions—well within the ability of the United States and its allies to provide within nine days—should give NATO high confidence of halting a frontal attack of this scale and speed. Moreover, if the Pact's overall effectiveness were reduced by as little as 20 percent to account for the lower readiness of some of the divisions used in the attack, NATO would need the barriers but only 31 divisions to achieve the same result (case B-5). If, in addition, the Pact's combat power were reduced by as little as 20 percent to correct for the exaggerated estimates of enemy firepower, NATO would need $31\frac{1}{3}$ divisions but not the barriers (case B-6).

Lest these results seem excessively optimistic, it must be stressed that they do not allow for the virtual certainty that the Pact commander would concentrate his forces heavily against one or more sectors of the allied front and attempt a breakthrough followed by the encirclement of major NATO units. With perfect information and a frictionless response to the Pact concentrations, the NATO commander could deal with this tactic as readily as with a steamroller assault undertaken uniformly all along the front. But conditions of perfect information and absence of friction are rarely met. Barriers could help to deal with these dangers in two ways—by compelling the attacker to concentrate his forces even more heavily if he is to achieve his breakthrough within a short time, and by permitting the defender to man the front more lightly and hold a larger proportion of his mobile forces in reserve. Barriers thus would ease the defending commander's uncertainty and facilitate his decision to reallocate his units and commit the reserve forces at his disposal.

But even with barriers, a NATO force of no more than $30\frac{1}{3}$ divisions will give Allied Forces, Center Region virtually no reserve to deal with enemy concentrations. Slipping forces laterally across the front to oppose them, especially an enemy adept at bluffs and feints, will not provide a defense of high confidence. At full strength and effectiveness, the Pact's 57 divisions in fact would have a 60 percent chance of defeating this force (case B-7). NATO might be able to withstand a frontal assault with slightly more than 1.8 times its own combat power, so long as barriers were in place. But the threat of concentrations and the need for uncommitted and mobile reserves, combined with the high probability of imperfect information and friction in the response, could drive the tolerable firepower ratio down overall to 1.45—which in this case would set the NATO requirement at 42 divisions (combined with barriers), rather than $30\frac{1}{3}$ divisions, after nine days of mobilization (case B-8).

A force of this size is well within NATO's current capabilities, although no more than 4 of the additional 12 divisions could be expected to come from the United States under existing plans. The European allies could and would have to provide the remainder. However, if the NATO response to warning were seriously delayed, the deployment of so large a reinforcement might prove impossible. Conceivably the total defending force would amount to no more than $36\frac{1}{3}$ divisions. In that event, if the Pact achieved tactical surprise with its concentrations, it could have perhaps a 50 percent chance of achieving its immediate objectives despite barriers on the NATO side (case B-9).

The Pact's 90-division attack, occurring after only fourteen days of preparation, is generally considered both the likeliest case and the one most dangerous for NATO. However, a third of the attacking force would be Eastern European and would probably contain 10 category 2 and 31 category 3 divisions, as shown in tables 4-6 and 4-7. During the same fourteen days, NATO (assuming no commitment of forces to other theaters) could probably put together a defending force of approximately 46 divisions. Given its cumbersome decisionmaking, however, the most likely eventuality is that NATO could place no more than $36\frac{1}{3}$ divisions in forward positions before the Pact attacked. Obviously a Pact force at fully estimated combat power and effectiveness would have a very high probability (as much as 70 percent) of defeating $36\frac{1}{3}$ NATO divisions with a frontal attack, even if the allies were shielded by barriers (case C-1). The standard expectation is that the Pact would have advanced more than 100 kilometers after seven days of fighting. But if the Pact's combat power is degraded by only 20 percent and its effectiveness is reduced by no more than 20 percent because of the number of low-readiness divisions, the $36\frac{1}{3}$ NATO divisions combined with barriers would have nearly a 70 percent chance of thwarting a frontal assault (case C-2). More realistically, if the same Pact force (with its reduced combat power and effectiveness) is allowed to concentrate in particular sectors for an attempted breakthrough, NATO would not have high confidence of controlling the situation, even assuming defenses in depth, with fewer than 43 divisions (case C-3).

The reductions made in Pact performance seem entirely plausible and warranted. That NATO could mobilize and deploy more than $36\frac{1}{3}$ divisions in fourteen days is quite obvious. The United States and France together can provide as many as $9\frac{2}{3}$ more, giving the Alliance a total of 46 divisions. A firm French commitment to provide at least 7 divisions fourteen days after mobilization would clearly be desirable. Moreover, if this kind of contingency is to be taken seriously, as it should be, NATO decisionmaking and alerting procedures will have to be improved. To the extent that allied nuclear capabilities are separated from the conventional forces the necessary improvements should be possible, particularly in the form of accelerated political action and alerting procedures tied to Pact behavior.

As has already been suggested, the designers of the three standard planning contingencies have envisioned large Pact forces with full combat power and effectiveness, and at the same time have put NATO in a position in which it could not possibly mobilize and deploy its full capability before the Pact attacked. The key assumption behind these contingencies has been that time would work to the advantage of NATO, and that the worst cases for the Alliance therefore would be the short-warning cases. The Pact thus has been credited with the ability to achieve feats of mobilization, deployment, and force performance that no one within NATO knows how to duplicate. To give only one example, U.S. National Guard divisions, which may be on a par with Soviet category 2 divisions and are certainly in better condition than the Pact's category 3 units, would currently require ninety days of additional organization and training before the Army would willingly commit them to combat. They could be deployed earlier, but only at the cost of reduced combat power, effectiveness, and tactical agility.

Apart from this kind of anomaly, there are grounds for questioning whether the current planning contingencies represent the most plausible worst cases confronting NATO. Considering the manifest problems the Soviet Union has with its Eastern European allies, would it not be more realistic to assume that Soviet leaders need time not only to bring the Pact forces to their full combat power and effectiveness, but also to create political conditions more conducive to the loyalty of these "allies" than would exist if the Pact were to attack NATO "out of the blue" and virtually without provocation? Might not those leaders also wish to build up the Pact attack force beyond the 90 divisions usually attributed to it? Certainly the Kremlin's behavior with respect to Czechoslovakia in 1968, Afghanistan in 1979, and Poland in 1981 suggests that both the political and the military leaders prefer to trade speed of action for confidence in the performance of their forces, and that they are willing to invest three or four months (at the expense of strategic but not tactical surprise) to achieve conditions they consider favorable to decisive action.

Standard military analysis, which may now be used more by Russian than by American staffs, would support the Kremlin in this predisposition.[13] Suppose for a moment that after about three months the Pact could have a fully ready and dependable force of 90 divisions. Such a force, combined with the tactics of concentration, would have better than a 90 percent chance of defeating even the NATO force of 46 divisions, assuming no major barriers had been built (case D-1). If the attacking force were built up to 110 divisions at full combat power and effectiveness in 120 days, its chances of defeating the 46-division NATO force would rise to about 95 percent (case E-1). NATO barriers would reduce these odds considerably—in the first instance to about 55 percent (case D-2) and in the second to 77 percent (case E-2). But if NATO wanted very high confidence in its nonnuclear deterrent under these conditions—say, less than a 10 percent probability that its defenses would fail—it would have to do much more than build barriers. Unless substitutes for standard armored and mechanized formations can be made acceptable to the military authorities—whether through new technologies such as Assault Breaker or more specialized units adapted to the terrain—at least 6 more standard divisions must be added to deal with the 90-division threat, for a total of 52 allied armored and mechanized divisions (case D-7), and another 10, for a total of 62, to contain the 110-division threat (case E-6). As many as 8 more divisions, for a total of 70, would be needed against the 110-division threat in order to gain high confidence of defeating Pact concentrations achieved with the advantage of tactical surprise (case E-7).

Ground Force Programs

The allies could not make available even the smaller total of 62 divisions in 90 to 120 days from their existing resources. Among them they have enough active-duty and reserve formations on the books to provide that total, but currently no more than 49 divisions would be available from Europe, Canada, and the United States. (See table 4-7.) The remaining 13 divisions—5 from the United States and 8 from Europe—would have to be drawn from the reserves of the various countries. In principle this would leave the U.S. Army and Marine Corps with 16 other divisions (mostly in the reserves) for contingencies in Norway, the Persian Gulf, and Korea. But as a practical matter, both Europe and the United States would have to invest considerably more in the equipment and training of their reserve forces—and in sealift—than they presently do. Assuming that standard armored and mechanized divisions would be required and that they would be given increased training, the six-year cost for this hedge of 13 divisions would come to $45.4 billion in 1983 dollars. To approach anything like the equivalent of 70 divisions, NATO would probably have to rely on substitutes for ground forces such as tactical aircraft.

Barriers and greater emphasis on equipped and trained reserve units do not exhaust the list of improvements NATO needs to ensure a high-confidence conventional defense in central Europe. In the event of an emergency, it is already planned to shift the U.S. line of communication from Bremerhaven to Antwerp, which can handle up to 340,000 tons of military cargo a day, or enough to supply 85 U.S. division slices. To provide for at least 62 divisions, air force needs, and the civilian economy, however, and to hedge against damage to Antwerp, restoration of the line of communication through France would be most desirable, preferably in peacetime. The move could entail a six-year cost of $2 billion in 1983 dollars.

Then there is the difficult issue of war reserve stocks. The United States is already engaged in a program to provide 60 days' worth, based on the belief that combat consumption will be high. These stocks consist of modern munitions, other combat consumables, and a number of capital items such as tanks and artillery for U.S. forces oriented toward Europe. The other allies have neither supplies nor plans for war reserve stocks of comparable size. What they or the United States, for that matter, should set as their objectives is by no means certain. The U.S. military services argue that since there is no assurance that either side will use nuclear weapons, plans must be made for a conventional war of indefinite duration. Traditionally this is assumed to require stocks sufficient to last 180 days—enough to sustain allied forces until production lines can keep pace with combat consumption.

A more important question is whether the forces of the Warsaw Pact have sufficient war reserve stocks to fight at high rates of consumption for an extended period of time. The prevailing wisdom holds that they do, although the evidence for that claim is quite thin. Given the uncertainties, it would be prudent for the European allies to increase their stocks to at least 45 days' worth of consumables for 42 divisions in order to have reasonable confidence of being able to outlast the Pact. This could require a total outlay, primarily for modern munitions, of up to $40.8 billion in 1983 dollars over a period of six years. If units are exercised more frequently and live ammunition is fired on a regular basis, current consumption probably would require that production lines be kept open even after war reserve stockpiles have been filled, thus preserving the ability to convert to high output with little delay. For a 42-division force, the incremental cost of such a policy for six years is estimated at $4.3 billion in 1983 dollars.

Uncertainty about the decision to use nuclear weapons and about the consequent length of a conventional war raises questions that go well beyond the size of the forces and the stocks that NATO should maintain. One of them concerns the possibility that the Pact might decide to use chemical weapons and the response NATO should make. The Alliance's position in the past has been that any resort to chemical weapons by the Pact would be met by nuclear retaliation. However, the growing emphasis within NATO on the acquisition of defenses against chemical agents, and the U.S. plan to stockpile binary chemical shells and bombs as replacements for older stocks, strongly suggest that at least implicitly the United States has decided that a "tit-for-tat" deterrent is more credible. Whether NATO should allocate additional resources to chemical weapons is by no means clear. Just as there is uncertainty whether the Soviet Union has actually stockpiled nuclear weapons in Eastern Europe, so there are debates about the extent to which the Russians have developed an operational capability for offensive chemical warfare. Consequently the case for going beyond current programs and outlays remains to be made.

A much more difficult question is whether, in the event of a conventional conflict lasting more than a month, NATO in general and the United States in particular could find trained manpower and units to replace individuals lost to combat and illness, and to allow for the rotation of battleworn divisions in need of rest and refitting. With the all-volunteer force, the United States can maintain an active-duty military establishment of slightly more than 2 million men and women, a paid reserve force of about 900,000, and an individual ready reserve (IRR) of 419,000. In the event of a small-scale conflict, this establishment can probably meet the manpower needs of its combat units by using active-duty forces in the initial stages of the conflict, the IRR for fillers, and the

National Guard and Reserve for unit replacement and rotation. If wars occurred more or less simultaneously in Europe and in some other theater of great importance, and if the Warsaw Pact mobilized the greater-than-expected threat of 90 to 110 fully combat-ready divisions, the personnel in the active-duty ground forces and the IRR would not suffice, short of conscription, to sustain combat beyond several weeks. Moreover, National Guard and Reserve units would be needed as part of the initial NATO defense.

The ground forces of the Pact would suffer equal if not greater attrition. But given the large number of reservists and stocks of older equipment at their disposal, they would be better able to rotate their divisions and bring them back to full strength. If the United States, on the other hand, were to reinstitute conscription at the outset of such a conflict, individual replacements would emerge from the training pipeline only after about four months and unit replacements could not be deployed for at least a year. To expect and plan for a high-confidence defense of much more than a month's duration in central Europe, along with the other contingencies for which the United States must prepare, thus strongly implies the reintroduction of peacetime conscription in America. The cost over a six-year period would be approximately $72 billion in 1983 dollars, with the burden falling entirely on the United States.

Berlin

The thorniest question of all concerns the fate of West Berlin under these conditions. It is widely assumed that, located as it is, the city is militarily indefensible. Yet despite the twists and turns in NATO policy, the western sectors of Berlin seem safer today than they were in the supposedly halcyon years of American strategic nuclear superiority. Conceivably that freedom continues to rest entirely on Soviet fear of allied nuclear action, although that threat (however latent) did not suffice to prevent the Berlin blockade of 1948. At least as conceivable an explanation is recognition by the Soviet leaders that a major move against West Berlin not only would have deep and lasting repercussions within NATO, but also could lead to immediate military reprisals by the allied powers responsible for Berlin. NATO prides itself, perhaps excessively, on being a strictly defensive alliance with restricted territorial responsibilities. Yet no alliance can forgo some degree of counteroffensive action, and the allied "occupying" powers (Great Britain, France, and the United States) in conjunction with West Germany have the capability to make imposing military demonstrations on the ground and in the air along the access routes to Berlin, and even to carve out salients within East Germany itself. For at least twenty years the responsible allied powers have in fact recognized that, at a minimum, preliminary measures such as these would have to precede the fateful nuclear decision. Thus, whether NATO remains committed to the possibility of first use or adopts NFU as its policy, any moves to strengthen allied conventional capabilities will contribute to the security of West Berlin.

The Contribution of Tactical Airpower

Although the U.S. Army usually considers the outcome of the conventional land battle to be solely the function of opposing ground forces and their interaction, tactical air power can influence the battle in four ways—by keeping enemy aircraft from disrupting NATO's ground and air operations, by eliminating the Pact's theater-based nuclear capability, by interdicting enemy lines of communication, and by providing close air support to allied ground forces. In the performance of these missions, there is a point at which tactical aircraft can substitute for additional ground forces, whether by directing highly mobile firepower against enemy units, or by eroding the performance of those units through the destruction of their supplies and the ability of the line of communication to deliver them. The enemy, of course, may have a comparable capability that would counterbalance the effects of allied air power.

It had been assumed until recently that NATO could compensate in part for its alleged weaknesses in ground forces by means of its tactical air forces. Now, however, there is a growing tendency to discount or dismiss that advantage on several grounds—the density and lethality of Warsaw Pact air defenses, the development by the USSR of the capability to conduct air superiority and interdiction operations of its own, the wholesale introduction of modern fighter-attack aircraft into the inventories of the Pact air forces, and the Pact's substantial numerical superiority in the air.

That the Pact has improved its capability for air defense and offense is hardly a matter for argument. That it threatens to eliminate NATO's advantages in tactical air power is more open to question. As the Israeli air force demonstrated against Syrian air defenses in June 1982, using largely U.S. equipment, Soviet-type surface-to-air missiles and radar-guided anti-aircraft artillery can apparently be neutralized or destroyed at extremely low cost to the attacker. As the Israelis also demonstrated in those engagements, front-line American aircraft armed with the latest air-to-air missiles can obtain extraordinarily high rates of kill against modern Soviet aircraft.

It will be argued that Syrians were operating the Soviet equipment, which in any event was less sophisticated than what NATO would encounter in central Europe, and that Israel may have the most highly trained and experienced tactical air force in the world. These arguments would be more persuasive were it not that Soviet personnel generally have had less combat experience than their Syrian counterparts, undergo much less rigorous (and less flexible) training than do U.S. and European air forces, and would be flying against more advanced U.S. (and possibly European) equipment than is being exported to Israel.

As to the Pact's numerical superiority, it comes from counting Soviet homeland air defenses as part of the threat, from omitting the French and Danish air forces altogether, and from failing to include the U.S. tactical aircraft that would be rapidly deployed to Europe in an emergency. When these unwarranted inclusions and exclusions are corrected, the expected tactical air deployments of NATO and the Pact in the central region are about equal in size but quite different in mission, as can be seen from table 4-11. NATO tends to invest less than the Pact in air defense and more in close air support, deep air superiority, and interdiction. It continues to have the superior tactical air forces, both in equipment and in skill.

Whether that superiority is sufficient in degree and kind to add to confidence in the allied conventional deterrent is more difficult to determine. As part of its blitzkrieg strategy, the Pact might well attempt to accompany its ground attack with a large-scale offensive against NATO air bases and nuclear capabilities. Because of low kill probabilities, poor maintenance, and allied air defenses, this attack would probably damage no more than 30 percent of an estimated 19,300 targets and collapse after about five days. (See table 4-12.) NATO more or less simultaneously would be committing roughly 16 percent of its offensive aircraft to close air support and the remaining 84 percent to the deep missions of air superiority, nuclear suppression, and interdiction. If the 441 aircraft flying close air support could make as many as three sorties

Table 4-11. NATO and Warsaw Pact Air Order of Battle in the Central Region of Europe

	M day			M + 14		
Alliance	*Fighter-attack*	*Fighter*	*Total*	*Fighter-attack*	*Fighter*	*Total*
NATO						
Belgium	90	36	126	90	36	126
Britain	228	112	340	228	112	340
Canada	42	...	42	66	...	66
Denmark	60	40	100	60	40	100
France	255	150	405	255	150	405
Netherlands	90	36	126	90	36	126
United States	612	...	612	1,572	...	1,572
West Germany	330	60	390	330	60	390
Total	1,707	434	2,141	2,691	434	3,125
Warsaw Pact						
Czechoslovakia	160	250	410	160	250	410
East Germany	50	300	350	50	300	350
Poland	220	430	650	220	430	650
Soviet Union	770	500	1,270	1,350	870	2,220
Total	1,200	1,480	2,680	1,780	1,850	3,630

Sources: IISS, *The Military Balance, 1981–1982*, pp. 5–37; and *Department of Defense Annual Report, Fiscal Year 1983*, p. III-38.

Table 4-12. Illustrative Air Superiority, Counter-Nuclear, and Interdiction Campaign in the Central Region of Europe

	NATO assets at:			Warsaw Pact assets at:		
Item	*D day*	*D + 5*	*D + 14*	*D day*	*D + 5*	*D + 14*
Fighter-attack aircraft	2,000	1,351	987	2,000	...	...
Aircraft shelters	2,000	1,821	1,821	3,500	2,099	370
Nuclear launchers	2,000	1,821	1,821	1,500	900	159
Surface-to-air missiles	1,500	1,365	1,365	3,000	1,798	319
Interdiction targets	300	274	274	200	121	22

Source: Author's estimates.

a day, they could provide the combat power, effectiveness, and mobility of more than 2⅔ standard U.S. divisions, an increment to allied ground forces that would go far toward neutralizing the Pact's efforts to deceive the allied commander, concentrate for a breakthrough, and achieve tactical surprise.

The NATO campaign to assure air superiority over East Germany and Poland, suppress targetable nuclear delivery systems, and interdict enemy reinforcements and supplies would have a good chance of achieving its first two objectives within fourteen days. The interdiction program, however, challenged to attack a relatively dense network of roads and railroad lines in Eastern Europe and supplies in East Germany for as many as two weeks of combat, would probably not have much effect on the combat power of the Pact ground forces until about the third week of the campaign. NATO air commanders could try for an earlier payoff from these sorties by reallocating some of them to close air support, but F-4s, F-15s, F-16s, and F-111s are not the ideal aircraft for this kind of mission.

It is frequently argued that NATO has overinvested in air superiority and interdiction at the expense of close air support. The U.S. Army in fact buys fragile and expensive attack helicopters to make up for what it considers to be Air Force neglect of close air support for the ground forces. Yet it would be difficult to argue that the allied forces should forgo the three main deep missions, especially if the suppression of enemy air defenses and sheltered aircraft can be accomplished using modern decoys, electronic countermeasures, and munitions at relatively low cost in allied aircraft—or possibly in the future with cheap cruise missiles as partial substitutes for manned aircraft. At a minimum, the threat posed by these missions forces the enemy to spread his defenses, shelter his aircraft, minimize the daylight movement of his reinforcements and replacements, protect his lines of communication, and maintain a major capability to repair damaged airfields, bridges, tunnels, rail lines, and switches. At a maximum, a successful campaign of air superiority and interdiction can substantially diminish the enemy's ability to continue an assault on NATO beyond a few weeks and can pave the way for an allied counteroffensive, if that should prove desirable. As the Israeli air force has persuasively demonstrated, waging such a campaign benefits from high technology incorporated into combat aircraft and combat support capabilities.

None of this is to say that NATO could not use a great many more close air support sorties for attacks on enemy ground concentrations, even allowing for the possibility of Pact attacks at night and in foul weather. To obtain them, however, would probably require the acquisition of more close air support aircraft rather than additional attack helicopters or the reallocation of aircraft poorly suited for the mission from the deep air superiority and interdiction campaign.

The U.S. Air National Guard and Reserve have more than enough units to provide the 9 additional wings of aircraft necessary to cope with the kinds of concentrations the Pact could develop with the greater-than-expected threat of 110 divisions. To gain still higher confidence in blunting the Pact air offensive, the European allies could usefully establish 21 reserve air squadrons of their own; they too have commercial pilots who would welcome the opportunity to fly military aircraft on weekends. These wings could be equipped with relatively short-range fighters such as the F-5G or the Mirage. To accommodate fully the planned U.S. aircraft reinforcements, the additional U.S. wings for close air support, and the new allied interceptor squadrons would necessitate completion of the program for collocated operating bases; access to bases in northeastern France would be desirable as well.

If these improvements were adopted, the United States should plan to spend a total of approximately $6.8 billion for additional A-10 aircraft. Over a period of six years, the European allies could expect to incur a cost of $22.3 billion (in 1983 dollars) for the reserve air squadrons and their aircraft. Completion of the program for collocated operating bases, including shelters for the reinforcing aircraft from the United States, would entail a one-time cost estimated at no more than $300 million in 1983 dollars.

NATO Budgets

What would these proposed changes imply for the cost of the allied deterrent? All members of NATO engaged in the defense of central Europe now spend about $263.2 billion a year (in U.S. prices) explicitly for that purpose. As can be seen from table 4-13, the U.S. share amounts to $138 billion, or about 52 percent of the total. If that share seems large, it is worth remembering that the United States produces roughly 55 percent of relevant allied national income. In the circumstances, the tax levied on Americans to support a longstanding mutual interest is not out of proportion to the levy imposed on allied citizens.

As the capabilities of the Soviet Union and to a much lesser extent those of Eastern Europe have improved, the members of NATO have pledged to seek an annual real increase of 3 percent in their respective defense budgets between 1979 and 1986. General Bernard W. Rogers, the current SACEUR, has suggested that a 4 percent real increase during each of the next six years would give NATO the kind of security it needs. Presumably his estimate omits naval augmentations, which fall within the province of SACLANT (Supreme Allied Commander, Atlantic).[14]

Table 4-13. NATO Resources Allocated to the Central Region of Europe[a]
Billions of 1983 dollars unless otherwise specified

Item	United States	Non-U.S. NATO[b]	Total
Poseidon warheads committed to SACEUR	1.0	...	1.0
Tactical nuclear capabilities	3.2	...	3.2
Ground forces	43.5	61.2	104.7
Naval forces	30.7	19.0	49.7
Tactical air forces	55.2	45.0	100.2
Long-range mobility forces	4.4	...	4.4
Total	138.0	125.2	263.2
Percent of total	52.0	48.0	100.0
National income	3,390.0	2,831.0	6,221.0
Percent of total	55.0	45.0	100.0

Source: Author's estimates.
a. The costs of all programs are calculated in U.S. prices.
b. Belgium, Britain, Canada, Denmark, France, the Netherlands, and West Germany.

How does an independent assessment of NATO's strategy and posture and of needed improvements in them fit with these official estimates? Whether the Alliance stays with MC-14/3 or adopts NFU as its basic guidance, the dimensions of the allied military problem and the means to its solution point in the same direction. The real issue is to determine what improvements legitimately can be charged to the NATO budget and how far to pursue them, recognizing that as higher confidence in the deterrent is acquired, the effort encounters diminishing returns to scale.

Strategic Nuclear Modernization

Such choices are particularly germane to the allied strategic nuclear forces. The United States, and Great Britain and France on a smaller scale, already possess second-strike strategic capabilities sufficient to deter attacks on their homelands. These capabilities and their Soviet counterparts are such that, although the nuclear powers profess to have no thought of a first strike, the mere possibility—and the consequences that would follow from its realization—causes all the members of this exclusive club to approach the nuclear threshold with fear and wariness engendered by the unknown.

To maintain fear and wariness might be said to constitute the main function of the strategic nuclear forces. Despite loose talk about Soviet strategic superiority, windows of vulnerability, or limited and protracted nuclear war, all the nuclear powers continue to have the gravest doubts about the feasibility of exercising much control over nuclear exchanges or of achieving an exploitable advantage from them. Short of agreements to reduce and control them, the strategic forces may require modest modernization and change. But it is simply not evident that any other additions or modifications will enlarge their role as part of the NATO deterrent or make their current role more credible.

However the NATO nuclear powers may choose to deal with the real or imagined problems facing the strategic forces, it seems fair to assume that these programs would be undertaken independently of NATO's existence. Thus, the costs of expanding or otherwise improving the American, British, or French strategic deterrents are not charged as increments to the current NATO budget.

Tactical Nuclear Modernization

The tactical nuclear forces deployed in and near Europe, primarily by the United States, are a different matter. Until recently their costs have been relatively modest because, except for the nuclear warheads themselves, their storage, and the special communications and custodial personnel that go with them, they rely primarily on launchers that have conventional warfare as their stated primary task. The main exceptions are the Lance and Pershing I missiles and, it can be argued, the Poseidon launchers committed to NATO. If the Pershing II and GLCM are deployed to Europe starting in 1983, they will significantly increase the cost to the United States of maintaining this part of the deterrent, now averaging $3.2 billion a year.

No matter how NATO may define the role of nuclear weapons in its strategy, it should be evident that the Soviet Union is at least as capable as the United States of using these weapons first. It should be equally evident that NATO's leaders will not arrive easily or quickly at a decision to release nuclear warheads to military commanders, whether for demonstrations or for wider use against military targets along the front or in Eastern Europe. In the circumstances, there is a strong case for worrying less about enhanced radiation weapons, earth penetrators, and other improved nuclear warheads, and for worrying more about the survivability of their launchers.

Pershing II and GLCM, at an estimated six-year cost of $8 billion (in 1983 dollars), are expected to be somewhat less vulnerable than currently deployed systems—Poseidon excepted. But no replacements are in sight

Table 4-14. **Incremental Resources Available between 1984 and 1989 for Strengthening the NATO Defense of the Central Region of Europe**
Billions of 1983 dollars

	Incremental resources available at an annual real increase of:	
Item	3 percent	4 percent
United States	90.7	123.9
Non-U.S. NATO	82.8	112.4
Total NATO	173.5	236.3
Modernization of the nuclear forces	12.7	12.7
Total for nonnuclear capabilities	160.8	223.6
Modernization of naval forces	32.8	32.8
Total for other nonnuclear capabilities	128.0	190.8

Source: Author's estimates.

for the shorter-range launchers, which not only are vulnerable to blanketing attacks by the relatively high yields of Soviet nuclear weapons but also interfere seriously with NATO's ability to establish and exploit its conventional defenses. To create a separate and mobile capability that would keep out of the way of the nonnuclear forces (perhaps by being based near the Rhine), that could survive a Soviet conventional or nuclear attack, and at the same time have the capacity on short notice to attack discrete targets at or near the front, will not be cheap. One way to meet these conditions is to deploy some 220 helicopters armed with 880 nuclear missiles, at a six-year cost of $4.7 billion in 1983 dollars. Other and cheaper methods may be found, particularly if the operational accuracy of cruise missiles lives up to the promise of development tests and ways to attack moving targets can be provided.

These outlays for the tactical nuclear forces, presumably to be incurred by the United States, would leave approximately $160.8 billion (in 1983 dollars) for the improvement of allied nonnuclear forces, assuming a 3 percent real increase each year for six years (table 4-14). If the average annual increase were 4 percent, the amount available would be $223.6 billion.

The case for making major improvements in NATO's conventional forces seems as persuasive under MC-14/3 as it would be under NFU. The Soviet Union, despite or perhaps because of the difficulties it has encountered in Eastern Europe, has been strengthening its ground and air forces oriented toward Western Europe. Because allied nuclear decisions are so likely to be slow in coming, if they come at all, NATO needs a powerful conventional shield behind which to consider its options. Since the strength of the Pact is exaggerated in many respects, to acquire the hedges necessary for a robust conventional defense does not appear to be an overwhelming task in terms of magnitude or cost.

Naval Modernization

The incremental cost of a stout conventional defense will depend on several considerations. The first is the extent to which the preferences and importunities of the U.S. Navy should be taken to coincide with NATO's highest-priority needs. If the ambitious naval shipbuilding program, centered as it is on additional attack carrier battle groups, is to be charged substantially against the Alliance obligations of the United States, either the American share of the NATO burden must rise, or the U.S. ability to provide additional ground and tactical air forces to the central region of Europe will be diminished.

The U.S. Second and Sixth Fleets, in the Atlantic and Mediterranean, respectively, will undoubtedly require new ships, but the case for expanding those fleets, particularly with more carrier battle groups, remains to be made. Much the same skepticism is warranted with respect to the navies of the European allies. What they need to protect the Atlantic and Mediterranean sea lines of communication is not more surface combatants, amphibious warfare ships, submarines, or patrol aircraft, but systematic replacement and modernization of the capabilities they already have. Thus, in addition to the $49.7 billion already allocated to the relevant allied navies in 1983, it is difficult to imagine how more than $32.8 billion (in 1983 dollars) could be usefully spent for NATO purposes over a six-year period.

A second consideration bearing on the incremental cost of these conventional hedges is the scale of the program on which NATO embarks. In the old allied defense plan for 1970 (ADP-70) and more recently in the long-term defense plan (LTDP), the Alliance committed itself to intricate and costly efforts that included not only programs to modernize and expand nuclear and conventional forces, but also to ambitious schemes to make the various national forces more integrated in their operations (interoperable), more standardized in their equipment and supplies, and more interdependent in their production of military goods and services.

Improving the Ground and Tactical Air Forces

An alternative and less costly approach is to postpone the effort to make NATO into a highly rational entity that can accomplish everything at once, and concentrate instead on a limited number of the most urgent military needs: barriers; war reserve stocks; an improved line of communication; expanded, better equipped, better trained, promptly available active-duty and reserve ground and tactical air forces; and an alerting procedure for the conventional forces that can operate independently of the system for alerting the theater nuclear forces and can respond promptly to mobilization and deployment actions by the Warsaw Pact.

A third consideration has perhaps the greatest budgetary importance for NATO, yet is seldom mentioned with respect to the conventional forces. It is the degree of confidence the allies want to have in their nonnuclear deterrent, given the uncertainties that exist about the intentions and capabilities of the Pact and about the length of time for which the conventional defense should be built to last. To provide a basis for determining levels of confidence, table 4-15 lays out five nonnuclear options containing a sequence of measures designed to increase the credibility of NATO's conventional deterrent. The options are arranged in order of their relative urgency. The costs are assumed to be cumulative.

The first option contains major barriers, an improved line of communication, fully funded collocated operating bases, and stocks for a total of thirty days of combat. It is intended to increase NATO's level of confidence against what might be termed the realistic threat, in which the Warsaw Pact forces are degraded in combat power and effectiveness because of their rapid mobilization and deployment and the conventional conflict lasts no more than thirty days.

The second option, which is incremental to the first and begins to hedge against the greater-than-expected threat, would increase NATO's probability of success by adding three allied divisions and their war reserve stocks for thirty days of combat.

The third option, also incremental, provides additional capabilities to hedge against the greater-than-expected threat: ten additional divisions and nine wings of close air support aircraft.

The fourth option further strengthens this hedge by acquiring forty-

Table 4-15. Options for Strengthening the Land-Based NATO Forces in the Central Region of Europe
Billions of 1983 dollars

Option and force sustainability	Six-year cost	Cumulative six-year cost
First: 30 days		
Barriers	1.0	. . .
Improved line of communication	2.0	. . .
Collocated operating bases	0.3	. . .
War reserve stocks and training: 34 divisions, 15 days	24.1	. . .
War reserve stocks and training: 25 wings, 15 days	8.9	. . .
Total	36.3	36.3
Second: 30 days		
Three allied reserve divisions[a]	9.3	. . .
War reserve stocks and training: 3 divisions, 30 days	4.3	. . .
Total	13.6	49.9
Third: 30 days		
Five allied reserve divisions[b]	15.5	. . .
War reserve stocks and training: 5 divisions, 30 days	7.1	. . .
Five U.S. reserve divisions	20.6	. . .
War reserve stocks and training: 5 divisions, 30 days	7.1	. . .
Nine U.S. reserve wings of close air support	6.8	. . .
War reserve stocks and training: 9 wings, 30 days	6.4	. . .
Sealift for 8 U.S. divisions	15.4	. . .
Total	78.9	128.8
Fourth: 45 days		
War reserve stocks and training: 47 divisions, 15 days	33.3	. . .
War reserve stocks and training: 34 wings, 15 days	12.1	. . .
Total	45.4	174.2
Fifth: indefinite		
U.S. conscription	72.0	. . .
Seven allied wings of interceptor aircraft	14.1	. . .
War reserve stocks and training: 7 wings, 45 days	7.4	. . .
Total	93.5	267.7

Source: Author's estimates
a. It is assumed that, of the 3 divisions, 2 come from West Germany and 1 from France.
b. It is assumed that, of the 5 divisions, ⅔ of a division comes from Britain, 3 from France, and 1⅓ from the Netherlands.

five days of war reserve stocks for all the allied ground and tactical air forces as well as for the U.S. reserve divisions and air wings.

The last option invests in additional hedges not only against the greater-than-expected threat but also against the possibility that the conventional phase of the conflict might last well beyond forty-five days.

Table 4-16. The Cost of the Incremental Options and Their Effect on the Balance of Forces in the Central Region of Europe

Costs in billions of 1983 dollars

Item	Incremental cost of option	NATO resources remaining at:		Force sustainability (days)	Forces available for combat at:				
		3 percent	4 percent		M + 4	M + 9ᵃ	M + 14ᵃ	M + 90	M + 120
Resources available (1984–89)	...	173.5	236.3	...	...	...	...	...	...
Nuclear and naval modernization	45.5	128.0	190.8	...	...	...	...	...	...
Current forces									
Warsaw Pact divisions	...	...	...	Uncertainᵇ	30	57	90	90	110
NATO divisions	...	...	...	15	30⅓	43	46	49	49
NATO close air support aircraft	...	...	...	15	252	252	441	441	441
First option	36.3	91.7	154.5						
Warsaw Pact divisions	...	...	...	Uncertainᵇ	30	57	90	90	110
NATO divisions	...	...	...	30	30⅓	43	46	49	49
NATO close air support aircraft	...	...	...	30	252	252	441	441	441

Second option										
Warsaw Pact divisions	13.6	78.1	140.9	Uncertain[b]	30	57	90	90	90	110 · 110
NATO divisions	...	...	...	30	30⅓	43	46	52	52	52 · 62
NATO close air support aircraft	...	...	...	30	252	252	441	441	1008	441 · 1008
Third option										
Warsaw Pact divisions	78.9	−0.8	62.0	Uncertain[b]	30	57	90	90	90	110 · 110
NATO divisions	...	...	...	30	30⅓	43	46	52	52	52 · 62
NATO close air support aircraft	...	...	...	30	252	252	441	441	1008	441 · 1008
Fourth option										
Warsaw Pact divisions	45.4	−46.2	16.6	Uncertain[b]	30	57	90	90	90	110 · 110
NATO divisions	...	...	...	45	30⅓	43	46	52	52	52 · 62
NATO close air support aircraft	...	...	...	45	252	252	441	441	1008	441 · 1008
Fifth option										
Warsaw Pact divisions	93.5	−139.7	−76.9	Uncertain[b]	30	57	90	90	90	110 · 110
NATO divisions	...	...	...	Indefinite	30⅓	43	46	52	52	52 · 62
NATO close air support aircraft	...	...	...	45	252	252	441	441	1008	441 · 1008

Source: Author's estimates based on tables 4-7, 4-8, 4-11, 4-14, 4-15.

a. Warsaw Pact forces are degraded by 10 percent in combat power and 20 percent in effectiveness at M + 9 and M + 14.

b. It is unlikely that the Warsaw Pact can sustain large-scale, intense combat for more than 30 days.

Planning for a nonnuclear war of that length would assume the renewal of peacetime conscription in the United States.

How the allied forces would change as a result of purchasing these options is summarized in table 4-16. The first option does not increase NATO's force structure, nor does the fourth. The main changes in force structure result from the second and third options. As the table indicates, NATO can acquire the programs for nuclear and naval modernization and essentially all of the first three options on the assumption of an annual 3 percent real increase in the NATO budget for the central region over the next six years. With a 4 percent real increase in each of those years, all but the last option can be afforded. Whether the fifth package is acquired will depend largely on the seriousness with which U.S. civilian leaders take the commitment to prepare for a nonnuclear war of indefinite duration.

The implications for deterrence of acquiring these incremental options are shown in table 4-17. The combination of the first three packages gives NATO high confidence of a successful defense for thirty days against both the realistic and the greater-than-expected threat, which could be a sufficient hedge, considering the rapid rates of consumption assumed in calculating war reserve stocks. Acquisition of the fourth option gives the Alliance high confidence of defending successfully against all five major attacks and somewhat less confidence of being able to outlast the Pact in a conflict lasting more than forty-five days. The consequence, even without the fifth option, should be a deterrent for the central region of Europe that provides substantially greater credibility, particularly in a crisis, than the present NATO posture, regardless of the strategy that is adopted.

How far NATO can go in purchasing these hedges will depend to a considerable degree on the economic health of its members.[15] As both the United States and the European members of NATO have discovered, to increase defense budgets in real terms during periods of economic recession is not only politically difficult but also damaging to the consensus for larger and more rational defenses. If it is to reach sensible goals for its collective military posture, the Alliance will have to combine increased spending for defense with economic recovery and sustained economic growth.

Adoption of something like the illustrative options will not prove easy, even with a rising economic tide that lifts all boats, especially since the options may understate the cost of instituting truly comprehensive

Table 4-17. The Probability of a Successful Nonnuclear Forward Defense of the Central Region of Europe by NATO as a Function of Incremental Options

Option and sustainability	*Probability of a successful forward defense after an attack at:*				
	M + 4	*M + 9*[a]	*M + 14*[a]	*M + 90*	*M + 120*
Current capabilities: 15 days					
NATO without close air support	.20	.50	.15	.15	.05
NATO with close air support	>.90	.85	.20	.15	.10
First option: 30 days					
NATO without close air support	>.90	>.90	>.90	.65	.30
NATO with close air support	>.90	>.90	>.90	>.90	.40
Second option: 30 days					
NATO without close air support	>.90	>.90	>.90	>.90	.35
NATO with close air support	>.90	>.90	>.90	>.90	.45
Third option: 30 days					
NATO without close air support	>.90	>.90	>.90	>.90	>.90[b]
NATO with close air support	>.90	>.90	>.90	>.90	>.90
Fourth option: 45 days					
NATO without close air support	>.90	>.90	>.90	>.90	>.90[b]
NATO with close air support	>.90	>.90	>.90	>.90	>.90
Fifth option					
NATO without close air support: indefinite sustainability	>.90	>.90	>.90	>.90	>.90[b]
NATO with close air support: 45-day sustainability	>.90	>.90	>.90	>.90	>.90

Source: Author's estimates based on tables 4-10 and 4-16, and on equations in the appendix.

a. Warsaw Pact forces are degraded by 10 percent in combat power and 20 percent in effectiveness at M + 9 and M + 14.

b. If the allied commander misallocates as many as three West German divisions because of tactical surprise, this probability falls to .65.

improvements in the deterrent for the central region. On the other hand, most of the options include the acquisition of orthodox and expensive ground and tactical air forces. Should the military authorities deem it feasible to combine barriers with lighter, less capital-intensive ground forces and to substitute cheaper missiles for penetrating manned aircraft against some targets in Eastern Europe, the options may overstate the resources that will be required.

To emphasize the importance of changing NATO's defense posture and to suggest the directions it should take if there is to be a highly credible deterrent in central Europe—and one that would remain credible in a crisis—is not to argue that a basic change of strategy is irrelevant to the problems of the Alliance. It is to argue that the benefits, externalities, and possible costs associated with NFU deserve separate and special analysis. Change is essential. It may be possible without NFU, although the record of progress is not encouraging. Whether it would founder on the rock of NFU remains to be examined.

Notes

1. *Annual Defense Department Report, FY 1976 and FY 197T*, pp. I-17–19.
2. *Annual Defense Department Report, FY 1978*, pp. 108–09.
3. *Department of Defense Annual Report, Fiscal Year 1981*, p. 108.
4. *Annual Defense Department Report to the Congress, Fiscal Year 1983*, p. II-18.
5. International Institute for Strategic Studies, *The Military Balance, 1981–1982* (London: IISS, 1981), pp. 12–13.
6. For a further discussion of the war at sea, see Charles DiBona and William O'Keefe, "Quantifying the Sealane Defense Problem," in Paul H. Nitze and others, *Securing the Seas: The Soviet Naval Challenge and Western Alliance Options* (Boulder, Colo.: Westview, 1979), pp. 337–82.
7. Alain C. Enthoven and K. Wayne Smith, *How Much Is Enough? Shaping the Defense Program, 1961–1969* (Harper and Row, 1971), pp. 132–42.
8. The standard tests assume that the Pact moves with such speed and efficiency that the Alliance can never catch up, but this assumption is misleading.
9. Strategic surprise is assumed to occur when the Warsaw Pact mobilizes and deploys its forces and attacks before NATO can realize its full potential for defense. Tactical surprise is achieved when NATO misjudges the location and magnitude of the main Pact concentration. Strategic surprise usually results from NATO's failure to respond promptly to a warning of Pact mobilization.
10. The results depend not only on firepower and effectiveness, but also on other factors such as division frontages, the length of the front, concentration, and mobility, and on the use of certain standard calculations about force engagements and movement of the front. An illustration of the methodology based on U.S. and Soviet sources is given in the appendix.
11. Malcolm W. Hoag of the Rand Corporation proposed such barriers in the early 1960s. Omar N. Bradley testified to the effectiveness of defensive obstacles during World War II in *A Soldier's Story* (Henry Holt, 1951), pp. 243–44. Such defenses can include sensors, minefields, tank traps, other man-made or natural obstacles, and protected firepower. They can be organized into one or more barriers arranged in some depth, and can consist variously of permanent installations or prefabricated and stockpiled components that can be emplaced in an emergency.
12. A concentrated attack is defined as one in which the Warsaw Pact commander covers the front with a screen of forces and concentrates his reserves in one or more sectors for a breakthrough attempt. A frontal attack, by contrast, assumes that the Pact commander distributes all his forces uniformly along the forward edge of the battle.
13. See Yu. V. Chuyev and Yu. B. Mikhaylov, *Forecasting in Military Affairs: A Soviet View* (Government Printing Office, 1980), brought to my attention by Professor Stephen M. Meyer of the Massachusetts Institute of Technology. The secretary of defense, however, has not yet announced an analytical window of vulnerability.
14. General Bernard W. Rogers, "The Atlantic Alliance: Prescriptions for a Difficult Decade," *Foreign Affairs*, vol. 60 (Summer 1982), p. 1155.
15. Robert W. Komer, "Maritime Strategy vs. Coalition Defense," *Foreign Affairs*, vol. 60 (Summer 1982), pp. 1136, 1141.

CHAPTER FIVE

PERSPECTIVES ON STRATEGY

Jonathan Alford

MILITARY alliances tend to be conservative rather than radical, and the way they arrive at a consensus is peculiarly sensitive to the relative political and military weight of their members. They are conservative because arriving at a consensus can be painful, involving as it must the reconciliation of conflicting interests. The members tend therefore to shirk fundamental revision of agreed policies even though the objective circumstances may have changed. Moreover, it is generally true, at least for NATO, that a consensus on common policies tends to be formulated in language that permits the maximum latitude for national interpretations of the policy. The reverse of that proposition is that a consensus is unlikely to be reached on the basis of language that is too precise, unduly binding, and incapable of multiple interpretations. Hence, for the Western Alliance, the doctrine of flexible response is permissive and remarkably unspecific as to the precise response the Alliance would be called upon to make to aggression. It is almost certainly best that it should be so.

The relative weight of the members of a formal alliance may, of course, change over time. An initially dominant member, able to dictate preferences to the rest and thus determine basic policy, may cease to be dominant as time goes by. When that happens, as seems to have happened in NATO, the process of arriving at agreed positions becomes slower and messier, which in turn makes the organization even more reluctant to undertake new initiatives or revise its policy. A relative shift in influence clearly has not occurred within the Warsaw Pact, although one must note that in more subtle ways the ability of the dominant partner, the USSR, to dictate policy has undergone a change. No longer can the Soviet Union demand and expect to receive unqualified support in Eastern Europe for its policies and preferences.

Alliance Dynamics

Within NATO, historic trends in postwar European security have undermined the basis for consensus. The first and arguably most important of these trends has been the relative shift in the strategic nuclear balance between the Soviet Union and the United States. It is fashionable to interpret this shift in the absolute numbers of strategic nuclear delivery systems or warheads and in their accuracy as if it were the state of the strategic balance alone that was important. In fact it is reasonable to argue that what matters has been the progressive reduction of American strategic nuclear options, beginning with the growing vulnerability of American cities to Soviet retaliation, a change that took place long before the Soviet Union attained anything approaching strategic parity. When the United States could no longer be certain of destroying Soviet intercontinental nuclear weapons before launch, the price for the United States of initiating nuclear strikes rose dramatically, and serious questions arose about the willingness of the United States to use nuclear weapons to defend Europe. While there probably was no precise moment of transition, it is reasonable to suppose that the perception of increasing American vulnerability began to be politically significant in about 1964.

The shift of itself did not increase the likelihood that the Soviet Union would attack the United States, for the levels of destruction that the one could cause to the other's homeland were by no means equal, and neither side doubted the outcome of a strategic nuclear exchange. Yet the belief that the American homeland was no longer safe affected both the American and the Western European calculus; American decisionmakers became fearful of any automaticity in nuclear escalation resulting from conflict in Europe, and Europeans grew fearful that an American president would not deliberately raise the level of nuclear violence if deterrence failed. Transferring that assumption to the Kremlin, Western Europeans began to sense the hollowness of deterrent threats that rested ultimately on threats to invoke nuclear attacks on the Soviet homeland in retaliation for conventional transgression in Europe. Soviet attainment of a survivable intercontinental nuclear capability thus had the effect of limiting Western retaliatory options while loosening the constraints on Soviet options in Europe, especially the conventional option. By the same token it increased the political and military importance of the conventional balance of forces in Europe. So long as the United States could credibly threaten to use strategic nuclear weapons against the Soviet Union if it invaded Western Europe, it was reasonable to suppose that the resulting asymmetrical deterrence would hold the Soviet Union in check. It mattered little that NATO's conventional forces were considerably weaker than the Soviet Union's so long as the continental United States was essentially invulnerable to strategic nuclear attack. With the advent of Sputnik I and the ensuing Soviet ability to hold a very few American cities hostage, the calculus changed; from hardly mattering at all, conventional force levels became critical in determining whether the Soviet Union had a conventional option in Europe.

It took much longer for an understanding of what had happened to permeate both political circles and the public consciousness. The United States still looked much more powerful than the USSR, and indeed was. And because of the cost implications, people preferred to pretend that the new strategic reality was something other than what it was. They were reassured in the knowledge that the possibility of nuclear escalation continued to restrain Soviet aggression in Europe. Just as Americans could no longer be certain that war in Europe would not escalate to the continental United States, so the Soviet leaders could not be certain that a conventional war in Europe could be kept conventional, with all the attendant dangers to the Soviet homeland if it could not. So long as the balance of probabilities was—and is—that a war in Europe would get out of control, both superpowers, sensing their mutual vulnerability, would be extremely chary of taking risks. Given the concentration of nuclear weapons based in and targeted on Europe, a war involving the alliances in Europe seems more likely to escape control than would a war in any other part of the world.

Therein is the fundamental paradox of European security. While deterrence of Soviet ambitions may prove quite durable in the sense that Soviet leaders appear unlikely, as a deliberate act of policy, to invoke the risk of nuclear escalation by invading Western Europe, some unintended crisis may nevertheless bring East and West to the brink. NATO then would have thrust upon it the choice whether to defend against conventional attack solely with conventional forces on the assumption that nuclear weapons are not used first by the aggressor, or to employ nuclear strikes to bolster a failing defense. NATO need not make that decision at the outset of a war, but unless the nuclear capability survives the conventional phase of a conflict, the Alliance will have no option to resort to nuclear weapons short of calling on U.S. intercontinental forces.

Nor does the Soviet Union necessarily have to decide now whether to resort to nuclear weapons at the outset of a war in Europe. Evidence about Soviet theater nuclear policies is scanty, but the patterns of procurement and deployment of conventional and nuclear systems over the past three decades seem to indicate a desire to retain a preemptive first-strike theater nuclear option, a secure second-strike theater retaliatory option, a tactical nuclear option, and a conventional damage-limiting option designed to reduce the theater nuclear threat to the USSR. These capabilities impute a purposefulness to Soviet nuclear and conventional programs that may in fact be absent, yet Soviet acquisitions are not inconsistent with such an interpretation. Soviet theater weapons have become more survivable and accurate, covering a longer range and a greater variety of potential missions over time. It seems prudent to assume that the longer-range nuclear delivery systems—aircraft and ballistic missiles—now have sufficient accuracy, yield, and number to preempt NATO's theater nuclear assets as they are currently disposed, and could make it virtually impossible for NATO to respond with in-theater weapons other than the sea-based Poseidon and Trident missiles allotted to the Supreme Allied Commander, Europe. Furthermore the SS-20 missile, unlike the earlier SS-4s and SS-5s, is a relatively secure second-strike system well able to ride out any Western nuclear or conventional attack through mobility and dispersal. By acquiring a variety of quite survivable shorter-range "battlefield" systems—missiles, nuclear-capable artillery, and nuclear-capable aircraft—the Soviet Union has become at least as able as NATO to use nuclear ordnance to affect the tactical outcome of a ground war. Finally, in anticipation of a period of conventional hostilities or of actively seeking to restrict a war to the conventional level, the USSR has acquired systems—mainly medium-range strike aircraft—that could destroy many if not all of NATO's theater nuclear assets by conventional means before they could be used, thus limiting the damage the Soviet Union might subsequently expect to suffer if the West did decide to resort to theater nuclear weapons. This capability is the result of NATO's excessive reliance on dual-capable aircraft tied to fixed bases that are vulnerable to conventional attack.

Recognizing the dangers arising from at least the first and last of these options, NATO determined in its December 1979 decision on intermediate-range nuclear forces to make its theater nuclear systems a great deal more survivable. Whatever the merits of "coupling" arguments and of the need to place the USSR itself at risk, it was surely prudent to attempt to deny, by dispersal of assets and by deceptive basing, both a preemptive nuclear and a preemptive conventional option to the Soviet Union. Related to the vulnerability argument was a recognition that Soviet defenses against NATO's current theater nuclear systems had been considerably improved.

NATO tends to conceive of itself as an exclusively defensive alliance, neither intending to attack nor capable of attacking the Warsaw Pact countries. Nor has it ever set out to acquire that capability. Yet few if any weapon systems are unambiguously defensive. There is simply no way of distinguishing satisfactorily between an intent to defend and an intent to attack when considering such things as long-range strike aircraft and nuclear weapons placed on long-range delivery systems. A main battle tank remains a main battle tank whether it is intended to buttress an antitank defense and counterattack, or to spearhead an attack. Moreover, it would be unrealistic for a group of nations determined to conduct a robust defense to deny itself some weapon systems that are as appropriate for the offense as for the defense, precisely because an effective defense will rely upon counterattack, interdiction, and destruction of the attacker's assets before they can be brought to bear on the defense.

While the kinds of systems that are purchased do not permit a distinction between defensive or offensive designs, the numbers of particular systems and their combination may indicate a desire to create a particular military option in war, as may officially enunciated doctrine or observation of the pattern of exercising from which doctrine can be inferred. Yet here, too, the possibility exists that states may prefer to deter a putative opponent by being prepared to attack first when threatened. An offensive defense has both logic to recommend it and, in certain circumstances, history and geography to justify it. It would be preferable for international stability were it not so, but possession of the ability to attack preemptively or preventively is a prudent protective measure, capable of deterring someone whose intentions are suspect.

In tracing the development of the military forces of the Warsaw Pact since its formation, it is at least arguable that fear of the West and of China may have helped drive the Soviet Union to acquire a rather impressive deterrent in the form of offensive conventional military forces of several kinds. The need to garrison the Soviet empire goes some way to explain the size and characteristics of its forces in Eastern Europe, which do not resemble what the West would consider to be internal security forces. Nonetheless, the high degree of mobility required to fit Soviet doctrine for conventional war is also an essential attribute of internal security forces. The Soviet Union has tended to quell dissent among its allies with massive deployments of armored firepower, which could account for Soviet tank and motorized rifle divisions structured for a rapid conventional assault. As Jacek Kuron has remarked, the "Soviet tank factor" has a powerful influence on Polish politics.

Moscow's Conventional Options

Whatever its motives, the Soviet Union has created conventional military options that are exploitable in war. The central question for European security is whether Moscow envisages three distinct options or only one. If there are three, they might be an unreinforced attack, a reinforced attack, and a maritime blockade.

An Unreinforced Attack

For some time the Warsaw Pact has been capable of mounting an attack against Western Europe with distinctly limited objectives in a comparatively short time and with a considerable prospect of attaining those objectives. One can debate whether the warning period for such an attack would be twenty-four, thirty-six, or forty-eight hours, whether all or only part of the Soviet forces permanently deployed forward in Eastern Europe would be used, whether any non-Soviet Warsaw Pact (NSWP) forces would participate, and whether the Soviet Union would simultaneously carry out air attacks well beyond the battle area. What is hardly debatable is that the Soviet Union, with the advantage of time and place, could seize and hold West Berlin and parts of Norway, Turkey, and West Germany to a depth of 50 to 100 kilometers. For NATO to have any hope of preventing such a "limited" assault on Western territory, it would have to position its standing forces much closer to the East-West divide in peacetime than it does, increase the readiness of those forces, and construct a wide belt of obstacles to delay the enemy advance. Moreover, it would have to do these things over most of the front, for there is no way of identifying in advance which areas would be singled out by the aggressor. None of these steps would be politically easy.

Such an assault might be conducted by the Group of Soviet Forces in Germany (GSFG), a limited strike force consisting of only nineteen divisions. On the assumption that the GSFG would have to move without pause from its peacetime locations some distance inside Germany, that hastily prepared NATO defenses, screening forces, and air attacks would take their toll, and that the weight of Soviet forces, aside from small diversionary attacks, would be concentrated on one sector, it is doubtful that any Soviet commander would assign objectives for such a force deeper than, say, 100 kilometers over a front 100 kilometers wide. With nineteen divisions at his disposal, the GSFG commander might allocate seven or eight divisions to each of two echelons, keeping perhaps five divisions to defend other sectors or for diversionary operations or in reserve. Soviet commanders normally are not expected to have local reserves but in this case—precisely because it is an unreinforced attack—a commander would be imprudent not to hold part of his force in reserve, having set the objectives at about 50 kilometers for the first echelon divisions and 100 kilometers for the second. Prudence aside, the GSFG is now much more capable than it was of mounting such an operation unaided by reserves. It is believed to have sufficient organic logistic support with stocks in place to sustain it; it seems to have enough mobility and firepower; and it now has its own helicopter and air support formations along with impressive ground-based air defenses. Even if precise figures are open to debate, the GSFG appears to be a largely autonomous offensive force designed for a limited purpose.

The question is whether the Soviet Union could envisage circumstances in which a limited operation of this kind would be politically useful, and useful at a level of risk acceptable to the Soviet leadership. The Soviet Politburo might be prepared to exercise the option in a crisis if it sensed that NATO was about to attack the Warsaw Pact, or as a prelude to massive political pressure on Western Europe in the absence of the United States. Much harder to imagine is that the Soviet Union would run the risk of escalation to general war that would attend even such a limited operation without preparing the whole military machinery of the Warsaw Pact.

A limited option in Europe exists both in theory and in capability, and that alone may be a source of satisfaction to Soviet leaders. The USSR appears to have an unquenchable thirst for an almost infinite variety of military options to suit all imaginable political eventualities. That it is hard to define the political circumstances in which an option might be exercised is no reason to dismiss it as a fantasy.

A Reinforced Attack

If in normal circumstances the conquest of Western Europe far exceeds the capabilities of Soviet forces positioned forward in Eastern Europe, how does the picture change when reinforcements from the Soviet Union are added? The bulk of those forces must fill 50 percent or more of their complement by calling up reservists, a task that will certainly take days and probably weeks if it is to be completed before Soviet divisions begin moving westward. It seems more likely that reserve divisions would begin to move at around three-quarters strength, relying on stragglers to catch up. Despite what one assumes to be extensive planning for mobilization in Soviet military districts, the process is unlikely to be tidy. Communications within the Soviet Union are sparse and distances great. Civilian vehicles must be pressed into service. The standard of training of reservists is uncertain. Moreover, if confusion in the allocation of rolling stock in the civilian economy is any guide, the assembly and routing of trains will severely tax logistics, despite considerable investment in such facilities as change-of-gauge stations at the Soviet-Polish border to ease congestion. Nevertheless, the USSR has the potential to bring as many as a hundred additional divisions to the European theater without drawing down forces in the Far East or the southern USSR.

In the considerable literature discussing projected rates of Soviet reinforcement, a middle view is that the first of the reinforcing formations will begin to reach East Germany in seven to ten days, with the flow building to a peak in about fourteen days. By the twenty-eighth day the bulk of the reinforcing divisions would be passing into East Germany and divisions at the head of the line of march would have moved on. These successive waves are known colloquially as the second (and possibly third) strategic echelons. While such an operation has not been tested in practice and the details remain conjectural, it seems clear that the Soviet forces already in Eastern Europe and those facing West Germany, Norway, and Turkey would become the first strategic echelon, deployable on a number of separate axes. Under Soviet doctrine, this echelon would be assigned objectives whose attainment is likely to exhaust it. The second echelon would then take over and push toward more distant objectives. Refining the concept further, each strategic echelon would be given intermediate and final objectives, and the echelons themselves be subdivided into operational and tactical echelons.

A major question remains, followed by two observations. Suppose that the Soviet Union for whatever reason had decided to conquer Western Europe and that the first strategic echelon could attack in, say, thirty-six hours. Would that echelon delay the attack until the second strategic echelon was on its tail? To attack when ready would entail some risk of piecemeal defeat, but would gain the advantage of surprise and perhaps disrupt NATO's defense. Waiting, on the other hand, would allow preparation of the defense but also permit elements of the attacking force to join loosely together, build momentum, and ensure that NATO would feel the full weight of the assault without intermission.

Whatever the answer, to coordinate such an operation, maintain orderly flows forward of men and matériel, and ensure the appropriate allocation of routes and transport would be extremely demanding. It would also be highly susceptible to disruption by air attack or local opposition. Indeed, few other military operations could present so many vulnerabilities and difficulties in execution. To assemble up to a hundred divisions and move them westward an average distance of some 1,500 kilometers before they even enter NATO territory on the central front— and in the face of hostile action—would be an extraordinary achievement. It would be unwise to claim that it cannot be done, though one might contend that no Soviet military planner can be entirely confident that it could be done according to plan.

The second observation is that NATO has no alternative but to assume that such an operation might be attempted, and that it would not necessarily dissolve in chaos. However slowly and haltingly the westward movement might proceed, the weight of Soviet forces would be felt sooner or later, and it would not be enough for NATO simply to have confidence that it could hold the first strategic echelon. If NATO exhausts itself in doing so and uses up its trained manpower and stocks of munitions and equipment, the pressure from succeeding echelons could prove decisive; for what is not seriously in doubt is that the Soviet Union has vast reserves of manpower and equipment, even if one discounts the

contribution of non-Soviet Warsaw Pact forces. This is the true significance of the late Chairman Brezhnev's remark that "quantity has a
quality all its own." In short, even if NATO's forces do not crack under
the leading Soviet echelons and Soviet conventional air power can be
kept in check, the Soviet Union appears to have sufficient resources to
maintain and even increase the pressure over time. It is small comfort
to NATO that the increasing pressure may be somewhat more gradually
applied than worst-case analysis predicts.

We cannot know when the point of exhaustion will be reached or even
that NATO will be able to contain the first Soviet strategic echelon, for
there are a great many variables. The evidence suggests, however, that
breakdown might occur somewhat later than is generally asserted—
perhaps after $M + 30$ days. This conclusion is important for NATO's
nuclear posture. "No early use" of nuclear weapons would imply that
NATO, if it is to retain any nuclear bargaining power and be capable of
exercising a nuclear option, must seek to preserve its theater nuclear
forces during a substantial period of fierce conventional war during
which the Soviet Union will be seeking to destroy those weapons by
conventional means. "No early use" (or even no first use) is thus likely
to demand much greater survivability of theater nuclear forces in
conventional war than would "early first use."

The preceding analysis is couched largely in terms of attrition because
NATO, however strongly it is urged to avoid a war of conventional
attrition, seems unlikely in the long run to be able to dictate how the war
is to be fought. That will be determined ultimately by the aggressor, and
the Soviet Union appears able to impose a war of attrition if it fails in a
war of maneuver. NATO cannot, just as the German army after 1943
could not, ultimately escape a war of attrition. If a Soviet multithrust
attack combining firepower and mobility does not succeed in breaking
up the Western defense—and some agility in the defense would help to
ensure that NATO is not broken up—the Soviet Union has the second
option of pinning NATO's forces down by sheer mass and imposing the
conditions of warfare that best suit the stronger opponent. If NATO
does not lose when battlefield densities are comparatively low, it can
hardly avoid the debilitating effects of attrition as densities build up.

A Maritime Blockade

Either in conjunction with or before a major land attack on central
Europe, the Warsaw Pact could attempt to impose a maritime blockade

of Western Europe, thereby isolating Europe from the United States and from the sources of its energy and other raw materials. It is a truism that sea denial is easier than sea control. The Soviet Union in general is not dependent on maritime access; it will not be dependent at all if it can use its air, surface, and subsurface antisubmarine warfare capabilities to secure certain continual contiguous sea spaces in which to operate its SSBNs. Beyond that, the Soviet Navy is presumed to have one overriding mission in general war: to deny the West the use of the sea. All other missions are either subordinated to that primary mission or contribute to it—for example, amphibious operations to secure access to open oceans. The mission of interdicting Western maritime traffic is assumed to be assigned primarily to submarines and secondarily to naval aviation and surface task groups. It implies engaging and destroying Western naval units assigned to open-ocean operations to protect maritime traffic, such as carrier task groups.

This summary description of Soviet maritime strategy is intended only to demonstrate that the maritime isolation of Western Europe is an option assiduously pursued by the Soviet Union, as evidenced particularly by the growth of the Soviet deep-water submarine force and long-range naval aviation. The obvious growth of Soviet surface capabilities to some extent has distracted NATO's attention from the increasing submarine threat, which should be taken very seriously indeed.

Given Europe's resource dependency, the Soviet maritime option of Persian Gulf oil denial is quite real. There is little doubt that the Soviet Union could prevent tanker sailings around the Cape of Good Hope or through the Red Sea to Europe (and through the Malacca Straits to Japan), using a relatively small number of nuclear-powered submarines armed with cruise missiles and torpedoes. Oil shipments through the Mediterranean might be interrupted to a lesser extent, given the hazards facing Soviet submarines in those waters. How quickly and completely the blockade would cause European economies to collapse is hard to predict, for the outcome would depend on stockpile policy, on rationing, on alternative sources of supply, and on the effectiveness of energy sharing arrangements. Nevertheless, Western Europe would be in a desperate situation after sixty days, and even thirty days of this kind of blockade would probably bring Europe to its knees. No other military action would be necessary, although the West should assume that the Soviet Union would at the same time complete a preventive mobilization and raise the readiness of its nuclear forces to meet Western military counteraction. While the use of nuclear weapons at sea to counter such a blockade is imaginable, it seems unlikely in that Soviet submarines will seek to operate in sea areas not patrolled by Western navies or aircraft.

The Soviet Union has a second option in the attempt to prevent transatlantic reinforcement. This operation could prove to be substantially more difficult than an oil blockade, since a considerable concentration of naval power would attempt to frustrate Soviet submarines or aircraft, and at least some of the faster U.S. ships would run singly, use evasive routing, and eventually carry a measure of self-protection. Some ships would be sunk, but a total blockade would be hard to enforce; a significant proportion of U.S. men and matériel would reach Western Europe, while Soviet submarines and naval aircraft would suffer substantial losses. Nevertheless, most analysts conclude that the major Soviet submarine and naval aviation effort would be devoted to Atlantic interdiction, a point confirmed by Soviet exercises. Depending on the success of its blockade, the Soviet Union would hope to adjust the rate of insertion of forces into the theater in its favor, thus affecting both force ratios and, most important, attrition and munition usage.

Thus there is a direct link between maritime operations in the North Atlantic and the use of nuclear weapons to avoid defeat. Inability to sustain the conventional war in Europe from the United States would surely advance the point at which the West might have to contemplate first use of nuclear weapons. Much more questionable is whether the West would consider using those weapons in the context of energy starvation. Hence an energy blockade would constitute a more independent option for the Soviet Union, weakening the West with less attendant nuclear risk.

In the evolution of its military power, the Soviet Union appears to have moved in directions that provide options to be exercised in the longer term should others fail in the shorter term. And it also has an option through the exercise of economic warfare—an energy blockade—that could decisively affect Western Europe's political will without risking an irreversible clash with the United States or military escalation. NATO must address Western vulnerabilities in both respects.

Conclusion

In outlining the way NATO and the Warsaw Pact arrived at their present positions, it is not hard to set out the trends in military capabilities measured in numbers of men and equipment. It is harder to add qualitative factors and to predict from those figures what might be the outcome of a military engagement between the two alliances. It is harder still to determine the answer to the key question: what is the driving force behind the patterns of military investment we observe? If Warsaw Pact, and especially Soviet, investment is intended ultimately to change the international environment through the use of military force, that conclusion will dictate one set of NATO responses, all of which must be bent toward denying the Warsaw Pact the attainment of its objectives. If, on the other hand, Soviet military investment is made through fear of an uncertain future and to assure Soviet security, an alternative set of responses may be appropriate, having more to do with reassurance, confidence building, and crisis management than with the simple aggregation of competing military power. A third possible intepretation is that the Pact's political unity flows from military power, without necessarily an intent to use that power in war against the West. NATO should make clear to its members and to its potential adversary that threats to use military power will not shake Western unity and resolve—a political response to an essentially political challenge.

Since there is no way of being certain which of the three interpretations of Soviet intentions is correct, prudence calls for a response to current problems that combines a degree of reassurance to the Russians with increased military and political self-assurance for NATO. Reassurance to the USSR would come from reorganizing NATO's defense so that it need not depend on early use of nuclear weapons, a step that would at least contribute to crisis stability and perhaps permit the deescalation of a crisis before the use of nuclear weapons made it virtually certain that control would be lost. In particular, a substantial reduction in the number of battlefield nuclear weapons could encourage the belief that pressures to use those weapons early would also be reduced. But military self-assurance can come only from confidence that NATO has the ability to deny all Soviet options—nuclear, conventional, and maritime—by combining nuclear risk with defense. To exclude nuclear risk altogether—by adopting a no-first-use doctrine or posture, for example—would encourage an opponent to believe that the risks of conventional operations might be limited and tolerable, thereby increasing his propensity for risk-taking in a crisis.

While it is impossible to determine precisely the level of deployed or deployable military power that will suffice to deny Soviet options, three factors lead to the conclusion that NATO in general and NATO Europe in particular must contribute more at the conventional level. The first derives from the change in the Soviet-American nuclear relationship. If the nuclear component of Western deterrence is generally acknowledged to have become less credible and if deterrence in Europe is the sum of nuclear risk and conventional denial, it is necessary to improve NATO's conventional ability to deny the Warsaw Pact all possible conventional objectives. Second, the Warsaw Pact in general and the Soviet Union in particular have shown no sign of reducing the rate of increase of their investment in conventional forces, reflected less in quantitative than in qualitative terms. Third, the United States, by assuming a wider conventional security burden outside Europe, tends to shift a somewhat greater security load onto European shoulders. In short, trends are at work that are changing the conventional balance in a direction favorable to the Warsaw Pact. If these trends are neglected, a situation that currently might not offer conventional options to the Pact could come in the future to tempt the Pact to action.

A number of constraints on conventional improvements are likely to operate for the next ten years or more: economic conditions, manpower availability, and defense cost inflation.

During a period of economic stagnation, defense appropriations are unlikely to rise dramatically. Most Western European states seem neither able nor willing to commit themselves to annual increases of more than one or two percentage points above the rate of general inflation. Such increases can do little more than compensate for the higher rate of defense cost inflation, and a pessimist would say that they cannot do even that. In the United States, real defense growth may be sustainable for some years to come, but a considerable part of that growth seems destined for missions not directly concerned with the conventional defense of Western Europe.

It is a simple demographic fact that manpower will become scarce in the late 1980s. Whether this trend becomes militarily significant will depend in part on unemployment levels, though the reduction in the size of the eighteen-year-old cohort seems certain to affect the conscripted element of NATO's forces, particularly in West Germany. At the present time, high unemployment has reduced somewhat the direct costs of manpower by lessening the need to link wage increases to inflation. If unemployment is reduced later in the 1980s, competition for scarce manpower might require governments to increase military pay in order to attract volunteers.

Partly as a result of expanding technological demands and partly because costs in the defense sector rise faster than costs in civilian industry, military hardware has shown a disturbing tendency to increase in cost with each generational change by a factor of 3 or more. For high performance jet aircraft and helicopters the factor can be as high as 5, while the *average* increase has been between 2.5 and 3 in recent years. Resolving this into annual rates of change, military equipment in general costs about 6 percent more in real terms each year. Since new equipment usually absorbs about one-fourth of most defense budgets, budgets must rise by 1.5 percent a year in real terms merely to compensate for defense cost inflation.

Ways may be found to reorganize Western conventional defenses and increase their capabilities without increasing their cost—to produce weapons more efficiently and economically, and to develop effective new weapon systems that cost less than those they will replace. But it is hard to be optimistic that NATO can substantially improve its conventional defense under the identifiable constraints. Of the various solutions being discussed, all more or less radical, none is without political cost. It is easy enough for political and military leaders to declare that NATO must improve its conventional capabilities and reduce its nuclear dependence; it is far less easy to determine precisely how that conventional improvement is to be attained.

CHAPTER SIX

NO FIRST USE
AND NATO'S NUCLEAR POSTURE

Leon V. Sigal

NATO's military forces are intended to deter war and maintain a stable balance of power in Europe by means that are politically acceptable to those who share the burdens and risks. In a fundamental sense, deterrence and stability are compatible objectives. The aim of deterrence is to convince a potential adversary that the cost of obtaining his political objectives by military means would be prohibitively high. When two adversaries deter each other from resorting to military force, then by definition the military relationship between them is stable. Yet not all weapons, force postures, or targeting plans designed to assure deterrence also promote stability. In 1914, for example, alliance obligations undertaken to deter war instead provoked it, and mobilization set in motion by Russia as a precaution prompted preemption by Germany.

In Search of Deterrence and Stability

NATO's efforts to build a posture of stable deterrence raise questions about the specific aims of deterrence and the possibility of achieving them without evoking a preemptive Soviet strike in a time of crisis. Nuclear weapons are expected to serve many purposes. In addition to discouraging Soviet use of nuclear, chemical, or biological weapons against Western Europe, the nuclear systems at NATO's disposal are intended to deter a Soviet conventional attack—both by warning of escalation and by their threatened use on the battlefield—and to deter a Soviet nuclear attack against the United States. Because an all-purpose nuclear deterrent does not exist, these varied objectives imply trade-offs among competing weapon systems, force postures, targeting doctrines, and declaratory policies.

To deter Soviet use of nuclear weapons against Western Europe, for example, requires invulnerable intercontinental and intermediate-range nuclear systems that can strike targets on Soviet territory after surviving a Soviet nuclear attack. Short-range or battlefield nuclear weapons cannot deter such an attack because they cannot reach the Soviet border from their positions in Europe; moreover, their own vulnerability might be an inducement to attack. The British and French nuclear forces might help to deter an attack against the respective home countries, but could they deter an attack against West Germany?

Since the advent of nuclear weapons, the conditions for deterrence and stability have become at once more urgent and more difficult to satisfy. Military stability now takes three distinct but related forms—strategic stability, which results when both sides have sufficient invulnerable nuclear weapons to inflict unacceptable damage on the other side even after suffering a nuclear attack; crisis stability, signifying that neither side's weapons present vulnerabilities that could attract a preemptive strike; and arms race stability, which prevails when neither side fears that its opponent is developing weapons that could endanger strategic stability or crisis stability. But stability does not signify the absence of change in the two sides' forces, nor does it refer to a mechanical "balance" in which "heavy" missiles weigh more. The concept of stability does suggest that a few nuclear weapons more or less do not make either side better or worse off. What matters more than numbers today is the quality of nuclear forces, in particular their accuracy and their vulnerability to attack.

As the conditions for stability have changed in the nuclear era, the scope and nature of deterrence also have undergone a transformation. Three levels must now be distinguished: deterrence at the intercontinental or strategic nuclear level; regional or theater nuclear deterrence in Western Europe; and deterrence at the level of conventional weapons. Stability at each level raises questions about the level below. Since the mid-1960s strategic stability, however precarious, has existed between the United States and the Soviet Union. But mutual deterrence between the superpowers has aroused concern about America's ability to extend deterrence to its allies in NATO. Although the superpowers are deterred from waging nuclear war directly against each other, what might prevent the Soviet Union from using or threatening to use nuclear weapons against Western Europe? Nuclear stability at the strategic level does not necessarily assure nuclear stability in Europe. And even if extended deterrence suffices to prevent a nuclear attack or nuclear blackmail in Western Europe, what might deter the Warsaw Pact from launching a conventional attack there? Stability between the superpowers need not exclude instability at the conventional level, either.

Attempts to assure regional deterrence have led down several paths. In one direction, European states might acquire nuclear weapons of their own. While that path was open to Great Britain and France, it was not open to West Germany because German acquisition of a nuclear force would undermine the postwar settlement in Europe, jeopardizing East-West, intra-European, and intra-German political relations. A second possibility was a Western European nuclear force. While the British or French forces conceivably could evolve in that direction, such a force implies a degree of political community that has yet to be attained in Western Europe. A third approach is to beef up U.S. nuclear capabilities to make extended deterrence seem more credible. The fourth option is to strengthen NATO's conventional defenses, relying on them—and on the risk of escalation to nuclear war—to deter an attack from the East. The choice between the third and fourth approaches has confronted NATO planners with difficult trade-offs between deterrence and stability.

Efforts to strengthen NATO's conventional forces for the most part can minimize those trade-offs. Emplacing physical barriers to retard Warsaw Pact advances, strengthening reserve units, and improving NATO's ability to mobilize its forces more rapidly are steps so patently defensive that they could hardly be construed as provocative. They would also buttress deterrence by increasing the prospects for repulsing an attack from the East, and by reinforcing the credibility of the nuclear deterrent: the more robust the conventional defense, the greater the risk that a conventional war might get out of hand. Escalation to nuclear war would seem far less plausible if NATO were to suffer a conventional collapse at the outset of hostilities.

As in the case of nuclear weapons, however, qualitative details of NATO's conventional force posture are important. For the sake of allied unity it has been essential that NATO adopt a strategy of forward defense, lest it seem willing to concede too much West German territory in order to conduct a defense in depth. Were NATO to undertake a force buildup sufficient to carry forward defense to its logical extreme, a threat to roll eastward once attacked, that posture might appear to be less a precaution than a provocation to the Warsaw Pact countries. Its adoption could lead to an offsetting buildup that would endanger arms race stability or crisis stability at the conventional level. Short of such an extreme, improvements in NATO's conventional posture contribute to deterrence without jeopardizing stability.

NATO's other option—buttressing U.S. nuclear capabilities to make extended deterrence somehow seem more credible—carries greater risk of instability. At the intercontinental level, acquiring a sufficient number of accurate warheads on MX or Trident II missiles to threaten the entire Soviet land-based missile force would contribute little to deterrence in Europe, but would impair crisis stability by giving Soviet leaders an overwhelming incentive to launch a preemptive attack if U.S. first use appeared imminent. Acquiring workable antiballistic missiles and embarking on civil defense programs might limit damage in the event of Soviet retaliation and thereby increase the credibility of U.S. first use. But those programs, if undertaken, would endanger all three forms of stability between the superpowers. So, too, would the deployment of antisatellite weapons to supplement other means of disrupting Soviet command, control, and communications (C^3). At the regional or theater level, Pershing II ballistic missiles, by virtue of their accuracy and rapid flight, would threaten Soviet C^3 from bases in West Germany. They would facilitate U.S. first use by reducing the possibility of a coordinated Soviet retaliatory strike, but at great cost to crisis stability. Another weapon, the ground-launched cruise missile (GLCM), is suitable for retaliation against a Soviet first strike, and its deployment in Europe might lessen allied misgivings about the American nuclear deterrent— provided ways are found to reduce GLCMs' vulnerability to attack. Owing to their subsonic speed to the target, GLCMs are not a first-strike weapon and their presence would not be destabilizing. Apart from GLCMs, however, other additions to the U.S. nuclear force could jeopardize stability without contributing much to deterrence.

NFU and Stable Deterrence

Stable deterrence need not be a contradiction in terms. NATO's current force posture only makes it seem so. The debate over NFU, if it is seriously joined, could illuminate the issues involved in a stable deterrent posture and encourage NATO to make some of the trade-offs it has too long avoided.

As declaratory policy, NFU presumably would alter perceptions in the East that a war in Europe would inevitably, rapidly, and deliberately become nuclear, without eliminating the fear that it could ultimately, gradually, or inadvertently do so. As strategic doctrine, NFU would direct NATO planners to prepare realistically for conventional defense without contemplating early use of nuclear forces. As a critical tool, NFU draws attention to the need to reconcile deterrence with stability in the European theater—to design force postures and targeting plans with an eye both to reducing the vulnerability of NATO's nuclear forces to attack and to retaliating in ways that would pose significant threats to the other side, thereby adding to deterrence without arousing fear of surprise attack. It is in its sense as a critical tool that NFU is discussed here.

NFU highlights four related aspects of NATO's nuclear posture that are of particular concern. First is the disproportionate number of short-range systems contained in NATO's nuclear arsenal. Second is the physical location of those weapons and the difficulty of dispersing them, both of which make them vulnerable to preemptive attack by either conventional or nuclear means. Third is the decision to use nuclear weapons and the process of making it, which cast doubt on whether the weapons would ever be usable. Fourth is the commingling of nuclear and conventional forces; far from supplementing NATO's conventional posture, much of the NATO nuclear force may actually detract from it. Whether or not NATO moves toward adoption of NFU, it cannot afford to ignore the questions NFU raises about these aspects of NATO's current nuclear posture and their effects on stable deterrence.

The Short-Range Emphasis in NATO's Present Posture

A differentiating characteristic of nuclear systems is the maximum range their means of delivery can project them. Since a delivery vehicle can reach targets at distances shorter than its maximum range, the distinction is somewhat arbitrary. Moreover, the results of test firings may vary with climatic conditions, force loadings, and, in the case of cruise missiles, fuel capacity. Nonetheless, the distinction remains valid. Short-range or battlefield nuclear systems are capable of a maximum range of 100 kilometers or less. Medium-range nuclear systems have maximum ranges of between 100 and 1,000 kilometers. Intermediate-range nuclear forces, also known as long-range theater nuclear forces, can travel from 1,000 to 5,500 kilometers, reaching Western Europe from bases in the USSR (or vice versa) but not the continental United States.

Public attention in Europe recently has focused on theater nuclear forces because of NATO's December 1979 decision to base new American ground-launched cruise missiles and Pershing II ballistic missiles in five Western European countries. While NFU holds implications for the doctrine and missions of those missiles, as well as for FB-111s and other aircraft in NATO's nuclear inventory, it has far more significance for NATO's nuclear forces of shorter range. Designed for use on or near the battlefield, those forces constitute the largest share in the mix of NATO nuclear systems and pose the most pressing problem for stable deterrence. Most are owned and controlled by the United States and attached to American forces in Europe. Others are U.S. owned but operated under various provisions for joint control by allied forces—so-called dual key systems. Still others are European owned and operated.

Of the 6,000 American nuclear warheads currently at NATO's disposal in Europe, as shown in table 3-1, some 2,250 are artillery shells that can strike targets at ranges of less than ten miles, roughly the distance from the White House to the suburbs of Washington, D.C. Some 700 are designed for air defense, detonating with a blast sufficient to knock a wing of enemy aircraft out of the sky. Another 300 are atomic demolition munitions, which can be installed in a few hours at previously dug sites—tunnels, mountain passes, and other topographically opportune locations—to retard the advance of tanks and other vehicles.

Though all of these weapons are referred to as deterrents, in a strict sense they are not. Short-range or battlefield nuclear weapons could be used against enemy forces in battle or to prevent their massing prior to an attack, thereby reducing their effectiveness. They do not suffice, however, to prevent either a conventional or a nuclear attack by imposing prohibitively high costs on the enemy. Nor could they deny the enemy gains without destroying what they are supposed to defend. Indeed, by virtue of their location and vulnerability, they, like the American fleet at Pearl Harbor in December 1941, are more a target for than a deterrent to enemy attack. Without exception, American exercises have shown that whenever NATO is about to use nuclear weapons, it prompts a Soviet preemptive strike.[1]

Location and Relocation

Nuclear weapons require special storage and handling facilities to protect them from accidents and terrorism. The trained manpower and extraordinary expense involved in maintaining these facilities has led the United States to economize on their number: most U.S. short-range warheads in central Europe are concentrated at just twenty-odd storage sites, all of which are recognizable and undoubtedly known to the Warsaw Pact countries. Protection of these weapons in peacetime thus increases their vulnerability to attack in war.

Dispersal poses other trade-offs in the choice of location. It is sometimes claimed that dispersing short-range warheads would not only reduce their vulnerability to attack but would also strengthen the adversary's perception of NATO's will to use them. Host governments, however, are reluctant to consider either relocation or peacetime exercises involving dispersal because the presence of nuclear weapons could arouse popular opposition in the immediate vicinity. Moreover, to affect Soviet perceptions of U.S. will, dispersal would require putting the weapons into the hands of commanders in the field—those who have an incentive to use them rather than lose them—thus raising the prospect of unauthorized employment and the risk of enemy preemption. Such an outcome is politically unappealing to publics fearful of nuclear war and politically unacceptable to leaders who would like to believe they retain formal control of the ultimate decision.

To leave the weapons where they are does not avoid the problem. Nuclear artillery shells, for example, are stored only a few hours' march from the intra-German frontier. To redeploy them into forward positions during a crisis might signal a hardening of NATO's will, but at the risk that the weapons might be preempted, overrun, or used prematurely. To hold them back would mean that if they were used at all, it would be on West German territory. Authority to use them in that case might be hard to obtain. Measures to reduce the collateral damage of NATO's nuclear weapons would not diminish the difficulty, since the collateral damage caused by a Soviet response or preemptive strike is unlikely to be low.

Atomic demolition munitions sharpen the dilemma of peacetime location and crisis relocation. ADMs are designed to be emplaced along access routes at or near the frontier to fill gaps in NATO defenses and retard Warsaw Pact advances into Western territory. Because of the time required to dig these weapons into tunnels, mountain passes, and other suitable locations, ADMs must be put into place well before use. But peacetime dispersal, in addition to risking accidental or unauthorized use or even seizure by terrorists, would make ADM sites more visible to enemy surveillance. In the event of war, ADMs could be overrun and captured or at least preempted, not necessarily by nuclear means. "Prechambering"—digging holes to accommodate ADMs at preselected sites without actually relocating the ADMs in forward positions—might enhance the security of ADMs in peacetime, but it would not avoid the dilemma of whether to pre-position them in a crisis. Forward deployment of ADMs during a crisis would have a more purely defensive character than redeploying other nuclear systems and should not prompt nuclear preemption by the other side. But redeployment would be visible to enemy reconnaissance and would leave ADMs in an exposed position, where they could be overrun. Fearing their loss, theater commanders would propose using them. Political leaders might well hesitate to grant authority, finding the first use of nuclear weapons on their own territory to be an uninspiring signal for all to see. For that reason, prechambering has never found favor with European governments.

Hobson's Choice in Nuclear Decisionmaking

The decision to employ nuclear weapons could prove to be as difficult for Europeans to make at the lower end of the spectrum of deterrence as it would be for the United States at the other extreme. The procedures for making the decision and the extraordinary circumstances in which the choice would arise do not bode well for timely action. A request for authority to use nuclear weapons on or near the battlefield would be transmitted up from corps commanders through Supreme Headquarters, Allied Powers Europe (SHAPE) to the North Atlantic Council and the National Command Authority. The council consists of representatives of all NATO member states except France; the National Command Authority is the president of the United States or his lawful successor. If both approve, orders are to be sent back down through channels to corps and division commanders, and ultimately to the commanders of nuclear delivery units. Even assuming no interruption in communications, the process would take about twenty-four hours, according to a U.S. Army estimate.[2] Any threat to circumvent the formal channels could disrupt allied unity.

While the channels of communication are well established, the rules governing the use of nuclear weapons are much less so. NATO agreed on political guidelines at Athens in 1962 and on procedures for consultation in 1969.[3] Guidelines on the initial selective use of nuclear weapons—including battlefield weapons, ADMs, and theater weapons—were adopted in the early 1970s, but ten years of negotiation within NATO have brought no agreement on rules governing follow-on use. Moreover, bilateral agreements between the United States and host countries define various release procedures for the U.S. nuclear warheads deployed in Europe under programs of cooperation.

Release procedures within the NATO Military Committee have never been spelled out in public. Indeed, prudence counsels silence. If it were clear to the Warsaw Pact countries that any member of NATO could veto the use of nuclear weapons, then the possibility of executing deterrent threats might seem too remote to be credible. On the other hand, if it were clear to domestic publics that no veto existed, then Alliance unity might break up on the shoals of national sovereignty. Yet the 1962 guidelines oblige the United States only to consult, "time and circumstance permitting."[4] Even the ability of host countries to prevent nuclear launches from their territory is left ambiguous, although they do have physical means to halt launches whether or not two-key arrangements exist.

Apart from the murky procedures, the strains of the moment of decision can readily be foreseen. Once a conventional war is under way in central Europe, the issue of nuclear use is unlikely to be settled by the cool, calculated decision envisioned by some strategists. Regardless of declaratory policy, the advantages of first use will be obvious to everyone. But some whose homeland would become a nuclear battlefield, as well as others on the periphery, will wish to avert nuclear war at almost any cost. Organizational as well as national differences will create confusion about enemy intentions. A shower of intelligence reports may only thicken the fog of war. While a few may demand adamantly that NATO use nuclear weapons before the Warsaw Pact does, some may shrink from the decision.[5] Others may improvise. Paralysis or fatalism rather than flexibility and resourcefulness may be the result. Command and control may also prove to be precarious: in some cases there are no physical impediments to stop division commanders from deciding on their own to use the nuclear artillery at their disposal in order to reverse a desperate tactical situation.

If military organizations follow their own doctrine, political leaders might well wonder how limited a nuclear war could be. Short-range or battlefield nuclear weapons are not prescribed for in SACEUR's nuclear operation plan. That being so, corps commanders are to propose pre-packaged options resembling those rehearsed in peacetime exercises. "A package," according to the U.S. Army manual on tactical nuclear operations, "is a group of nuclear weapons of specific yields for use in a specific area and within a limited time to support a specific tactical goal." It would consist of 100 to 200 warheads programmed for an objective that is neither specific nor limited: "Each package must contain nuclear weapons sufficient to alter the tactical situation decisively and to accomplish the mission."[6]

The decision to use short-range nuclear weapons will sorely test NATO's target acquisition and intelligence capabilities. The prime targets for those weapons—Warsaw Pact tank and troop concentrations and short-range nuclear forces—will be difficult to locate and harder still to pin down. Enemy forces already engaged in battle are not suitable targets in that short-range nuclear weapons do not discriminate between enemy and friendly forces. (Indeed, the enemy might take advantage of this fact by adopting "hugging" tactics, remaining in close proximity to NATO forces, and by timing his attacks to take advantage of prevailing winds.) Intelligence about potential targets beyond the forward edge of battle is likely to come through separate channels, from aerial or satellite reconnaissance or from special teams on the ground behind enemy lines. Realtime or instantaneous transmission, processing, and coordination may prove unattainable in battle; indeed, too much haste might well seem undesirable. To transmit intelligence through channels, evaluate it, and bring it to the attention of relevant commanders could take an hour or more; in the meantime, the targets will have moved out of range. A tank column, for example, can attain speeds of ten to fifteen miles per hour against minimal resistance; short-range nuclear artillery, if self-propelled, can move even faster. If nuclear release is yet to be authorized, even more time will elapse between spotting enemy forces and reacting to their presence. In these circumstances, intelligence is unlikely to close the gap between the time urgency of the targets and the measured pace of deliberation and decision.

Theater commanders may wonder whether they will receive timely authorization to use short-range nuclear weapons. Thirty years of experience with war gaming shows how difficult it is to get the participants to decide on first use. When allies are among the players, authority to use nuclear weapons has seldom been granted, however hypothetical the situation. In a crisis, even a decision to move nuclear forces out of garrison might be difficult to obtain because of the increased risk of preemption. Simple logistics might dictate the ultimate decision if clogged roads prevent subsequent redeployment of the weapons.

Commingling of Nuclear and Conventional Forces

Not only do short-range or battlefield nuclear weapons add little to nuclear deterrence and defense; they also detract from NATO's conventional posture as a result of increased commingling of nuclear and conventional capabilities. In addition to aircraft on quick reaction alert (QRA), other medium- and short-range systems are dual capable: the M-109, M-110, and M-114 155mm howitzers can fire either nuclear or conventional shells; the F-4 and F-16 fighter aircraft and the A-6, A-7, and F-111 fighter-bombers can carry either nuclear or conventional ordnance; so can Lance and Nike-Hercules missiles. Hunter-killer submarines, when nuclear-armed with sea-launched cruise missiles (SLCMs), will also be dual capable.

While the delivery vehicles for all nuclear-capable systems are under the control of NATO field commanders, the nuclear warheads are not. Except for warheads assigned to aircraft, to surface-to-surface missiles on QRA, and to SLCMs when deployed, the warheads for use by allies remain at special storage sites under U.S. custody. Some of those for use by American forces are in the hands of battalion commanders; others are in separate units supervised by corps, division, or brigade commanders, depending on the geographic proximity of the unit to the storage site. Regimental or firing unit commanders take possession of the warheads once they are dispersed from storage, though authority to use them remains at the corps or division level.

Dual capability puts field commanders in a predicament. Anticipating escalation, they might withhold or withdraw dual-capable forces from the conventional battle in order to ready them for nuclear missions. The temptation would be greatest when the conventional conflict is most intense and its outcome most uncertain—precisely when the maximum conventional effort is most urgently needed. At that point, the commander of a submarine with nuclear SLCMs on board might be uncertain whether to hide or seek. To compound the predicament, if field commanders withdraw dual-capable systems from battle, the Warsaw Pact might interpret the redeployment to mean that nuclear war is imminent, prompting it to preempt when NATO is most vulnerable and least able to respond in kind. Moreover, if allied commanders withhold or withdraw these forces and have their requests for nuclear authorization refused, enemy preemption might still occur even though NATO's intention was to avoid nuclear war. Worst of all, the Pact might mistake preparations for conventional use of dual-capable systems as indicating a decision to use nuclear weapons and preempt with its own nuclear forces. Paradoxically, then, the commingling of conventional and nuclear forces that is intended to strengthen NATO in fact leaves it muscle-bound or paralyzed.

By the same token, integrating conventional and nuclear warfare in the tactics, planning, and training of NATO ground forces, while essential to prepare troops for nuclear battle if it should occur, may have the perverse consequence of leaving them less prepared to wage war without resorting to nuclear weapons for tactical ends. Drill does more than prepare troops for expected contingencies; it also leaves them less prepared for other eventualities. Forces that have practiced dispersing for a nuclear attack are less adept at massing for a conventional response. Forces trained to expect nuclear use in the event of an enemy breakthrough may be unprepared to regroup if that expectation is not fulfilled.

The dilemmas of nuclear location, relocation, and dual capability suggest that if, as the saying goes, armies are designed by geniuses to be run by idiots, the reverse is true for short-range nuclear forces in Europe. The hard choices posed by introducing short-range nuclear weapons into a war in central Europe make clear why exponents of nuclear warfighting strategies seek to erode any firebreak, physical or psychological, between nuclear and conventional weapons, and would predelegate authority for first use of nuclear weapons to commanders in the field. It is equally clear why heads of government, wishing to maintain political control, have ample reason to resist such efforts and why some might be drawn to NFU.

The political difficulty of getting the allies to agree on using nuclear weapons and the vulnerability of NATO's nuclear arsenal to Soviet preemption make it virtually impossible for NATO to use its short-range nuclear forces first in a calculated response to a Soviet conventional attack. In practice, if not in theory, NATO has already adopted a no-first-use policy with respect to those weapons. A formal declaration would reconcile policy and practice. It would also provide a rationale for reducing drastically, if not eliminating, short-range nuclear forces—at a minimum, ADMs and artillery and air defense rounds—and for ending commingling by reassigning dual-capable systems to purely conventional roles and missions.

The analysis suggests taking these steps whether or not the United States formally adopts NFU as declaratory policy: short-range and dual-capable systems are ill suited either for first use or for retaliation, and commingling depletes NATO's conventional strength. Using NFU as a critical tool indicates that, whether or not NFU is adopted as declaratory policy or as strategic doctrine, NATO's nuclear posture stands in need of correction.

Removal of short-range nuclear weapons from Western Europe should not be made contingent on reciprocal moves by the USSR or on arms control. The difficulty of verifying any agreement on short-range forces—or, indeed, of discovering the physical location of Soviet short-range nuclear warheads—would prolong any negotiation and jeopardize concrete results. Moreover, the political advantages of unilateral action by NATO outweigh the value of any negotiated quid pro quo from the Warsaw Pact. A reduction in NATO's short-range nuclear arsenal could mitigate public unease in Europe as the deployment of a modest number of intermediate-range weapons goes forward. It would also increase the political price the Warsaw Pact must pay if it upgrades or expands its own short-range nuclear forces. Drawing down NATO's short-range forces and ending commingling are in NATO's own political and security interests; otherwise these measures would not be worth instituting. They should not be delayed by becoming involved in arms control negotiations with the USSR.

Technological fixes will no longer suffice to make short-range nuclear forces more usable. Those who advocate the deployment of enhanced radiation warheads, for instance, overlook the possibility that a reduction in blast effects and collateral damage may be more than offset by unknown radiation effects and by innocent casualties. In any event, the usability of battlefield nuclear weapons is an issue that transcends the technicalities of weapon design. Strategists may theorize, but political leaders and generals are unlikely to forget that nuclear weapons are different and carry with them a risk of escalation beyond the endurable.

French and British Nuclear Forces

The composition, targeting doctrine, and declaratory policy of the French and British nuclear forces differ from those of the United States, as do the respective national interests and calculations of the circumstances in which these weapons might be used. What the French and British forces can or cannot deter has implications for NFU, just as U.S. consideration of NFU has implications for those forces.

The revival of American interest in NFU may seem to confirm what some Frenchmen have long contended—that no nation should be counted on to risk its own destruction to protect anyone but itself. Yet France, in its own force posture and declaratory policy, has at least a residual capacity for extending deterrence to West Germany. Even though France's nuclear forces are less formidable than those of the United States, geographic contiguity lends a certain credibility to the French guarantee.

French declaratory policy on extended deterrence has always been somewhat ambiguous. Part of the ambiguity is deliberate, part circumstantial. Deliberately, no French government has ever specified the vital interests for which it would be prepared to invoke a nuclear threat. In particular, no French government has excluded West Germany from those vital interests. What gives this silence meaning—and extended deterrence some credibility—are the circumstances in which France might have to consider using nuclear weapons. Were France to come under conventional attack by the Warsaw Pact, that attack would probably follow from the expansion of a war in West Germany. Since West Germany is no more than 275 miles wide—130 miles at its narrowest—France, acting solely to preserve its own territorial integrity and survival, would have to consider using its nuclear deterrent before Germany was overrun. Extended deterrence is, at least to this extent, unavoidable.

Beyond this zone of ambiguity, those in a position to speak authoritatively on behalf of France in recent years have on occasion openly embraced an expanded area of vital interest. In the mid-1970s General Guy Mery, the armed forces chief of staff, sparked considerable controversy by referring publicly to *sanctuarisation élargie*—enlarged sanctuary—by which he implied extending France's deterrent beyond its borders to its European neighbors, in particular West Germany.[7] The government retreated under heavy fire, particularly from right-wing Gaullists who denounced the idea of extending deterrence to West Germany as being beyond France's capabilities and hence lacking credibility—the same view they have held about the American deterrent. Yet the Giscardists eventually settled on a declaratory policy of Meryism without Mery, and that policy continues in effect under their Socialist successors. President Valéry Giscard d'Estaing, announcing tests of France's enhanced radiation weapon, told a June 26, 1980, press conference, "In our reflections about the employment of this weapon, we will take account of the following assumption: France is directly concerned with the security of neighboring European states."[8] Defense Minister Yvon Bourges later traced this line of policy to a 1972 White Paper, which stated that

though deterrence is reserved for the protection of our vital interests, the limits of the latter are necessarily somewhat hazy. . . . France lives in a network of interests which go beyond her borders. She is not isolated. Therefore, Western Europe as a whole cannot fail to benefit indirectly from French strategy.[9]

In his first formal statement on defense, Socialist Prime Minister Pierre Mauroy made the point somewhat more unequivocally when he stated that "an attack against France does not begin when an enemy enters her territory."[10] Even Jacques Chirac, keeper of the flame of Gaullist nationalism, has called for a "strategic nuclear guarantee" for Western Europe involving French nuclear forces along with the British and American.[11] In the light of recent European history, extending a French nuclear guarantee to West Germany has political meaning transcending military matters. Since strategy is only intermittently a subject of public discussion in France, public support for it is largely untested and French officials are hesitant to put it to a test.

Yet today, more than ever before, the dominant view of France's strategic doctrine, widely shared among French officials in and out of uniform, contemplates first use of nuclear weapons. In a conventional war against the Warsaw Pact, they would be prepared initially to use tactical nuclear weapons to warn of impending strikes by their strategic nuclear forces and to demonstrate their resolve, then attack the Soviet Union itself. They insist on distinguishing their strategy from the flexible response of NATO, which they continue to disparage as being too flexible to assure a response. They remain skeptical of controlling escalation once the nuclear threshold is crossed. They see a continuing role for land-based intermediate-range ballistic missiles (IRBMs) to underline the risk of any attack on France and to shift the assumption of that risk to the attacker, who would have to eliminate those IRBMs, presumably by using nuclear weapons first. Were it to try, France would have submarine-launched ballistic missiles in reserve.

Current French nuclear weapon programs, begun under Giscard and continued, indeed expanded, under President François Mitterrand, seem consistent with this strategic doctrine. Modernization of France's strategic forces will reduce somewhat their vulnerability to enemy attack while nearly doubling the number of warheads they can deliver against Soviet targets. A new missile, the M-4, with up to six warheads not independently targetable, will replace the sixteen single-warhead M-20 missiles aboard France's five nuclear submarines (SSBNs). A sixth SSBN is under construction, and a seventh, the first of a new generation, is scheduled to be launched in 1984. The latter will carry a new MIRVed missile, the M-5, as yet of undecided specifications though undoubtedly of longer range. France's IRBM force, consisting of eighteen S-3s with a range of 3,500 kilometers, is based in vulnerable fixed sites in the Albion Plateau of Haute-Provence in southern France. A new mobile IRBM, the SX, is being designed to replace them and the aging Mirage IV force by 1992. In the meantime, the thirty-three Mirage IVs will be armed with air-to-surface cruise missiles to enhance their penetrativity and prolong their usefulness at least until the new IRBM is deployed, if not beyond. Command, control, and communication facilities will also be hardened. France's strategic forces will then have the combination of range and relative inaccuracy appropriate for attacking Moscow and other cities and soft targets in the USSR, yet pose no serious threat to the Soviet land-based ICBM force. Improved survivability will enhance their deterrent capacity.

Modernization of France's tactical nuclear forces is not incompatible with their role in signaling escalation as well as in extending deterrence. A new tactical nuclear missile, Hades, with nearly triple Pluton's range of 120 kilometers, could reach Warsaw Pact territory from either side of the Franco-German border, thereby conveying seriousness of purpose without jeopardizing West German territory. Enhanced radiation weapons (ERW), tested but not yet deployed, could, French officials argue, be used against Warsaw Pact forces in West Germany more readily than other tactical nuclear weapons because they reduce collateral damage somewhat. Although ERWs are designed to stop tank attacks in densely settled areas, that is not the purpose that the French claim to have in mind for them. As Defense Minister Bourges said shortly before the ERW tests were announced,

They show that our wish is to warn, to reprimand, to say: Stop, our vital interests are threatened; we cannot accept this aggression and we are ready to raise the battle to the strategic nuclear threshold. . . . In the hypothesis that you have to use these arms on a friendly territory which has been invaded, the advantage is that you may perhaps avoid killing your friends at the same time as the enemy's army.[12]

His Socialist successor, Charles Hernu, less concerned about arousing the ire of the Gaullists, could afford to be more explicit about the implications of ERW. Acquiring the weapon, he told an interviewer in September 1982, would mean that France "was prepared to enter a war not only as soon as our territory was threatened (since, in that case, we have the deterrent force), but as soon as enemy tanks entered Germany. France would, therefore, be prepared to take part in a 'forward battle.' "[13] The implication of Hernu's remark, that France was contemplating early first use of nuclear weapons, is less than wholly credible. It also runs directly counter to NFU.

NFU has already been the object of scathing criticism, not all of it confined to Gaullist quarters, from those who see the threat of first use as essential to France's security. American adoption of NFU would only underscore what already needs little emphasis in France: the value of independence. "France is developing its own deterrent strategy," Defense Minister Hernu explained last year, "because when the time comes to make decisive choices a great country is alone."[14] Yet great countries may make decisive choices to cooperate as well as to disassociate. NFU, especially against a background of rising American unilateralism and impatience with burden bearing, could confirm the belief of some Frenchmen, on the left as well as on the right, that the long-term solution to both East-West and Franco-German security relations lies in a European, not an Atlanticist, direction, and that extending a French nuclear guarantee is part of an inevitable evolution in that direction. As symbols of France's independence from the United States, the *force de frappe* and the declaratory policy of first use are unassailable at home. An American declaration of NFU might bolster support for what has more doubtful standing in France: extending deterrence as well as security cooperation to West Germany.

Great Britain's strategic nuclear deterrent resembles France's insofar as the decision to use it does not require American assent. There the resemblance ends. Britain's declaratory policy, strategic doctrine, and force posture all differ from France's. So, too, does the breadth of domestic support for remaining a nuclear power; the independent deterrent is not "above politics" as it is in France.

France's rejection of NATO's doctrine of flexible response precludes France from formally committing its nuclear deterrent to the Alliance—or from formal reintegration with NATO. By contrast, the British deterrent is formally tied to NATO. The link may be mere formality; coordination of targeting may in practice prove to be purely coincidental, and even the terms of the Nassau agreement dedicating Polaris submarines to NATO permits them to be used independently when Great Britain's "supreme national interests are at stake"—presumably the only circumstances in which their use would be considered. Yet government after government has reiterated the commitment of Britain's deterrent to NATO.

The British reconcile "independence" with the dedication of their deterrent to NATO by stressing the need for a "second center" of decision, a rationale originated by General André Beaufre to justify France's deterrent. As stated in the 1980 British White Paper justifying the decision to acquire Trident,

A Soviet leadership . . . might believe that it could impose its will on Europe by military force without becoming involved in strategic nuclear war with the United States. Modernised U.S. nuclear forces in Europe help guard against any such misconception; but an independent capability fully under European control provides a key element of insurance. A nuclear decision would of course be no less agonising for the United Kingdom than for the United States. But it would be the decision of a separate and independent power, and a power whose survival in freedom would be directly and immediately threatened by aggression in Europe.[15]

In the British case, the "second center" argument—a polite way of making the point about independence—seems intended more to deflect domestic criticism than to devise a sound strategic doctrine. Unlike France, the United Kingdom is set apart by its insular position. No less is at stake than a fundamental purpose of British foreign policy for the past three centuries—discouraging hegemonic drives on the Continent. Yet the prospect of Soviet retaliation might seem a more imminent threat to the survival of that tight little island. It is not apparent why the Warsaw Pact, in contemplating a conventional attack on central Europe, would consider British use of nuclear weapons more likely than American use of them.

The "second center" rationale subsumes two other possibilities: that British first use would somehow act as a powder train to set off American nuclear forces, or that British strategic forces would deter Soviet retaliation against the British Isles in the event that Britain used its battlefield nuclear forces on the Continent, alone or in concert with its allies. The British White Paper on Trident addresses the second possibility:

British nuclear forces include both strategic and lower-level components. If we had only the latter they could not serve the key "second-centre" deterrent purpose, since the threat of their use would not be credible. An aggressor faced with an armoury comprising only non-strategic nuclear weapons would know that he could if necessary use strategic nuclear weapons to overbear it without risking strategic retaliation upon himself. . . .[16]

Yet the "second center" rationale assumes that, whether as catalyst or as sanctuary, the United Kingdom would act before and independently of the United States. Why the British would risk going it alone in either case—and in circumstances in which the United States was reluctant to join—is not at all clear. First use of nuclear weapons by Britain alone, especially of its "lower components," hardly seems credible under these conditions. Indeed, if first use *by NATO* were to involve the "lower components" of British nuclear forces on the Continent, London could hardly view that step with detachment despite its independent strategic deterrent.

What the independent deterrent can do more credibly than the American guarantee is to deter a Soviet attack on Great Britain, period. How much the added insurance is worth and whether the country can afford it are likely to remain issues of heated parliamentary debate in London.[17] NFU, to the extent that it cast doubt on the American nuclear commitment, could make that insurance seem more worthwhile.

Britain's "lower level" nuclear components include one regiment equipped with twelve Lance missiles and three regiments armed with dual-capable artillery, whose nuclear warheads are controlled under two-key arrangements with the United States, as well as gravity bombs for its medium-range dual-capable aircraft, Buccaneers, Jaguars, and Tornadoes. The arguments against U.S. dual-capable and short-range nuclear systems apply with at least equal force to their British counterparts.

Britain's strategic nuclear forces currently consist of four SSBNs, each carrying sixteen missiles. Each missile can carry up to three multiple reentry vehicles, which are being equipped for advanced penetration and a capacity to maneuver in space, though not to be targeted independently. Its fifty-seven Vulcan bombers armed with gravity bombs are to be retired within the year. What remains is consonant with a minimum deterrent capable of surviving a Soviet first strike and retaliating against Soviet cities or soft targets, especially by attacking the center of Soviet power in Moscow itself. But Great Britain cannot credibly extend deterrence to its continental allies: it has too few submarines on patrol to make possible withholding warheads in a limited attack, and those warheads are too inaccurate to threaten most other targets. Indeed, current British targeting doctrine is probably somewhat incompatible with the extended deterrence provided by American strategic forces.

British acquisition of Trident D-5 missiles will make independent deterrence only marginally more feasible. The D-5 has twice the range of the Polaris A-3 missile, allowing the SSBN to patrol in a much greater area. Increased range not only increases its survivability but also may make withholding more feasible. Each D-5 can carry up to fourteen independently targetable warheads, although the British currently intend to put no more than eight MIRVs on each missile. MIRVing the sixteen missiles on each submarine would increase the number of targets they could strike by an order of magnitude. And the accuracy of the D-5 would enable the British to attack hard targets, including Soviet ICBM silos, although not in sufficient numbers to give Britain a first-strike capability against the entire Soviet land-based missile force unless they were used as part of the American SIOP. The D-5, in short, in addition to increasing the credibility of minimum deterrence, might enable Great Britain to withhold an attack on cities and strike a variety of other targets. The British White Paper on Trident hints at this prospect in justifying acquisition of the earlier generation of Trident missile, the C-4:

Successive United Kingdom governments have always declined to make public their nuclear targetting policy and plans, or to define precisely what minimum level of destructive capability they judged necessary for deterrence. The Government however thinks it right now to make clear that their concept of deterrence is concerned essentially with posing a potential threat to key aspects of Soviet state power. *There might with changing conditions be more than one way of doing this, and some flexibility in contingency planning is appropriate.*[18]

The British government originally made the case for Trident as a hedge against Soviet antiballistic missile and antisubmarine war threats, but in the event of an NFU declaration it might shift its ground to make Trident a hedge against American disengagement.

Domestic support for Britain's nuclear posture is less than enthusiastic. Unilateral disarmers question the nation's possession or basing of nuclear weapons no matter who owns them. Doubts about Trident are more widespread, ranging from those of military men and their Conservative supporters who see the program as a diversion of scarce resources from other, more urgent military needs, to those of Labourites and Social Democrats who worry about the social consequences of so large an expenditure on military hardware. An American NFU declaration, some feel, might further polarize the British polity on the issue of nuclear weapons by hardening the Tory faith in the independent deterrent as insurance against U.S. disengagement while giving new inspiration to the unilateralists on the left dedicated to ridding themselves of these weapons, without reassuring the center about American reliability and steadfastness.

Adoption of NFU by the United States, either as declaratory policy or as the basis for its posture and plans, would be unlikely to alter one fundamental element of French and British nuclear policy: that in the event of conventional war in Europe, both nations are prepared to consider first use of their nuclear forces on or near the battlefield and ultimately against targets in the Soviet Union. NFU thus might reduce somewhat the risk of nuclear war but not eliminate it—a fact that Soviet planners are likely to take into account in considering changes in their nuclear posture.

But even if France and Great Britain continue to rely on a declaratory policy of first use, they are unlikely to acquire the nuclear wherewithal to carry it out. Nor will their threat to respond to conventional war in central Europe with nuclear means be any more credible than America's. Beefed-up conventional capabilities will remain necessary to buttress their nuclear postures. In a strategic environment in which nuclear forces check each other, the conventional balance becomes critical to any calculation of risk. Moreover, the circumstances in which first use of nuclear weapons might seem credible do not arise at the very outset of war in Europe, but only after the conventional battle has gathered intensity over time. Steps to enhance conventional forces and prevent a rapid collapse of NATO's forward defenses do not undermine the nuclear guarantee; they reinforce it—no less so for the French and British than for the Americans. Hence, regardless of their stances on NFU, Britain and France would do well to consider measures to improve their conventional capabilities in support of NATO. Britain's acquisition of Trident, for example, if it came at the expense of withdrawing the British Army of the Rhine, would add little or nothing to NATO's or Britain's overall security.

Cross-pressures on French defense policy leave the possibility of substantial conventional force improvements in doubt. On the one hand, economic recession has put added strains on a budget already stretched by the need to carry out long-standing policy pledges of the Socialist party. With its unshakable commitment to nuclear modernization, the government has been forced to retrench on conventional force improvements. It has put as good a face as it could on the cutbacks by restructuring the armed forces, putting greater emphasis on the reserves and on lighter, more mobile standing forces to counter a tank assault.[19] On the other hand, some French officials, mainly but not exclusively in the Quai d'Orsay, are uneasy about growing neutralism and pacifism on the German left and eager to draw their neighbors into a "strategic dialogue" as a way of ensuring against any reorientation in German outlook. While the most visible aspect of this dialogue has been France's willingness to inform the Germans of its nuclear thinking, the more significant step has been improved Franco-German cooperation on the conventional side.[20] This context has also facilitated greater French cooperation within NATO, including restoring lines of communication and joint force planning, without raising the question of formal reintegration. These moves could help to reduce reliance on nuclear weapons while protecting against any adverse political side-effects in Bonn, but only if they are accompanied by improvements in French conventional forces, a point made by those who object to cutbacks in the army budget.[21]

Chemical Weapons

Consideration of NFU focuses attention on what nuclear weapons can and cannot deter. Chemical warfare is a case in point. What are the implications of NFU for NATO's use of nuclear weapons to deter chemical warfare in Europe?

Chemical weapons have much in common with nuclear weapons.

Both differ qualitatively from conventional weapons in that they are intrinsically indiscriminate. Their use inevitably causes collateral damage, regardless of the precautions taken to prevent it. Moreover, what may disturb people most about nuclear weapons is the effect that most closely resembles that of chemicals: radiation, like gas, diffuses almost imperceptibly through the air and kills slowly, silently, randomly. There are of course important differences between chemical and nuclear weapons. It is possible to protect military forces against the effects of chemicals in ways that are not available against nuclear or, for that matter, conventional weapons. Moreover, the sheer mass of chemical stocks required to have effects equivalent to those of a single nuclear explosion poses formidable problems of logistics and delivery. These differences notwithstanding, the perceived similarity between chemical and nuclear weapons necessitates consideration of the links between the two when considering an NFU declaration for nuclear weapons.

To the extent that chemical and nuclear weapons are perceived as two of a kind and qualitatively distinct from conventional weapons, initiating chemical warfare would be tantamount to crossing the nuclear threshold rather than taking an intermediate step on some hypothetical ladder of escalation. In that case, nuclear retaliation would seem a proportionate response. Threatened first use of nuclear weapons could thus deter the use of chemicals in a war in Europe. When Great Britain decided to destroy its chemical weapon stocks and renounce chemical warfare in 1970, Defense Minister Denis Healey appeared to endorse this logic before the House of Commons: "If the House really considers the situation, I believe it will recognize that it is almost inconceivable that enemy forces would use chemical weapons against NATO forces except in the circumstances of mass invasion—in which event more terrible weapons would surely come into play."[22] This principle, however, has never become formal NATO—or British—policy.

Instead, NATO along with the United States continues to base its policy on the prenuclear premise that it takes chemicals to deter the use of chemical weapons. That policy stipulates no first use of chemicals. In the United States it was first promulgated by President Franklin D. Roosevelt in June 1943, when reports of Japanese use of gas in China were circulating in Allied capitals: "I state categorically that we shall under no circumstances resort to the use of such weapons unless they are first used by our enemies." He accompanied this pledge with a threat: "Any use of gas by any Axis power, therefore, will immediately be followed by the fullest possible retaliation upon munition centers, seaports, and other military objectives throughout the whole extent of the territory of such Axis country."[23] NFU remains the U.S. policy on chemical warfare to this day. When the United States became a signatory of the Geneva Protocol in 1975, fifty years after initialing it, the Senate qualified the treaty's absolute prohibition of the use of chemical and biological weapons by attaching a reservation that in effect reiterated Roosevelt's policy.

That policy permits the Army Chemical Corps to continue stockpiling chemical agents as a deterrent to enemy use. Yet chemicals have seemed ancillary to the Army's essential mission, ground combat, and at least partially competitive with the principal capabilities for carrying out that mission, firepower and mobility. Moreover, many Army officers remain skeptical that chemicals would be usable by either side in central Europe. Consequently the Army has always stinted on its chemical warfare effort and never fully integrated chemicals into its forces and plans. The chemical capability it has acquired consists largely of quick-acting agents in bombs and artillery shells, the least incompatible with other Army capabilities. The United States has not added to those stocks since 1969.[24]

Those who advocate new deployments of chemical weapons would doubtless seize on a nuclear NFU declaration to press their case. That case rests on three arguments: that chemicals alone deter the use of chemicals; that the Warsaw Pact has a substantial chemical capability, both offensive and defensive, thoroughly integrated into its force structure and plans; and that, to judge from reports of toxic "yellow rain" in Afghanistan, the Russians are prepared to engage in chemical warfare. The case is less than wholly convincing.

First, little is known about Soviet chemical capabilities. In 1975 the chairman of the Joint Chiefs of Staff acknowledged that "it is not possible with any reasonable degree of assurance to predict or estimate the size of the Soviet Union's agent stockpile."[25] Nor is there much basis for firm conclusions about the quality of Soviet efforts. The pattern of Soviet deployment yields no definitive clues about their intended use: they could serve as an offensive threat or a retaliatory capability. Far from indicating preparedness to wage chemical warfare, the extensive precautions the Soviet Union has taken against chemicals in Europe may well be the by-product of an earlier preoccupation with protecting troops in a nuclear environment.[26] Any use of chemicals in Afghanistan is not germane to the question of deterring their use in Europe because of the asymmetry of forces in Afghanistan.

Second, any disadvantage NATO may have in chemicals does not stem from the size or age of its chemical inventory, but from the politics and logistics of deploying chemical munitions in Western Europe. U.S. stocks are plentiful and many of them are years away from deterioration or obsolescence.[27] That they are not located where they might be needed is a legacy of World War I, when gas warfare in Europe caused 1.3 million casualties, including 91,000 deaths. Time has not dispelled the specter of Ypres. As a result, in NATO Europe only West Germany permits American forces to store chemical weapons on its territory, only France still manufactures them, and NATO has never agreed to integrate such munitions into its force posture and plans.

Redeployment of NATO's chemical stocks, many of them in the United States, to central Europe under wartime conditions would be a feat of logistics. To facilitate redeployment, the Army's chemical warfare specialists want to produce a new generation of chemical munitions. Called binary weapons, they are bomb or artillery shells containing two substances that are relatively harmless if kept apart in separate canisters but combine chemically to form nerve gas when the munition is fired and the canisters burst. The two ingredients would be manufactured, transported, and stored separately; the canisters would be mated on the battlefield just before use and their contents combined only upon firing.[28] While binary munitions would substantially reduce the risks of transportation and storage, their greater weight and volume, as well as the complexity of mating canisters on the battlefield, would hardly eliminate logistical difficulties. An attempt to ease those difficulties by deploying binaries to the U.S. forces in West Germany under present political conditions would probably backfire, perhaps forcing the withdrawal of existing stocks.

Lastly, new chemical weapon deployments would add little to deterrence. Even in retaliation, chemicals do not seem very usable amid the densely settled areas of central Europe. And defenses against chemicals are feasible, at least for military forces. Respirators and special clothing can substantially reduce troop contamination, although they limit mobility and exertion, especially in hot weather. Modern tanks are equipped with seals and filtered air supplies to protect their crews. Antidotes administered by the troops themselves can save the lives of those exposed to nerve gas. Decontamination kits are also standard equipment. These means of protecting troops against chemical attack by and large would be reasonably effective if widely instituted. Given the vagaries of wind and weather, the principal victims of chemical attack are thus likely to be unprotected civilians, not enemy forces. That would undoubtedly be the case if NATO were to retaliate in kind for enemy first use of chemicals. Hence the authority to retaliate in kind is likely to be granted grudgingly, if at all.

In any event, adoption of an NFU declaratory policy for nuclear weapons would require no compensatory change in the size or composition of NATO's chemical stockpile. Along with appropriate defensive countermeasures, the present stockpile should suffice to deter limited use of chemicals, leaving nuclear weapons to come into play in the event of large-scale or indiscriminate chemical attacks. Lest anyone misunderstand U.S. intentions, the adoption of a nuclear NFU policy could be combined with the present policy on chemicals by stipulating that the United States will not be the first to use nuclear or chemical weapons, but is prepared to respond to an adversary's first use of either with appropriate means.

NFU outside Europe

An NFU declaration would have implications for American strategy beyond the confines of Europe. While U.S. policy in recent years has emphasized equipping allies to defend themselves, treaty commitments as well as ties of history and common interest oblige the United States to do more. Ultimately those obligations extend to nuclear deterrence. That is why the United States has maintained a few hundred nuclear artillery shells in South Korea. The Reagan administration seeks to expand theater nuclear forces elsewhere by deploying sea-launched cruise missiles aboard surface vessels and submarines. But the efficacy of a nuclear response to a conventional challenge in Northeast Asia or the Persian Gulf is open to doubt.

Just how nuclear weapons would prove useful in the Persian Gulf has never been clear. A demonstrative use against Soviet forces would invite counterdemonstrations against the U.S. fleet and against ports, bases, pre-positioning sites, and other U.S. facilities in the region. The exchange could easily escalate, and the net result seems hardly to America's advantage. A threat to attack Soviet territory assumes an added risk of retaliation against the United States itself. If that threat is less than wholly credible in the European context, it is far less so elsewhere. While the mere presence of SLCM-armed ships might provide visible reassurance to some, it might also be a visible source of anxiety to others in a region menaced more by internal unrest than by external aggression. Ship visits and home-porting could not allay that anxiety.

Even in Northeast Asia, keeping an SLCM fleet on station will be difficult without access to neighboring ports. Most countries are unlikely to prove more hospitable than Japan, and land-based nuclear weapons are out of the question outside Korea. The nuclear artillery shells kept there create many of the dilemmas presented by short-range and dual-capable systems in central Europe. Moreover, they are unnecessary. With American help, South Korea's conventional forces seem adequate to deter a North Korean attack.

A discussion of the conventional capabilities needed to maintain U.S. commitments outside Europe and the contribution the NATO allies can make lies beyond the scope of this analysis. Yet one conclusion seems hard to dispute: nuclear weapons cannot substitute for conventional strength.

Notes

1. *Department of Defense Authorization for Appropriation for Fiscal Year 1979,* Hearings before the Senate Committee on Armed Services, 95 Cong. 2 sess. (Government Printing Office, 1978), pt. 9: *Research and Development,* pp. 6559–61.

2. U.S. Department of the Army, *Operations: FM 100-5* (Dept. of the Army, 1976), p. 10-9.

3. North Atlantic Treaty Organization, *Facts and Figures,* 10th ed. (Brussels: NATO Information Service, 1981), pp. 152–54.

4. Cited in footnote 8, North Atlantic Assembly's Special Committee on Nuclear Weapons in Europe, *Second Interim Report on Nuclear Weapons in Europe,* Committee Print, Senate Committee on Foreign Relations, 98 Cong. 1 sess. (GPO, 1983), p. 8.

5. On this point, see Fred Charles Iklé, "NATO's 'First Nuclear Use': A Deepening Trap?" *Strategic Review,* vol. 8 (Winter 1980), p. 20.

6. U.S. Department of the Army, *Operations: FM 100-5* (Dept. of the Army, 1982), p. 7-12.

7. "The Purpose of Pluton," Address by the French Prime Minister, M. Chirac, February 10, 1975, published in *Survival,* vol. 17 (September–October 1975), pp. 241–43; and "French Defence Policy," Comments by General Guy Mery, March 15, 1976, published in *Survival,* vol. 18. (September–October 1976), pp. 226–28.

8. "La Conférence de Presse," *Le Monde,* June 28, 1980.

9. Michel Debré, *French White Paper on National Defense,* vol. 1, *1972* (New York: Service de Presse et d'Information, 1972), p. 13. Cf. "Yvon Bourges Interviewed on

Defense Capabilities" in Foreign Broadcast Information Service (hereafter FBIS), *Daily Report: Western Europe,* May 9, 1980, p. K7.

10. Speech before the Institute of Advanced National Defense Studies, September 14, 1981, quoted in François de Rose, "Updating Deterrence in Europe: Inflexible Response?" *Survival,* vol. 24 (January–February 1982), p. 22.

11. "Politicians Plan Group to Counter Socialists," *International Herald-Tribune,* July 6, 1982.

12. "Yvon Bourges Interviewed on Defense Capabilities," p. K6.

13. *Le Figaro Magazine,* September 4–10, 1982, pp. 54–55.

14. Charles Hernu, "Une défense, des choix, des moyens," *Le Figaro,* January 30–31, 1982.

15. "The Future United Kingdom Strategic Nuclear Deterrent Force," Defence Open Government Document 80/23 (Ministry of Defence, 1980), pp. 3–4.

16. Ibid., p. 4.

17. A lucid and authoritative discussion of the debate over British nuclear posture and policy is found in Lawrence Freedman, *Britain and Nuclear Weapons* (London: Macmillan Press for the Royal Institute of International Affairs, 1980).

18. "The Future United Kingdom Strategic Nuclear Deterrent Force," p. 6. Emphasis added.

19. Jacques Isnard, "Le Général Delaunay dévoile les grandes lignes du nouveau modèle d'armée de terre proposé par M. Hernu," *Le Monde,* November 30, 1982; "Nuclear Forces to Receive Priority in 1983," in FBIS, *Daily Report: Western Europe,* October 8, 1982, p. K1; and "M. Hernu: Ne pas manquer les grands rendez-vous technologiques de demain," *Le Monde,* December 7, 1982.

20. Bradley Graham, "French to Share A-Plans with Bonn," *Washington Post,* October 23, 1982; and "Stratégie Franco-Allemande," *Le Monde,* October 24–25, 1982.

21. Confidential letter from Army Chief of Staff Delaunay to Armed Forces Chief of Staff Lacaze, leaked Washington-style and excerpted in *Le Matin,* December 6, 1982.

22. Stockholm International Peace Research Institute (SIPRI), *The Problem of Chemical and Biological Warfare,* vol. 2: *CB Weapons Today* (Stockholm: Almqvist and Wiksell, 1973), p. 189. The Thatcher government has since renewed British interest in chemical weapons.

23. Franklin D. Roosevelt, "Use of Poison Gas: Statement by the President," *Department of State Bulletin,* vol. 8 (June 12, 1943), p. 507. Reports of Japanese use of gas dropped off thereafter.

24. J. P. Perry Robinson, "Chemical Arms Control and the Assimilation of Chemical Weapons," *International Journal,* vol. 36 (Summer 1981), pp. 522–24, notes some institutional constraints on integrating chemical weapons into U.S. forces.

25. Wayne Biddle, "Restocking the Chemical Arsenal," *New York Times Magazine,* May 24, 1981, p. 37. A recent British estimate, the first ever made public by that government on its own authority, puts Soviet chemical munition stocks at 300,000 tonnes. U.K., Secretary of State for Defence, *Statement on the Defence Estimates, 1982:* vol. 1, cmnd. 8529-1 (London: Her Majesty's Stationery Office, 1982), p. 21.

26. C. N. Donnelly, "Winning the NBC War: Soviet Army Theory and Practice," *International Defense Review,* vol. 14, no. 8 (1981), p. 989.

27. "Would War with Gas Mean Holocaust?" Roundtable with Maj. Gen. Niles J. Fulwyler, director of the Army's Nuclear and Chemical Directorate, and Matthew Meselson, *New York Times,* May 2, 1982.

28. Matthew Meselson and Julian Perry Robinson, "Chemical Warfare and Chemical Disarmament," *Scientific American,* vol. 242 (April 1980), p. 40.

CHAPTER SEVEN

POLITICAL PROSPECTS
FOR NO FIRST USE

Leon V. Sigal

EUROPEAN and American reactions to proposals for no first use, whether as declaratory policy or military doctrine, should be viewed in the context of persistent ambivalence and sporadic outbursts of concern about nuclear weapons.

The current nuclear distemper in Europe began with the so-called neutron bomb controversy in 1977. Public opposition to the neutron weapon was muted at the time, but European governments were under no misapprehension that it would remain so, once they decided to deploy enhanced radiation weapons on European soil. Their reluctance to be seen embracing deployment was one reason for President Jimmy Carter's abrupt reversal on the issue. Following NATO's decision to deploy Pershing II and ground-launched cruise missiles in West Germany, Great Britain, Italy, Belgium, and the Netherlands, protest movements against nuclear weapons gained adherents throughout Western Europe. The reaction was not confined to activist circles, for public opinion showed signs of restiveness as well. While support for continued membership in NATO held firm in all five prospective basing countries, opposition to the missile deployments mounted and with it, fear that war was more imminent.

Antinuclear tremors reverberated through European politics, destabilizing governing coalitions, exposing fault lines within parties, especially on the center-left, and setting off a scramble for solid ground among politicians of all persuasions. No government has collapsed over the missile issue alone, but it has been a precipitating factor in changes of government in Belgium and the Netherlands. Splits have developed within the British Labour party, the German Social Democratic party (SPD), and most Belgian and Dutch parties on the moderate left. At its party conference in September 1982, British Labour reverted to the

134

unilateralist stance it had abandoned twenty years before by incorporating into the party's official program a pledge to cancel GLCM and Trident deployments and to close all nuclear bases in Britain, American and British alike.[1] The German SPD shows signs of moving in the same direction. Socialists in the Low Countries, Denmark, and Norway have also backed away from the NATO nuclear deployments. If this trend were to continue, it would narrow considerably the hitherto broad base of political support for NATO and threaten to turn the Alliance into a right-wing club.

Europe's Dependence and the Dilemmas of Deterrence

In diagnosing the current nuclear distemper, it is essential to recognize that neither the issues nor the policies proposed for dealing with them are new, including NFU. The issues have always been divisive, and they remain so today. No consensus has ever existed in Europe on the place of nuclear weapons in NATO strategy. Instead there has been public and parliamentary acquiescence by silence, punctuated by occasional outcries. Publics for the most part have left the debate up to experts in government who argue over technicalities in muffled tones and arcane language inaccessible to most laymen. Once public controversy has broken out—as it has from time to time in every NATO country except France—it has aroused intense moral anxiety that bureaucrats and strategists cannot address, much less allay. Yet past episodes of public controversy have been followed eventually by the restoration of popular acquiescence.

When considering the present nuclear anxiety, it is also worthwhile to recall the quite different anxiety that gave rise to NATO's decision to deploy new nuclear missiles in 1979. Then, some Europeans were worried by the growth of Soviet nuclear capability against Western Europe in the context of nuclear parity between the superpowers. The shift of mood over the next two years was a manifestation of the underlying causes of European unease.

The presence of nuclear weapons in Europe is more a symptom than a cause of that unease, for the weapons symbolize Europe's dependence on the United States for its ultimate security. Dependence breeds paranoia. A Europe caught between the superpowers can never feel wholly secure. As hostility rises between the two rivals, so does the risk of war, and with it the fear that the threat of nuclear retaliation may be invoked. As hostility subsides, so does the risk of war, and with it the assurance that the threat of nuclear retaliation remains reliable. A dependent Europe cannot be reassured. The swings in mood are most pronounced in West Germany and the Low Countries, where no illusion of political control can ease the anxiety of dependence.

That dependence rests ultimately on nuclear weapons adds to Europe's discomfort. Even if they do not follow the logic of deterrence in all its tortuous complexity, many Europeans grasp the paradox at its core: how can NATO deter the Warsaw Pact by retaliatory threats that it manifestly has little or no incentive to carry out? There is no sidestepping the dilemmas of deterrence that flow from this paradox—dilemmas in the strict sense of the term, posing unavoidable choices among alternatives, all of which are unsatisfactory. They are of long standing, recurring again and again without being resolvable once and for all.

Chapter 4 proposes a way out of these dilemmas: to base deterrence primarily on conventional capabilities so robust that the Warsaw Pact will either doubt its chances for victory in a conventional conflict, or fear that a conventional war in Europe might escalate to nuclear war. Yet to some Europeans, the emphasis on conventional deterrence merely poses the dilemma in a new form: how can NATO enhance deterrence by a threat that, however more likely to be carried out, reduces potential damage to the Soviet Union?

Geography makes this dilemma all the sharper. From the vantage point of West Germany, any step that reduces the potential cost of war to the Warsaw Pact would seem to increase the chance of its outbreak, and that is intolerable. Conventional weapons have become so destructive that the prospect of any war is too grim to bear for anyone situated near the front lines. What threatens to destroy West Germany is not nuclear war, but war. As a consequence, German strategists have tended until recently to emphasize deterrence rather than defense and to speak only of forward defense if they speak of defense at all, while many of their American counterparts have seen advantages in waging a conventional defense in depth, allowing NATO forces to fall back into Germany and wage a sustained conventional war.

From the vantage point of Washington, short-range or battlefield nuclear weapons, which offer at least some possibility of limiting nuclear war to Europe, may seem more usable than nuclear weapons capable of striking the USSR, which invite an immediate Soviet counterattack against the United States. Some American strategists make a distinction between what they call tactical and strategic nuclear weapons. Yet what appears to be tactical an ocean away from the battlefield is strategic to those living where the warheads would explode. Europeans might prefer to have the United States use intermediate-range nuclear weapons against the Soviet heartland in hope that the Soviet response would take place over their heads. Precisely this prospect, however, would probably make the United States no more willing to use those weapons than its own strategic forces.

Anxiety induced by dependence, compounded by the dilemmas of deterrence, lies at the source of the current malaise no less than of similar unease during the past thirty years. Yet the basis of dependence has undergone significant changes over the course of those years. If Europe remains ultimately dependent on the American nuclear deterrent for its security, that dependence now seems more remote than before. The change came about with mutual vulnerability, which has been a fact of life for the superpowers since the mid-1960s. While Charles de Gaulle and other Europeans expected this development, the strategic arms limitation talks brought it home to everyone. The shock of recognition led some Europeans to conclude that the American presence was less a source of reassurance, committing America irrevocably to Europe's defense, than a source of peril that could entangle Europe in the American-Soviet rivalry. A second change was the postwar economic recovery, which restored Europe's self-confidence. If the basis of dependence was eroding, so, too, was the feeling. But dependence would remain so long as Europe could not provide wholly for its own security. For some Europeans, the implication was that European states must have nuclear forces of their own; for others, that a European defense of Europe could not be nuclear alone, that conventional defense was the way to ease the anxiety of dependence.

Amid these crosscurrents lies the Federal Republic of Germany. West Germans, precluded by recent history from having nuclear forces of their own and thus ultimately dependent, yet deriving little reassurance from new nuclear deployments on their soil, wish to raise the nuclear threshold without putting it out of reach. Many are prepared to do more for conventional defense but are worried about the domestic budgetary cost and the commitment of others. West Germany is moving toward greater defense cooperation with France but within the framework of NATO, seeking to be more European without seeming less Atlanticist, perhaps to ensure against too close an embrace with America without feeding American doubts or loosening American ties.

Since there is no escaping the dilemmas of deterrence, neither the deployment of new American missiles nor the withdrawal of all U.S. forces from the Continent could put an end to European anxiety. The decision to deploy new intermediate-range nuclear missiles forced to the surface the latent fear that the threat of nuclear retaliation might be invoked. Yet NFU, if it came to be seen in Europe as an American attempt to avoid sharing the risk of war, could give rise to the opposite fear—that the threat of American nuclear retaliation could not be counted on. The withdrawal of short-range nuclear weapons would not have these connotations if it were done in the context of successful implementation of both tracks of NATO's December 1979 decision: a modest deployment of some new missiles within negotiated limits on the nuclear forces of both sides.

The persistence of the underlying dilemmas suggests that policies proposed to ease present European anxieties might give rise to the opposite anxieties a few years later. Implementing NFU, for example, would require a sustained effort that is bound to slacken if NFU were presented as a cure for the present nuclear distemper. For dependence also affects the level of conventional effort in Europe. To the extent that it has fostered the conviction that Europeans themselves can do little to improve NATO's defenses, dependence puts the Alliance in a political quandary. If the United States should threaten to withdraw its conventional forces from the Continent, Europeans would despair of offsetting the threat from the East through efforts of their own. If the American conventional effort should slacken, instead of compensating by increasing their own defense efforts, Europeans would ask why they should take the threat any more seriously than the United States. But if the United States were to step up its efforts, Europeans would conclude that they need not do more themselves. The increased conventional effort required of all the allies can be sustained only if NFU does not appear to be a purely American initiative.

American Challenges to NATO's Working Premises

While the current disquiet in Europe is largely attributable to conditions there, it has been aggravated since 1979 by a dramatic if perhaps impermanent shift in the American stance. The United States has begun posing a rather direct challenge to three working premises of its military cooperation with Europe.

One premise is that NATO is a military alliance for the common defense in Europe. The United States has sought to expand NATO's mission beyond Europe's boundaries. Yet allied involvement outside Europe has always been divisive, whether it has been Franco-British intervention over Suez or American engagement in Vietnam or differences in the Middle East. Despite talk of a division of labor, agreement on a common course of action has seldom been possible. As Henry Kissinger observed in 1965, "Sharing our burdens would give impetus to Atlantic cooperation only if our Allies have the same view as we of what is at stake outside of Europe and if they believe that the United States would curtail its commitments but for their assistance. Neither condition is met today."[2] Or since, one might add. American efforts to foster those conditions after Afghanistan and Iran, whether by lectures on the common cause or threats of unilateralism, have only exacerbated relations among the allies.

A second challenge from the United States is to the Alliance's shared image of the Soviet threat. American hyperbole about the magnitude and imminence of that threat is greeted with incredulity in Europe, where exposure to Soviet power has been a constant since World War II. Nothing short of a drastic overturning of the military balance is likely to alter European perceptions very much. Moreover, Europeans have sensed a diminution of the threat as a result of the erosion of the Soviet position in Eastern Europe, the diversion of military resources to the Far East and Afghanistan, and continuing economic weaknesses at home. The discrepancy between the European and American assessments has aroused more suspicion about American than about Soviet intentions. Suspicion is not allayed when the United States rationalizes its attempts to expand NATO's mission beyond Europe by attributing security threats elsewhere to Soviet manipulation and by proclaiming the "indivisibility" of détente. European support for countervailing pressure against the USSR in Europe has continued to be forthcoming; enthusiasm for an anticommunist crusade has not. Americans who fostered an inflated image of the Soviet menace feel let down by the European response. Exaggerated threat assessments discourage European defense efforts, in turn stimulating American impatience and pressures to withdraw from the Continent. Unilateralism in America and neutralism in Europe feed on each other.

Third and more fundamental is the American challenge to Alliance policy for meeting the Soviet threat: deterrence and détente. Western Europe has few war-fighters, nuclear or otherwise. To most Europeans, the only rationale for NATO's military capability is deterrence—a rationale rooted in the events of this century. The European experience, Fritz Stern has pointed out, has not been one of "the triumphant use of power" but "of brute and futile power, blindly spent and blindly worshipped."[3] That experience shaped the reaction of many Europeans to strategic parity, when they recognized American nuclear superiority to be a thing of the past and extended deterrence as less than certain. They became skeptical of American attempts to restore superiority, and with it the certainty of extended deterrence. Most are prepared to live with less than certainty. Loose talk from Washington about limited nuclear war, exchange ratios, and prevailing in protracted conflict only arouses their fear of war without reassuring them of its outcome. Those who do not dismiss this rhetoric as meaningless deem it unduly provocative.

From a European perspective, Americans have said far too much about moving beyond nuclear deterrence and too little about détente, none of it positive. While continuing to sell wheat to Moscow, Washington accused Europeans of being bought off by the gas pipeline and other commercial deals with the East. Apart from its inconsistency, to trivialize and demean the European conception of détente in this way is an affront. To the "great simplifiers" in America, détente is an unspeakable French word; to sophisticated Europeans, détente reinforced by deterrence holds the best hope for survival against an implacable foe in a nuclear world. Historical experience has taught them that neither deterrence nor détente by itself will suffice: the lesson of the interwar period is that conciliation not backed by strength is a flawed policy; the lesson of the years before World War I is that strength without conciliation is no better.

These lessons are not lost on the current generation of European leaders or on NATO itself. As the Harmel report noted in 1967, "Military security and a policy of détente are not contradictory but complementary."[4] For many Europeans, détente means more than trade with the East; it also signifies a gradual evolution in the two Europes, perhaps leading to a partial restoration of historic ties on the Continent. For some in Germany, it holds the possibility that the division of Europe is not permanent; for others, it makes permanent division more tolerable, enabling families separated by the postwar partition to resume normal contacts as well as commerce.

In Europe, the perceived effect of all three American challenges to accepted NATO premises is to heighten the risk of war, and with it the fear that nuclear weapons might be used. The challenges have also raised the prospect that Europe might be drawn into a war on the periphery. NFU might ease fears of entrapment, only to reawaken fears of abandonment.

The Domestic Politics of NFU in Europe

An NFU declaration would bring little more than temporary relief from the distress arising from Europe's dependence on the United States and from the dilemmas of deterrence. Unless the declaration were taken seriously and translated into changes in NATO's conventional and nuclear postures, it could do little to damp the swings of mood in Europe. But effectuating those changes will be difficult unless they have a European constituency—and that constituency does not now exist. NFU is unlikely to exert mass appeal, though it could prove attractive to some parliamentarians and attentive publics.

The pool of nuclear discontent is fed by several streams emanating from diverse sources. NFU would have marginal appeal for the antinuclear activists, though it might enlist the sympathies of some who would otherwise gravitate toward that movement. Among the activists are a great many pacifists who renounce the use of force on religious and ethical grounds. For them the distinction between nuclear and conventional forces is insignificant. Yet to deny that distinction is to condemn NFU to irrelevance. Most pacifists want nuclear weapons to be removed from Europe and nothing put in their place. The movement also includes environmentalists, who are as opposed to nuclear power as they are to nuclear weapons, and a small minority of parliamentarians, strategists, arms controllers, and others who harbor doubts about NATO's strategy and wish to reduce its reliance on nuclear weapons. The withdrawal of short-range nuclear warheads from Europe might find favor among these groups.

Other activists have joined with antinuclear groups as a means to other ends. For some the end is a reduced American presence in Europe or none at all; since nuclear weapons are both the symbol and embodiment of that presence, they want them removed. The reasons behind their common stand are varied. For a few the motive is a mixture of nationalism and neutralism. In Germany, for example, some believe that the only chance for reunification lies in loosening West Germany's ties to NATO and the United States. In the Low Countries, for reasons rooted in a history of neutrality, the drive for denuclearization is associated with nationalistic neutralism. For radical leftists the American presence in Europe forecloses the possibility of reorganizing political and economic relations at home along socialist lines; they seek to capitalize on an unpopular manifestation of that presence—nuclear weapons—to rally others to their cause. For still others the motive is little more than visceral populist anti-Americanism. These factions and others that wish to disassociate Europe from America would find little to gain from NFU.

For every European who sees nuclear weapons as a surrogate for American links to Europe and wants them removed, many others see a connection and want to maintain it. NFU could dismay the latter unless it were made clear that the changes in NATO's force posture would strengthen transatlantic military bonds. The less NFU seems a purely American initiative, the more reassuring it may be to these Europeans. It is among this large centrist group with representation in parties of both left and right, not among the antinuclear activists, that reduced reliance on nuclear weapons might have considerable appeal.

NFU of course implies more than reduced reliance on nuclear weapons and a drawdown of short-range warheads, for it would also entail an increase in conventional capabilities. Especially in times of economic recession, the cost of those capabilities could give pause to those who might otherwise be drawn to NFU. Given their traditional commitment to fiscal prudence and the welfare state, Christian Democrats in general and those in West Germany in particular might decline to pay the costs of NFU until economic recovery is assured. It would make sense to allay concerns about cost at both ends of the political spectrum—on the right, mindful of fiscal prudence, and on the left, protective of social welfare programs. But it would be politically unrealistic during a recession to expect any European parliament to authorize higher taxes, deeper deficits, or cuts in social programs for the sake of NFU.

The Bureaucratic Politics of NFU

Proponents of a no-first-use declaration argue that bureaucratically the best way to persuade American military planners in Washington and SHAPE to take NFU seriously is to proclaim it. Once the policy is announced, they will feel obliged to put it into practice. But policy is seldom, if ever, self-implementing. To translate NFU into NATO force postures and plans would require bureaucratic support. An NFU declaration will be resisted or supported according to the organizational interests of the military services and their relevant constituent parts; it will not alter those interests.

Which interests are at stake in the proposed changes? Since the end of World War II, nuclear roles and missions have had a special aura; otherwise it would be hard to explain why the U.S. Army and the Tactical Air Command, the two American military organizations responsible for nuclear roles and missions in Europe, would attach so much significance to these tasks. For years the Tactical Air Command has sought capabilities for delivering nuclear weapons against deep interdiction targets, preferably inside the Soviet Union. By contrast it has taken less pride in close air support. The Army's essential mission remains ground combat, yet it has been reluctant to relinquish its residual nuclear responsibilities in the form of battlefield systems in Europe and antiballistic missiles at home.

The Army and the Tactical Air Command would be the principal beneficiaries of NFU in practice. Their capabilities for fulfilling conventional roles and missions would increase significantly under the proposals made in chapter 4, as would their shares of the defense budget. Yet this prospect leaves them in doubt. The forces needed to carry out conventional tasks cost considerably more than nuclear forces to buy and maintain. Under current economic conditions, it would be virtually impossible to raise tax revenues or cut back on other programs—whether for social welfare or defense—to pay the cost. The competition for scarce resources reinforces their doubts: better to hang on to what we've got, they may reason, than to risk coming up empty-handed. A firm commitment to allocate the resources necessary for bolstering conventional defenses might well reassure them. Without it, they will be reluctant converts to NFU.

The competition for military resources affects rival services' calculations of organizational interests as well, and not only in the United States. Throughout NATO, nuclear forces help the other armed services to put a lid on army budgets, thereby allowing them to maintain their budget shares against army claims. They are likely to resist any change as a threat to the status quo with no offsetting advantages to their roles and missions, capabilities, or budgets.

Dual capability evokes still other bureaucratic interests. For the guardians of allied treasuries as well as Pentagon systems analysts, dual capability seems cost effective—getting two weapons for more nearly the price of one. But the accountant's preference for not buying two aircraft or howitzers when one might do discounts the pernicious effect of commonality on strategy and choice in the event of war.

Because the United States cannot implement NFU alone and needs Alliance cooperation, opponents of NFU in Washington can be expected to make common cause with like-minded organizations in other NATO capitals. An NFU declaration could facilitate the formation of an alliance within the Alliance by explicitly making an issue of NATO doctrine.

At best, doctrine is difficult to change within any military service. For NATO to reformulate its doctrine requires agreement from all the services and all the defense ministers of all the participating countries. Changes in MC-14/3, the strategic guidance to NATO commanders that codifies flexible response, could be proposed by the Supreme Allied Commander, Europe. They would then be considered by the NATO Military Committee, composed of the chiefs of staff of all the member states except France or their permanent representatives. The chiefs of staff presumably would have to coordinate the changes with the other military services in their respective countries. The Military Committee itself is supported by an international military staff whose plans and policy division would review the proposal. With the approval of the Military Committee, the new guidance would then be put before NATO's Defense Planning Committee, which meets frequently at the ambassadorial level and twice a year at the ministerial level. A change of this magnitude would undoubtedly require approval by the defense ministers themselves. The process is elaborate, time-consuming, and prone to deadlock.

To ask NATO to revise its doctrine of flexible response as a first step toward changing its force posture and plans would inject an imponderable question into an interminable process. Flexible response is deliberately ambiguous precisely because the dilemmas of NATO's strategy cannot be resolved. Attempts to change the doctrine could reopen a potentially divisive theological dispute about the role of nuclear weapons and allow opponents of any change to take refuge in existing doctrine.

A better way to implement NFU arises from the fact that doctrinal change is neither necessary nor sufficient to alter NATO practices. The proposed changes could readily be accommodated within the existing doctrine of flexible response. Instead of changing NATO's declaratory policy to NFU as the first step toward changing the force posture and plans, it might be easier to gain agreement on the practical steps to be taken with NATO's conventional and nuclear forces without raising doctrinal issues.

Lastly, the adoption of NFU in practice might be more attainable if it were not labeled "made in America." In November 1982 the North Atlantic Assembly, composed of parliamentarians from the NATO nations, adopted a resolution urging "appropriate High Level Group studies" and the implementation of policies "reducing the Alliance's reliance on short-range nuclear weapons."[5] Other Alliance-wide initiatives and a somewhat less visible American role might reassure those whose agreement must be sought and cannot be compelled.

NFU has value as a critical tool, exposing faults in NATO's current conventional and nuclear posture that NATO will have to remedy regardless of its declaratory policy. The question to be addressed in weighing the adoption of NFU as NATO's declaratory policy is whether NFU can be a creative as well as a critical tool, promoting the necessary changes in force posture. Alliance politics suggests that it cannot. To many Europeans, NFU is disturbing because it calls into question America's ultimate willingness to use nuclear weapons in Europe's behalf. Because NFU arouses anxieties on this point and NATO's Byzantine procedures for changing its doctrine give undue advantage to those who would oppose any change whatever, an attempt to alter declaratory policy first might only delay the implementation of essential changes in NATO's posture and plans. For that reason, NFU might be best left unsaid.

Notes

1. R. W. Apple, Jr., "Labor Party Reinforces Stand on Disarmament by Britain," *New York Times,* September 30, 1982; and "Labour Asserts Unilateral Pledge in New Policy Paper," *The Guardian,* June 18, 1982.

2. Henry A. Kissinger, *The Troubled Partnership: A Re-appraisal of the Atlantic Alliance* (McGraw-Hill for the Council on Foreign Relations, 1965), p. 231.

3. Fritz Stern, "A Shift of Mood in Europe," *New York Times,* September 2, 1981.

4. "Report on the Future Tasks of the Alliance," *NATO Letter,* vol. 16 (January 1968), p. 26.

5. North Atlantic Assembly's Special Committee on Nuclear Weapons in Europe, *Second Interim Report on Nuclear Weapons in Europe,* Committee Print, prepared for the Senate Committee on Foreign Relations, 98 Cong. 1 sess. (Government Printing Office, 1983), p. VII.

CHAPTER EIGHT

THE NO-FIRST-USE QUESTION
IN WEST GERMANY

Gert Krell
Thomas Risse-Kappen
Hans-Joachim Schmidt

MORE than fifteen years have passed since defense policy and military strategy were last on the public agenda in West Germany. Renewal of the defense debate was prompted in the first instance by highly visible nuclear decisions, first on the enhanced radiation weapon and then on the deployment of new "Eurostrategic" missiles—the Pershing II and ground-launched cruise missiles. The debate has moved beyond the peace movements, reaching the established social and political institutions, the churches, the unions, and above all the political parties. Divisions cut across all major camps. Peace and security have become controversial issues within not only the Social Democratic party (SPD), but also the Free Democratic party (FDP) and even the Christian Democratic Union and the Christian Social Union (CDU/CSU). This is the backdrop against which to view West German reactions to the no-first-use idea.

The debate over NFU has only begun. As yet, no parties have adopted formal positions on NFU, not even the Greens, nor has the peace movement. Generally, the CDU/CSU is opposed to the idea. NFU is not even supported by the leading CDU critic of nuclear weapons, Kurt Biedenkopf, who speaks for a very small minority in the party representative of the *Evangelische Arbeitskreis,* a circle of Protestant Christian Democrats. There is, however, support within the CDU for strengthening conventional deterrence and thereby raising the nuclear threshold. Manfred Wörner, the former parliamentary spokesman for the CDU and now the minister of defense, has indicated that he would like to move in that direction. The FDP has not yet discussed NFU extensively in its national committees dealing with foreign policy and defense policy. It does not consider NFU to be a realistic option, at least for the time being, although it is willing to discuss measures that could raise the nuclear threshold. Only the SPD has formally committed itself to studying the adoption of NFU as party policy. In April 1982, the party convention asked its executive to report on alternative defense strategies, including NFU, by the summer of 1983. A commission chaired by Egon Bahr will present its analysis and proposals to a special party convention in the fall of 1983 that is to decide the SPD's position on the deployment of intermediate-range missiles. Within the SPD attitudes towards NFU range, left to right, from Oscar Lafontaine's unconditional support and Egon Bahr's combined NFU–arms control approach, to Erwin Horn's conventional rearmament position similar to that of Wörner, to Georg Leber's outright opposition to the idea. The peace movement and the Greens seem to have no unified position on the issue. Some support NFU, or at least its basic direction, but most warn against increasing conventional arms. The following statement may be representative of their attitude: "We support a Europe free of nuclear weapons with the lowest possible level of purely defensive conventional arms."[1]

In sum, the spectrum of stands on NFU to be found in West Germany includes:

—Unconditional unilateral NFU. This position claims the support of a small minority within the SPD and sections of the peace movement.

—Unilateral or bilateral NFU accompanied by an increase in NATO's conventional forces to restore the conventional balance in Europe. Several defense experts across party lines consider this a good idea in principle, but they question the chances for realizing it because an NFU declaration would require a considerable buildup of conventional forces in order to be meaningful. They doubt that the necessary financial and manpower resources are available for such a buildup and they fear its possible consequences, such as a militarization of West German society and strains on the domestic political and social consensus.

—Bilateral NFU combined with a balance of conventional forces in Europe to be achieved through arms control. This essentially is Egon Bahr's position, which envisages NFU as part of a long-term comprehensive strategy for security in Europe. It will probably find broad support within the SPD. So, too, would an NFU agreement covering conventional as well as nuclear weapons. Experts in other parties may find such assessments basically acceptable, but they do not regard them as realistic.

—Rejection of NFU. Outright opponents not only believe the requirements necessary for NFU do not exist, but would also oppose NFU even if conventional compensation were possible. They fear an increased risk of conventional war and of decoupling the American nuclear deterrent. As will be explained in a moment, the West German "Gang of Four" has taken this line, as has former Defense Minister Hans Apel.

—Options short of the formal adoption of NFU, such as raising the nuclear threshold and increasing conventional flexibility. A rather broad consensus to move in this direction is emerging across all parties. The threat of an early use of nuclear weapons is no longer considered necessary. Significant reductions in battlefield nuclear weapons are regarded as possible by some.[2] No agreement yet exists, however, on measures to be taken in the conventional area.

The basic problems of security policy raised in the current debate have existed since West Germany became a member of NATO in 1955.[3] Since then, three constants have characterized the German security debate. One is the dilemma of deterrence and defense that arises from Germany's exposed geographic position. Second is the problem of risk-sharing—of coupling German security to the American deterrent. Third is the political requirement for détente.

The Dilemma of Deterrence and Defense

Because West Germany is highly industrialized and densely populated, any defense of its territorial integrity risks the destruction of what is supposed to be defended. Simulations of tactical nuclear as well as conventional war leave no doubt about that. To prevent war, *any* kind of war, in central Europe has thus always claimed undisputed priority in West German defense policy and in the political system, far outranking considerations of damage limitation.

An unqualified preference for war prevention does not resolve the dilemma, of course. All weapons have an inherent capacity for use, and if deterrence is to be credible, they must be designed for specific uses. The security debate in Germany nevertheless has tended to put so much emphasis on deterrence that even conventional forces are discussed mainly in terms of their war-preventing function. The German debate has concentrated on the issue of which combination of defenses would most credibly present the adversary with unacceptable risks and thus most reliably prevent war. The main dividing line has been a difference in emphasis between conventional and nuclear forces, with political parties and individuals sometimes shifting allegiance according to circumstances.

When the CDU/CSU government presented its proposals for the introduction of military conscription in 1956, it emphasized the importance of the army—the Bundeswehr—for strengthening the conventional component of the deterrent, since the employment of strategic nuclear weapons would spell death for the German people in the first hour of a conflict. The SPD concentrated its fire on the nuclearization of NATO doctrine in 1954, which provided for early use of tactical nuclear weapons, and on its possible consequences, which became known to the general public in the wake of the Carte Blanche tactical air exercise in June 1955.

At the end of the 1950s, when the Bundeswehr was about to receive its own nuclear-capable delivery vehicles, the federal government under the strong influence of Defense Minister Franz-Josef Strauss supported the concept of graduated deterrence, which still emphasized nuclear retaliation. West Germany's acquisition of nuclear-capable systems, Strauss argued, would make the risk of escalation incalculable for the enemy. Conventional forces were considered necessary, but their deterrent value was regarded as low. Strauss was highly critical of the concept of flexible response introduced by the Kennedy administration and accepted by NATO in 1967. He warned against the "Vietnamization of NATO strategy" and the new "doctrine of controlled war-fighting."[4] Fritz Erler and Helmut Schmidt from the Social Democratic opposition, the main exponents of conventional defense at the time, supported the new strategy on the grounds that the approaching nuclear stalemate between the two superpowers was making the threat to use nuclear weapons increasingly doubtful.[5]

The West German preference for war prevention is evident in all contributions to the current debate as well. The German "Gang of Four" —Karl Kaiser, Georg Leber, Alois Mertes, and Franz-Josef Schulze— responding to the NFU proposal by the American "Gang of Four," made a pointed allusion to West Germany's geographic position in arguing, "What matters most is to concentrate not only on the prevention of nuclear war, but on how to prevent *any* war, conventional war as well."[6] They also asked whether explicit renunciation of first use would reflect on the credibility of the general renunciation of violence contained in the United Nations charter or on NATO's stated intention not to be the first side to use any kind of weapon. In this debate it is not atypical for West Germans to accept uncritically the belief that deterrence will always work reliably to prevent war.

Others, like Egon Bahr, insist that a dilemma is involved in trying to combine the prevention of war with the capability to fight a war if it cannot be prevented.[7] Bahr does not believe in everlasting deterrence. He sees two facets to NATO's strategy of flexible response: it seeks to present an attacker with a complete spectrum of possible reactions at all levels and thus deter him, but it also seeks to limit the conflict if deterrence fails. Bahr concludes that because of its inherent contradictions, deterrence can never end the arms race. He is willing, however, to have flexible response remain in effect until a new strategy can be found.

Aside from such rare expressions of doubt about the reliability of nuclear deterrence, the debate remains one between advocates of a conventional emphasis and a nuclear emphasis. The German "Gang of Four" offers a classic exposition of the latter position, emphasizing the special deterrent effects of nuclear weapons. The indissoluble association between conventional and nuclear weapons on the Continent and their connection to U.S. strategic nuclear weapons present the Soviet Union with the unacceptable risk that any military conflict between the two alliances will escalate into nuclear war. Limited use of nuclear weapons, they say, is an important component of NATO doctrine, meant to deter and thus prevent even "small" wars. NFU would destroy the very essence of the strategy. It would enable the Soviet Union to calculate the risk because it would not have to fear the unacceptable damage inflicted by nuclear weapons: "We therefore fear that a credible renunciation of the first use of nuclear weapons would, once again, make war more probable."[8] Elsewhere, Alois Mertes has warned against another danger arising from a deterrent rendered incredible by NFU—a "climate of preventive accommodation" that might encourage the Soviet Union to use its military force for political blackmail, for instance, in Berlin. Those favoring a nuclear emphasis contend that conventional rearmament would not solve the problem since it would exempt the Soviet Union from the risk of nuclear war. The assumption that in the end only nuclear weapons can really deter Moscow takes its most extreme form in the assertion of the new minister of the interior, CSU member Friedrich Zimmermann, that even one less nuclear weapon could make an attack easier for the Soviet Union.[9]

Those who favor a conventional emphasis wish to raise the nuclear threshold, arguing that to threaten first use of nuclear weapons has become increasingly less credible. NATO's conventional weakness has made it necessary to contemplate early employment of nuclear weapons, but NATO would be self-deterred from using them because of their destructive effects. A clear break must be made between conventional and nuclear weapons, for only strong conventional defense capabilities can make deterrence credible. Conventional options, including interdiction strikes deep into Eastern Europe, increase the risks to the enemy. Manfred Wörner, the CDU defense minister, denies that a conventional balance in Europe would reduce the credibility of the deterrent. Credible deterrence to him must essentially be based on an effective conventional defense; war cannot be prevented simply by threatening to commit nuclear suicide. Wörner's emphasis on conventional defense does not extend to renouncing first use of nuclear weapons, however. Threatening first use remains a necessary evil that could be used to influence Soviet behavior in a conflict, according to Wörner.

Egon Bahr contends that his proposals for a nuclear-free zone in Europe and for NFU, combined with an approximate conventional balance, would not reduce the risks for the Soviets. There were no nuclear weapons in West Berlin, he argues, and if the risks for an attacker were obviously too great even there, then a Western Europe without nuclear weapons other than Britain's and France's should fare much better.[10] Even those who emphasize nuclear deterrence admit, says Bahr, that the United States might not use nuclear weapons after all if deterrence fails; they consider the fact that the USSR could be less than fully confident about American unwillingness to use them to be sufficient for deterrence.

Risk-Sharing and Coupling

As a "child of the cold war," West Germany alone cannot provide for its own security. It is dependent on NATO and especially on the American nuclear umbrella. Geostrategic asymmetry underlines German dependence, conjuring up fear of American "decoupling" from the European continent. The fear of decoupling has two aspects. On the one hand, West Germans are afraid that the United States might be unwilling to risk New York or Chicago in order to save Cologne or Frankfurt and not commit itself. On the other hand, West Germans fear the United States might be willing to limit a nuclear war to Europe, which would neither risk Chicago nor save Frankfurt. Fear of "decoupling by nonintervention" has alternated with fear of "decoupling by limited intervention."[11]

Chancellor Konrad Adenauer's conduct of German foreign policy between 1955 and 1963 can be understood only with the fear of decoupling in mind. Adenauer was convinced that Germany was critically dependent on U.S. security guarantees, but he became highly skeptical of U.S. foreign policy and its fluctuations and remained so—especially after the Radford plan of 1956 to reduce the number of U.S. troops in Europe and offset the reduction by increasing the number of tactical nuclear weapons. He frequently asked the Kennedy administration for reassurances on U.S. commitments to the Alliance. Strauss was also skeptical of U.S. guarantees. One of the reasons he demanded nuclear-capable delivery systems for the Bundeswehr was that they seemed to be the only means of securing a reliable U.S. commitment.

The policy of nuclear control-sharing that Germany sought in the late 1950s and early 1960s was rooted in the same ground. The multilateral nuclear force (MLF), originally conceived by the U.S. State Department as a device to prevent the buildup of French national nuclear forces and to satisfy German desires for nuclear participation, was greeted with enthusiasm by the West German government. But its strong support provoked French mistrust and then resistance, since France did not wish the Germans to have access to nuclear weapons. When the MLF became a controversial issue between the "Gaullist" and the "Atlanticist" factions within the CDU/CSU, the Americans dropped the project—all the more readily in that they had embarked on détente with the Soviet Union in the meantime. Instead of a "physical" solution to the issue of German participation, NATO opted for a political solution by establishing the Nuclear Planning Group in 1966.[12] This forum gave West Germany its first opportunity to participate in NATO's nuclear planning.

Decoupling—both the fear of it and the ambiguity of it—was an important consideration in NATO's decision to modernize its long-range theater nuclear forces. In October 1977, Helmut Schmidt warned against neglecting Western European security interests in the strategic arms limitation talks. The regional imbalance in Europe would weaken extended deterrence in an age of negotiated strategic parity if SALT remained isolated from the tactical nuclear and conventional levels.[13] The planned deployment of intermediate-range missiles in Europe is meant to assure continued U.S. involvement in deterrence and the defense of Western Europe. Land-basing was chosen as a visible testament to that commitment, yet this very visibility arouses opposition to the deployments.

NFU, the German "Gang of Four" charges, is antithetical to risk-sharing within the Atlantic Community in that conventional conflict in Europe would not pose the serious risk for the United States that the nuclear guarantee does. NFU would gamble with the unity of the Alliance and of Western Europe. West Germany can resist Soviet attempts at political blackmail only if it can depend on U.S. security guarantees. Social Democratic arms control expert Karsten Voigt has also voiced these concerns. While he does not favor a purely nuclear deterrent or defense, he also believes that West Germany could have no interest in promoting the idea or illusion that a prolonged conventional war in central Europe is possible without involving the territories of the two superpowers.[14]

Egon Bahr disagrees. With a conventional balance to be achieved through arms control, NFU would hardly affect the problem of coupling. Since deterrence would become more credible, coupling between Europe and the United States might even be reinforced. Bahr has evaluated two hypothetical options for coping with the coupling-decoupling dilemma. One is to integrate the American and European military forces that compose the NATO triad, thereby coupling America's fortunes almost automatically with those of Europe. But the United States rejected automatic coupling when it abandoned massive retaliation. Flexible response, adopted in its place, allowed for coupling as well as decoupling. The alternative to the NATO triad of nuclear and conventional forces is a conventional balance that would deter conventional attack by means of conventional forces only. Even then decoupling would remain a possibility, since a purely conventional war might leave the superpowers untouched. Neither solution could resolve the dilemma. Bahr concludes that the only way out is a political strategy of common security that takes into account the interests of both the adversary and the Alliance partners.[15]

Détente

By virtue of its exposed geographic position and its dependence on the United States, West Germany is vitally affected by changes in East-West relations. An increase or reduction in tension between the two blocs has consequences that are palpable to any citizen living in or traveling to Berlin. The division of Germany has created sensitivity to and responsibility for East-West relations; indeed, the postwar constitution requires that special attention be paid to conditions in East Germany. Defense policy decisions thus have always been made in the context of Ostpolitik—West Germany's relations with East Germany, Eastern Europe, and the Soviet Union.

The controversy over West German rearmament in the 1950s reflected this imperative. The Social Democratic opposition criticized rearmament less from a pacifist than from a nationalist point of view: rearmament and the integration of West Germany into the Western Alliance would make reunification impossible and ratify the division of Germany for good. The Adenauer government responded that only a position of strength would allow Germans to bargain with the Soviet Union on reunification.

Whenever nuclear decisions had to be made, the balance to be struck between defense and détente became an issue. The SPD opposed the Bundeswehr's acquisition of nuclear delivery vehicles on grounds that "the urge to acquire nuclear weapons and participation in the nuclear arms race" were incompatible with "the goals of détente and with comprehensive disarmament in connection with German reunification."[16] The Social Democrats instead supported the Rapacki plan for a nuclear-free zone in central Europe and made suggestions for conventional disengagement. Helmut Schmidt, the SPD's leading defense expert at the time, objected to a nuclear defense posture that the Soviets would regard as provocative, and even supported no first use of nuclear weapons. In 1957 he was sharply critical of a NATO decision to deploy intermediate-range missiles that could reach the Soviet Union and opposed their basing on West German soil. There is some evidence that Adenauer himself finally turned against deploying these missiles in Germany because of Ostpolitik considerations.[17]

NATO's twofold decision of 1979 shows the continuity of the defense-détente connection in West German foreign policy. West Germany was instrumental in putting this decision on a double track, embracing both modernization and arms control. Bonn also insisted that Germany not be the only NATO member on the Continent to accept basing, a principle of nonsingularity that dates back to the Adenauer era. Neither the government's efforts to make the modernization of intermediate-range nuclear weapons compatible with détente nor its pressures on the United

States to resume arms control negotiations with the Soviet Union have satisfied opponents of new nuclear missiles in the peace movement. They consider the decision to be a major threat to détente, which they want to see resuscitated and strengthened by unilateral restraint in armaments.

Controversial at its inception, détente is still a source of partisan division today. The SPD is more inclined than the CDU/CSU to support the view that there are no clear-cut military solutions to the West's security problems. In the Social Democratic view, those problems cannot be "armed away," whether by unilateral armament or by unilateral disarmament, and can be resolved or ameliorated only through political efforts. Thus Bahr's support for NFU differs from that of the American "Gang of Four" in regarding NFU as having political and psychological effects far beyond its effects on military strategy. In Bahr's view, NFU would signify a willingness to lower tensions that could facilitate détente.

Today the policy of détente has wide support among the West German electorate, even among conservative voters. The new conservative-liberal coalition of the Free Democrats and the CDU/CSU is not going to challenge that consensus. It has changed the tone of détente but will continue to support a policy of moderation toward the East. Even the CSU, despite its occasional invective against the "illusionary policy of détente," supports arms control as a part of security policy—though defense experts in the CDU/CSU are skeptical about the chances for actually achieving arms limitation. In other respects, differing assessments of the threat and of Soviet foreign policy in general largely account for current disagreements among the parties.

The New German Consensus: Raise the Nuclear Threshold

All but a handful of West German parliamentarians and specialists continue to regard NFU as being either infeasible or undesirable. Yet informed opinion has modified its stance to provide broad support for the second-best solution proposed by the American "Gang of Four." The established political parties, the government, and leading military men agree that raising the nuclear threshold is not only possible but necessary. There is disagreement about the possibility of attaining a balance of conventional forces in Europe in the near future, but many German leaders wish to increase the range of conventional options available to NATO. Some defense analysts close to the SPD have come out in support of recent American assessments of the conventional balance that are much more optimistic than the official ones. Many experts, however, even in the SPD, remain skeptical of what they regard as "best-case analysis."

Egon Bahr finds real hope for establishing a conventional balance within the framework of arms control. He believes that when all of the asymmetrical strengths and weaknesses in the whole of the Warsaw Pact and NATO forces are taken into account, they add up to a low risk of conventional aggression. His calculations include Soviet and American reinforcements and French forces along with estimates of the time needed for their redeployment. In contrast to most Americans, Bahr and large sections of the SPD take seriously the role of arms control in stabilizing the conventional balance in Europe. Bahr has suggested that as a first step the West should announce its willingness to accept NFU as the outcome of negotiations providing for a conventional balance.[18] While concentrating on central Europe, those negotiations should include Soviet and American reinforcements and French forces as well. The USSR would have the choice of reducing its own forces or agreeing to increases in Western forces. As a result of this agreement on a conventional balance, Bahr would have all land-based nuclear systems currently deployed in nonnuclear countries withdrawn from Europe. Some sort of "minimum sea-based extended deterrent" could remain in place.

Others are less sanguine about the prospects for restoring a conventional balance, though they disagree about the size of the buildup required to offset the Warsaw Pact. Manfred Wörner and Peter Kurt Würzbach of the CDU/CSU define a full conventional option as the "assured capability to arrest *and repel* a Soviet attack."[19] They contend that the Soviet Union will be deterred only if it must fear serious damage from conventional weapons in Eastern Europe and in its own hinterland. Deterrence thus would require NATO to maintain peacetime forces of thirty-six divisions for front-line defense and nine to twelve divisions in reserve, tantamount to doubling the size of the Bundeswehr. To provide enough money and manpower to satisfy this requirement in the 1980s would be politically impossible; it would come close to militarizing the Federal Republic, with negative consequences for German democracy. Erwin Horn, deputy chairman of the armed services committee in the Bundestag, agrees that attaining a conventional balance would require strengthening NATO's offensive capabilities against the Warsaw Pact's hinterland, but he draws the line short of mounting a conventional threat to the Soviet Union itself. Moscow, he believes, should not get the impression that the West could conquer extensive territories in Eastern Europe. To raise the nuclear threshold significantly by strengthening conventional defenses and reducing the number of battlefield nuclear weapons might provide a strong enough basis for NFU.

Even the sharpest critics of no first use agree that early first use should be dispensed with. The CSU, which at first had objected to Wörner's ideas, seems to have accepted the official Christian Democratic argument that raising the nuclear threshold and NFU are completely different issues. It is also widely agreed that part of the short-range nuclear battlefield weapons can be withdrawn. Most of them were meant to compensate for a lack of conventional firepower and could be replaced by adequate conventional reinforcements. Because the collateral damage they would cause makes them unusable in military operations, their employment would make sense only as a political signal and would have to be combined with the use of nuclear weapons against the enemy's hinterland. These short-range nuclear weapons could be reduced unilaterally, leaving some for symbolic purposes only.

Within the Social Democratic party, a nuclear-free zone 150 kilometers deep along the borders, as suggested by the Palme Commission, and the complete withdrawal of chemical weapons have some support as possible unilateral measures. The Free Democrats suggest raising the nuclear threshold in the context of mutual and balanced force reduction (MBFR) by unilaterally withdrawing 1,000 short-range warheads as a first step. If the Soviets made a corresponding withdrawal of tank units, another 2,000 warheads could be removed, thus reducing the total number of U.S. tactical nuclear weapons in Western Europe by 50 percent.[20] The CDU also considers a significant reduction in tactical nuclear weapons to be both possible and necessary, perhaps even if made unilaterally.

It is widely believed within all the established political parties that the trend in conventional weapon technology favors the defender. So-called smart weapons are sometimes greeted with enthusiasm as representing a "revolution" on the battlefield. What Karsten Voigt has called "conventional illusions" have caught the imagination of large segments of the SPD, the left, and the peace movement. While it is often assumed that these weapons can be used only in defense, modern technologies might usefully be employed in offensive tactics as well. They are certainly not a magic formula for stability in Europe. The embrace of conventional technology is motivated in part by a desire to legitimate defense policy: nonnuclear weapons that can be depicted as purely defensive would gain the widest political support.

Wörner and Würzbach, for example, call for increasing the conventional threat to the Warsaw Pact's rear areas by preparing to isolate its first-echelon forces through battlefield interdiction while conducting deep interdiction air strikes against the second and third echelons. Drawing heavily on the "extended battlefield" concept developed by Senator Sam Nunn and his group, they envisage interdiction options that require modern capabilities for battlefield management and target acquisition. Fixed targets such as bridges, railway stations, depots, and airfields are to be destroyed by unmanned vehicles such as drones, conventionally armed cruise missiles, and rockets armed with submunitions, which would be terminally guided by the mid-eighties. These new technologies could reduce significantly the amount of firepower necessary to destroy Soviet battle groups. As for strengthening NATO's front-line defenses, Wörner and Würzbach mention automatically guided ("smart") antitank mines to be distributed by multiple rocket launchers. While NATO cannot do without tanks in the future, they see no point in copying the Soviet spectrum of weapons. They also contend that NATO has placed too much emphasis on large weapon systems and should invest more in ammunition. Wörner and Würzbach are widely supported within the CDU and seem to be gathering support in the CSU.

Wörner opposes border fortifications on the ground that they could not withstand modern weapons. Apart from that, fortifications in West Germany evoke images of another Berlin wall and of Startbahn West, the new runway of Frankfurt airport, both symbolic of landscape paved with concrete. Together these images will assure the broadest conceivable resistance.

Outside the established circles, other military and nonmilitary forms of defense are being discussed. Some peace researchers and members of the peace movement as well as conservative military figures are working on concepts of territorial defense.[21] Their common point of departure is the deterrence-defense dilemma, which in present circumstances implies the destruction of what is supposed to be defended if deterrence fails. Contending that the present military strategies of NATO and the Warsaw Pact are a potential threat to crisis stability, these analysts advocate reducing NATO's dependence on military use of nuclear weapons and even on large conventional combat units. Horst Afheldt, for example, would replace flexible response with a territorial network of "technocommands"—small units consisting of about twenty-five men armed with antitank, light infantry, and anti-aircraft weapons. It is assumed that the attacker would have to overwhelm command after command and could not achieve a quick breakthrough. J. Löser suggests combining improved front-line defenses with a territorial defense mounted by small squadrons of fighter aircraft (*Jagdverbände*), and he supports a buildup of civil defense within his concept of "comprehensive defense." All of these proposals strive for a military posture that is more clearly defensive than the present one but also militarily effective. Some analysts who work on these questions wish to dispense with nuclear deterrence altogether, while Afheldt as well as Löser accept the political function of the strategic nuclear umbrella.

The established parties and the government are skeptical about these defensive concepts, the Christian Democrats emphatically so. Experts in the CDU argue that as long as the other side has theater nuclear weapons, the West needs them too, and territorial defense would lead to a militarization of society. Arms control experts within the Social Democratic party contend that these schemes are too narrowly military, offering unilateral military solutions to bilateral political problems.

Domestic Constraints on Change

Domestic constraints on strengthening the conventional forces have increased dramatically, even though pressures to reduce reliance on the nuclear leg of the NATO triad have never been greater and technological developments have brought significant changes in conventional weaponry. In West Germany the future of flexible response and the associated role of conventional defense will depend on some critical variables: the fiscal priorities of the government, trends in the defense budget and its controllability (especially in procurement), the supply of manpower for the Bundeswehr, the state of the economy, and the domestic consensus on budget priorities.

Europe is undergoing its most serious economic crisis since the Great Depression of the 1930s; in Germany the "economic miracle" has finally come to an end. As budgetary deficits continue to grow, the allocation of budget shares visibly strains the political system. A Reaganite shift of resources away from social welfare to defense is doubtful in Western Europe, even under conservative governments—all the more so in view of the American experience, in which domestic support for such a shift proved short-lived.

The defense component of the German federal budget has decreased over the past decade. In 1970, defense was still the single largest item, claiming 22.1 percent of the total; social expenditures followed closely with a 20.6 percent share. The order was reversed in 1975, when social expenditures claimed 22.8 percent and defense 20.0 percent. Since then the share of defense has declined, reaching 18 percent in 1982, while social expenditures have fluctuated between 22 and 23.5 percent. A comparison of the growth rates of various budgetary sectors shows that in the 1970s several kinds of nondefense expenditures grew faster than GNP and the total federal budget. But what appears to be a shift in priorities resulted not only from increased appropriations for welfare, research, and education, but also from a countercyclical policy designed to head off the 1975–76 recession by strengthening demand. If the effects of federal laws enacted in the 1970s to shift responsibilities from the *Länder* to the federal government are discounted, defense spending has grown at about the same rate as the total budget in recent years.[22]

West Germany's fiscal crisis, marked by sharp increases in the deficit and resulting public debt since the mid-1970s, has been intensified by the worldwide recession that began in 1980. Cyclical as well as structural, the current stagnation has added to strains on the budget and prevented a reduction of the burden of interest payments, although the first steps in the latter direction have been taken. The present crisis reflects the results of growing unemployment and bankruptcy, which reduce federal revenues while requiring larger outlays for unemployment benefits, social security, and loan guarantees.

There was real economic growth of 1.8 percent in 1980, but 1981 brought a negative growth rate of -0.5 percent followed by -1.5 percent in 1982.[23] Negative growth has created a familiar fiscal dilemma: on the one hand, deficits should be reduced in order to regain latitude for fiscal and economic initiatives; on the other hand, the government is pressed to increase expenditures to stimulate the economy and support the social security system. Efforts to consolidate government finances and the budget receive the highest political priority among all parties in the Bundestag. No one expects a vigorous revival of the domestic economy in the near term: real growth of 1 to 3 percent annually is the most to be hoped for over the next few years.[24] Even if there is a continuing economic recovery, it will do little to relieve strains on the social budget because unemployment will remain high even though its growth rate may slow.

There are basically two ways to deal with the general fiscal crisis: cutting expenditures by reducing individual budget items and government responsibilities, and increasing revenues by reducing government subsidies and raising taxes. The former CDU/CSU coalition government combined the two approaches but was very restrained in both. The new CDU/CSU/FDP government may come down somewhat harder on welfare expenditures in an effort to improve the climate for new business investment, but it is extremely unlikely that it will seek welfare cuts comparable to President Reagan's or Prime Minister Margaret Thatcher's—certainly not while increasing defense expenditures.[25] The ideology of Christian democracy in West Germany rests on the *soziale Marktwirtschaft,* a market economy tempered by the welfare state. The Christian Democratic Union has a strong tradition of social policy dating back to the Weimar Republic; with its sister party, the Christian Social Union, it wove today's network of social programs during their years as the governing coalition, 1949 to 1969.

Any cuts in welfare that are politically feasible will not be large enough in themselves to reduce budget deficits in the short run. Deep cuts in other areas such as government investment would be detrimental to the economy and will be made with great selectivity. What remains is to increase revenues by cutting subsidies or raising taxes. While these measures might also have adverse consequences for the economy, the tax burden in the Federal Republic is still fairly low compared to that in other industrialized countries. But large tax increases as well as sharp cuts in welfare would encounter massive resistance, especially from the trade unions.

Since consolidation of government finances has top priority, there will be no latitude for increasing defense expenditures at least until 1985. The new minister of defense is well aware of that, although he would like to restore the defense share of the budget to its former range of 20 to 22 percent. Attainment of that share is more likely to occur through reduced growth of nondefense spending than through a genuine shift of resources. How much more room for maneuver the government will have by 1987 is hard to predict, and it is harder still to foresee whether greater latitude would be used to increase the defense budget.

As for the defense budget itself, the biggest share is consumed by personnel costs, which increased from 38.6 percent in 1970 to 44.4 percent in 1977, when they started to decline to an estimated 41.8 percent in 1982. Investment, which includes expenditures for military construction, procurement, maintenance, and research and development, reached a low point of just over 30 percent in 1975, but has since increased to an estimated 33.6 percent for 1982 and to 34.4 percent in the budget draft for 1983. The increase is due to the so-called general renovation (*Runderneuerung*) of the Bundeswehr, which claimed considerable resources and still does. Procurement took an average of 57 percent of total investment annually between 1970 and 1975, but an estimated 72 percent between 1979 and 1983. Procurement expenditures increased by 60 percent in real terms between 1970 and 1982 (189 percent in current prices); even if one uses a special defense price deflator, the real increase was about 36.2 percent.

Unanticipated cost increases have created serious shortfalls in the defense budget and have led to demands for better defense management. The prices of technologically advanced systems will almost quadruple in fifteen years if one assumes an annual inflation rate of 4 percent. As early as 1975–76, several Social Democratic members of the armed services committee in the Bundestag warned against the rising costs of major weapon systems, especially the Tornado aircraft. By 1979 canceling or stretching out the procurement of several items had been proposed in order to bring defense expenditures under control. In 1980 several smaller economy measures reduced the defense budget deficit, but in 1980 and 1981 some DM 1.24 billion had to be provided through supplemental appropriations. In 1981 the medium-term defense budget estimate through fiscal year 1984 nonetheless showed a deficit of DM 2.3 billion.

In March 1981, Defense Minister Apel convened an urgent meeting with the military leadership to resolve the latest defense budget crisis. The new deficit had been caused by the unanticipated cost growth of Tornado, the AIM-9L Sidewinder air-to-air missile, the Leopard II tank, and SETAC, a bad-weather landing aid, as well as by increased expenditures for operations, maintenance, infrastructure, and ammunition storage. It was agreed to save DM 1.3 billion by canceling an order for

Milan antitank missiles and a navy–air force version of the Roland II mobile air defense system, by deferring the delivery of two frigates from 1985 to 1987 and of the Patriot air defense system from 1984 to 1986, and by stretching out the completion of other systems. The balance of DM 1 billion is to be covered by additional appropriations during 1982–84.[26]

Although these measures have relieved the immediate pressure on the defense budget, expenditures for the stretched-out and deferred procurements will rise in the long run. The exorbitant cost growth associated with deployment of the second generation of weapons for the Bundeswehr clearly demonstrates that another quantum jump to the third generation, to be deployed after the mid-1990s, cannot be afforded. Barring another economic miracle, no present or future West German government could increase the defense budget sufficiently to pay the price.

The Bundeswehr currently has a peacetime strength of about 495,000 and a mobilized strength of 1.25 million men.[27] The latter will increase to 1.34 million men by 1990 as a result of the Wartime Host Nation Support agreement, which spells out arrangements for manpower contributions and cost sharing between the United States and West Germany in the event of war. The present peacetime strength includes about 62,000 professional soldiers, about 180,000 conscripts who have volunteered for long-term service, and about 225,000 conscripts. The balance, which fluctuates, comes from up to 30,000 former conscripts in the ready reserve who have recently finished their service and can be called back within one year by the minister of defense without special authorization. In addition to the 225,000 drafted for the Bundeswehr each year, about 27,000 more men are required for the border patrol service, police, disaster control units, and development assistance. To maintain quality, some 25,000–50,000 men from the eligible pool are rejected annually.

Since 1968 the birth rate in West Germany has dropped sharply. As a result, the manpower pool available for conscription will start to decline in 1984 and fall short of the size required by 1987. At the current rate of decline, there will be a deficit of 104,000 conscripts by 1995. If no countermeasures are taken, the Bundeswehr's peacetime strength could fall to 290,000 men—a loss of one quarter of its fighting strength—and require the complete dissolution of nine field army brigades and the partial dissolution of another eight brigades, if the air force and navy are to be spared. The Bundeswehr could no longer perform its part in NATO's common defense, which includes immediately countering a surprise attack with its on-line forces, repelling limited attacks, and at least delaying large-scale attacks with conventional weapons.

To cope with the manpower shortfall, the Bundeswehr's Long-term Planning Commission has considered a number of measures, many of which raise sensitive political and legal questions. The following among its proposals would be the most effective:

Increasing the number of long-term conscript-volunteers. During the last twelve years about 9.1 percent of all conscripts volunteered for long-term service and remained in uniform for an average of 7.4 years. In hope of increasing the enlistment rate to 12 percent and extending the average length of service to 8.8 years, the commission proposed introducing additional financial incentives and improving the status of volunteers and their opportunities for advancement. Since the number of available conscripts will start to decline in 1984 and with it the number of conscript-volunteers, it will be necessary to enlist a large number of long-term conscripts as soon as possible in order to relieve the manpower shortage expected in the 1990s. This will cost a lot of money.

Extending basic service. At present basic service lasts fifteen months. Extending it to eighteen, twenty-one, or twenty-four months could reduce the requirements for conscripts by 32,000, 56,000, and 73,000 men, respectively. Extension would require a two-year transition to accommodate changes in the organization and planning of military training, but training could become much more effective as a result. Any extension would be extremely unpopular and certain to encounter serious political difficulties.

Replacing manpower with technology. By investing in technology as a partial substitute for manpower, all three branches of service could reduce their personnel by as much as 5 percent without impairing their combat effectiveness, and thereby reduce total manpower requirements by as many as 24,000 men. The resultant savings in manpower costs would be offset to some extent by increased expenditures for research and development.

Reducing impediments to service. Currently an average of 73.9 percent of each year's class of potential conscripts is found qualified for military service. Lowering the standards could increase the induction rate by 4 to 5 percent. Since not all conscripts would be fit for all tasks, special modifications in training would be required. Stricter administration of exemptions could also increase the number of conscripts, and conscripting men up to age 28 could postpone the onset of the manpower shortage until the early 1990s. Such changes would have costs: conscripting older men would involve a larger proportion of husbands and fathers—not a popular step—and require increases in military pay and social benefits.

Expanding military options for women. West Germany's basic law bars women from combat assignments and limits them to positions in which they will not have to use weapons—as medical officers or orderlies, for example, or in communications. Increasing opportunities for women could reduce the personnel gap by 10,000 to 20,000 at some additional cost for living quarters and social benefits (for example, maternity leave). Opening up long-term volunteer careers for women might add another 9,000 to 18,000 positions and would require additional incentives, principally monetary.

Many military experts fear that the reorganization of army field units (*Heeresstruktur 4*) will stretch the Bundeswehr's on-line strength to the limit. The corps groups will have a peacetime manpower complement of 40 percent, the divisional troops of 60 percent, and the field army brigades of about 90 percent, thus raising the demand for reserves considerably above previous levels. Starting in 1989 at the latest, a shortage of reservists will appear unless the length of reserve commitment is increased from six to eight years to ten to twelve years.

Arms control agreements might ease the strain. Manpower reductions have long been under consideration in the negotiations on mutual and balanced force reductions. According to the latest Western proposal, only U.S. and Soviet manpower would be reduced in the first phase of an MBFR agreement. Such an agreement, however, would contain commitments for a second phase that would include manpower reductions in the allied forces. The opposing alliances would agree to a general reduction of, say, 5 percent and then decide among themselves how to allocate it. An agreement along these lines might reduce the Bundeswehr's requirements by as many as 20,000 men, but it does not seem to be a near-term prospect.

The coming shortage of conscripts and reservists means that there will be no pool of personnel from which to form additional combat units in the foreseeable future. (Similar though less severe problems exist in the Belgian and Dutch forces.) The only way to increase force levels is to raise the army's peacetime strength, which will be feasible only if additional professional soldiers can be enlisted and trained and additional financial resources found to pay for them and for the associated weapons and command systems. Since moderate real growth in the defense budget will be absorbed by expenditures for research, development, and the procurement of weapon systems already planned, an expansion of West Germany's forces would require a reallocation of resources from other parts of the federal budget.

While the manpower shortage, contrary to earlier alarms, will probably not decrease combat effectiveness if appropriate countermeasures are taken and the necessary financial resources made available, the situation may be different with respect to military equipment. High cost growth has resulted in cancellations, deferrals, and stretchouts of weapon acquisitions that may eventually affect combat effectiveness.

Despite these problems, the Bundeswehr's overall combat effectiveness will increase considerably in the 1980s. The "general renovation" that began in the 1970s has made the Bundeswehr one of the most modern and best-equipped armies in the world, surpassing even U.S. qualitative standards in many respects. The reorganization of field units (*Heeresstruktur 4*) will create 3 additional brigades, 45 additional battalions, and 135 additional companies.[28] By the end of the 1980s, the new organizational structure will have added the equivalent of more than a division.

The Future of Flexible Response in West Germany

Defense policy in West Germany is entering a new phase. Defense, which has enjoyed broad support or at least acquiescence since the late 1950s, is now controversial. Four conceptions are emerging, the first of which might be called "flexible response with a nuclear emphasis." Its adherents, ranging from the Christian Socialists to the German "Gang of Four," consider tactical nuclear weapons to be indispensable for deterrence and for coupling. Given the current unpopularity of nuclear weapons, however, onetime proponents of heavy reliance on the nuclear component of NATO's triad are prepared to accept some deemphasis and even reductions in nuclear weapons. They are moving toward a second conception, "flexible response with a conventional emphasis." This position is advocated by a perhaps growing number of politicians from all parties as well as by military men who believe either that the conventional leg of the NATO triad is already much stronger than most assessments give it credit for, or that it can be strengthened further.

Minister of Defense Wörner seems to belong to this group, which is willing to reduce the number of tactical nuclear weapons and to increase NATO's conventional capabilities, including offensive capabilities, and thus raise the nuclear threshold. They stop short of NFU, however, contending that NATO would weaken deterrence if it unilaterally or even bilaterally declared NFU as its policy, the more so since full conventional compensation is not considered feasible. Some proponents of "conventional emphasis" would support higher defense expenditures, but they consider the 3 to 4 percent increases mentioned by U.S. experts to be both too high and too low—too high to be economically and politically feasible at home, yet too low to meet the full requirements of NFU. Exponents of both "conventional emphasis" and "nuclear emphasis" may support plans such as the one advanced by General Bernard W. Rogers, though for different reasons and only in financially restrained versions.[29] NATO might end up with increased conventional strength but no fewer nuclear weapons in Europe.

Proponents of the third conception emphasize arms control. They wish to move away from tactical and theater nuclear weapons through negotiation and to some extent unilaterally, and toward a negotiated conventional balance. Some might support increased expenditures on conventional weapons in an arms control context, but generally the SPD seems strongly opposed to defense increases and especially to strengthening offensive capabilities. Egon Bahr is the best-known representative of this group, and his position will probably gain wide support among SPD politicians and especially the SPD's rank and file. The fourth conception, "unilateral defensive conventionalism," calls for unilaterally banning nuclear weapons from West Germany and from Europe without increasing defense expenditures. Its proponents, mainly parts of the peace movement and some on the SPD's left, opt for a form of minimum conventional deterrence.

While the general trend is to reduce reliance on nuclear weapons and to emphasize conventional defense, it is by no means clear in what direction conventional defense will go, even if the economic situation were to allow more freedom of maneuver. For various reasons, three of the four groups mentioned above are opposed to full conventional compensation even if it were feasible. The one group that would like to go in that direction realizes that not much can be done, at least in the near future. Yet all the groups are moving toward support of reductions in nuclear weapons, especially battlefield weapons, and are opposed to their early use; meanwhile, they express more confidence in the conventional leg of the NATO triad.

Support for NFU does not come from those who were the audience for the American "Gang of Four." German supporters of NFU oppose conventional compensation, especially unilateral compensation or compensation attained by strengthening offensive capabilities. Changes in flexible response are likely, but they will not be large or sudden. Support for a deemphasis of nuclear deterrence is more readily mobilized by appeals that emphasize reliance on so-called defensive technologies and arms control. The current status and prospective development of West Germany's military forces support a shift toward conventional deterrence, but within limits. NATO's and the Bundeswehr's conventional strength need not be underrated in view of the improvements made in the last ten years and the others under way. Most of the improvements envisaged by the present force goals can probably be attained, with some delays. Fiscal and manpower constraints, however, will not permit the Federal Republic to do much more.

The list of obstacles to changes in flexible response by no means justifies the complacency of those favoring the status quo. As if to exacerbate the inherent inconsistencies of NATO doctrine, the crisis of détente and the nuclear posturing of the Reagan administration have turned uneasiness about tactical nuclear weapons into alarm. For substantive as well as political reasons, NATO will have to reduce its reliance on nuclear weapons in both doctrine and military posture. Conventional compensation, however, faces serious constraints in West Germany. Hard facts of fiscal and manpower limitations and of demography and geostrategy make the way out seem to many extremely difficult, if not unacceptable. Quite apart from questions of feasibility, strengthening NATO's offensive conventional capabilities in Europe threatens an already tenuous stability that is of great importance to West Germany. And there are limits to "defensive" conventional rearmament as well. A densely populated democratic and essentially nonmilitaristic society must not strain the level of tolerance that the common defense requires. Those who acknowledge the weaknesses of flexible response and the constraints that prevent a technological solution have no alternative but to look for political strategies to preserve peace and freedom. Their protection cannot be entrusted to deterrence or defense alone.

The Federal Republic of Germany has a genuine and vital interest in tension reduction and arms control. It is in such a context that NFU may become most useful.

Notes

1. Quotation attributed to Volkmar Deile (secretary of the Aktion Sühnezeichen, a Protestant peace group) in Gert Bastian and others, "Droht die 'Nachrüstung' noch?" *Blätter für deutsche und internationale Politik* (June 1982), p. 680.

2. Horst Ehmke, SPD deputy chairman in the Bundestag, has suggested no first use of battlefield nuclear weapons. "Wir müssen das nukleare Risiko teilen," *Der Spiegel*, vol. 36 (June 7, 1982), pp. 45–56.

3. See Thomas Risse-Kappen, "Déjà Vu: Deployment of Nuclear Weapons in West Germany," forthcoming.

4. Franz-Josef Strauss, *Herausforderung und Antwort* (Challenge and Response) (Stuttgart: Seewald Verlag, 1968), p. 197. See also Catherine McArdle Kelleher, *Germany and the Politics of Nuclear Weapons* (Columbia University Press, 1975), pp. 64–74.

5. See particularly Helmut Schmidt, *Defense or Retaliation: A German View* (Praeger, 1962).

6. Karl Kaiser and others, "Nuclear Weapons and the Preservation of Peace: A German Response," *Foreign Affairs*, vol. 60 (Summer 1982), p. 1158. Similarly, Hans Apel (former SPD minister of defense), "Zur Diskussion über die Strategie der NATO: Überlegungen zu dem Beitrag, Kernwaffen und das Atlantische Bündnis," *Europa-Archiv*, vol. 37 (June 10, 1982), pp. 353–56.

If not indicated otherwise, the following remarks on the attitudes of West German politicians refer to interviews with Egon Bahr (SPD), chairman of the subcommittee for disarmament and arms control in the Bundestag; Erwin Horn (SPD), deputy chairman of the armed services committee in the Bundestag; Karl Kaiser, director of the research institute of the Deutsche Gesellschaft für Auswärtige Politik; Friedrich Wilhelm Krüger-Sprengel, former adviser for defense and security affairs of the CSU group in the Bundestag, now in the Ministry of Defense; members of the planning staff in the Ministry of Defense; Alois Mertes (CDU), former foreign policy spokesman of the CDU in the Bundestag, now minister of state in the Foreign Affairs Ministry (Staatsminister); Uwe Stehr, adviser for arms control and security affairs of the SPD group in the Bundestag; Karsten Voigt, chairman of the SPD foreign policy working group; and Manfred Wörner (CDU), former chairman of the armed services committee in the Bundestag, now defense minister. The interviews were conducted in September 1982.

7. Egon Bahr, "Neuer Ansatz der gemeinsamen Sicherheit," speech at Rastatt, published in *Die Neue Gesellschaft*, vol. 29 (July 1982), p. 660.

8. Kaiser and others, "Nuclear Weapons and the Preservation of Peace," p. 1160.

9. Friedrich Zimmermann, "Frieden nur durch Stärke," *Bayernkurier*, May 29, 1982.

10. Bahr, "Neuer Ansatz der gemeinsamen Sicherheit," p. 667.

11. See Jane M. O. Sharp, "Nuclear Weapons and Alliance Cohesion," *Bulletin of the Atomic Scientists*, vol. 38 (June 1982), pp. 34–35, for a description of cycles in European-American relations over the coupling-decoupling issue.

12. D. Mahnke, *Nukleare Mitwirkung* (Nuclear Control-Sharing) (Berlin: de Gruyter, 1972), p. 219.

13. Helmut Schmidt, "The 1977 Alastair Buchan Memorial Lecture," *Survival,* vol. 20 (January–February 1978), pp. 2–10. For the INF debate in general, see Gert Krell and H. J. Schmidt, *Der Rüstungswettlauf in Europa* (The Arms Race in Europe) (Frankfurt: Campus, 1982); and David S. Yost and Thomas C. Glad, "West German Party Politics and Theater Nuclear Modernization since 1977," *Armed Forces and Society,* vol. 8 (Summer 1982), pp. 525–60.

14. Karsten Voigt, "Die Weltmächte mit unserem Risiko verkoppeln," *Vorwärts,* April 15, 1982. Cf. "Längerfristige Perspektive: Die Strategiedebatte muss Realitätsbezogen bleiben," *Sozialdemokratischer Pressedienst,* vol. 37 (January 6, 1982); and Kaiser and others, "Nuclear Weapons and the Preservation of Peace," pp. 1160–62.

15. Bahr, "Neuer Ansatz der gemeinsamen Sicherheit," p. 664.

16. Fritz Erler, Speech in the Bundestag, May 10, 1957.

17. Schmidt, *Defense or Retaliation,* passim. Concerning NFU, see H. Schmidt, quoted in K. v. Schubert (ed.), *Sicherheitspolitik der Bundesrepublik Deutschland: Dokumentation 1945–1977* (Security Policy of the Federal Republic of Germany), 2nd part (Köln: Wissenschaft und Politik, 1979), p. 139. Concerning the IRBM problem in 1957, see Kelleher, *Germany and the Politics of Nuclear Weapons,* pp. 130–34; and Harold Macmillan, *Riding the Storm, 1956–1959* (London: Macmillan, 1971), p. 335.

18. Bahr, "Neuer Ansatz der gemeinsamen Sicherheit," pp. 662–63. See also Egon Bahr, "Gemeinsame Sicherheit: Gedanken zur Entschärfung der nuklearen Konfrontation in Europa," *Europa-Archiv,* vol. 37 (July 25, 1982), pp. 421–30.

19. Manfred Wörner and Peter Kurtz Würzbach, "Studie einer Expertengruppe zur Verbesserung der konventionellen Verteidigung" (Study by a Group of Experts on Strengthening Conventional Defense), Press Office, CDU/CSU parliamentary party in the Bundestag, May 21, 1982, p. 4.

20. "Position Paper on Arms Control and Disarmament," Federal Expert Committee on Peace and Security, presented by J. Möllemann (former defense policy spokesman of the FDP in the Bundestag, minister of state in the first Kohl government), May 23, 1982, p. 4.

21. See Horst Afheldt, *Verteidigung und Frieden* (Defense and Security) (Munich: Carl Hanser, 1976); J. Löser, *Weder rot noch tot: Überleben ohne Atomkrieg—Eine Sicherheitspolitische Alternative* (Neither Red nor Dead: Surviving without Nuclear War—An Alternative for Defense) (Munich: Olzog, 1981); E. Spannocchi and G. Brossolet, *Verteidigung ohne Schlacht* (Defense without Battle) (Munich: Bernard & Graefe, 1980); and Franz Uhle-Wettler, *Gefechtsfeld Mitteleuropa: Gefahr der Übertechnisierung von Streitkräften* (The Battlefield in Central Europe: The Danger of Over-technology in Armed Forces) (Munich: Bernard & Graefe, 1980).

22. Kommission für die Langzeitplanung der Bundeswehr (Report of the Bundeswehr Long-Term Planning Commission), *Bericht* (Bonn, 1982), pp. 114–15 (hereafter Langzeitkommission).

23. Figures quoted from "Schwachstelle ist das Management," *Der Spiegel,* vol. 36 (August 16, 1982), p. 26; and Deutsches Institut für Wirtschaftsforschung, Wochenbericht 33/1982. See also "Jahreswirtschaftsbericht 1983 der Bundesregierung," *Bulletin des Presse- und Informationsamts der Bundesregierung,* 13 (February 2, 1983), p. 120.

24. Estimates in Langzeitkommission, p. 113. Cf. the study by Wirtschafts- und Sozialwissenschaftliches Institut der Gewerkschaften (WSI), which posits 2–3.5 percent real growth, quoted in *Frankfurter Rundschau,* October 2, 1982, p. 6.

25. Because of severe strains on the federal budget, the CDU/CSU/FDP coalition government raised the defense budget by only about DM 100 million above the draft budget of the former Schmidt government.

26. The data are from Bundesminister der Verteidigung, ed., "Ergebnisse der Rüstungsklausur (Defense Minister, Results of the Special Session on Defense, Bonn 1981), pp. 1–3; and *Wehrdienst,* XVII, 759 (1981), pp. 1–2.

27. The following data are from the Langzeitkommission, *Bericht,* pp. 45–72, 119–27.

28. Bundesminister der Verteidigung, ed., *Weissbuch 1979,* pp. 147–52. Since the strength of the new battalions and companies is reduced, the increase in fighting power is less than the increase in the number of units.

29. See General Bernard W. Rogers, "The Atlantic Alliance: Prescriptions for a Difficult Decade," *Foreign Affairs,* vol. 60 (Summer 1982), pp. 1145–56.

CHAPTER NINE

MOVING TOWARD NO FIRST USE IN PRACTICE

Johan Jørgen Holst

THE CONCEPT of no first use is currently receiving renewed attention in the debate about a nuclear strategy for the West.[1] It is a controversial concept, and much of the discussion has been stronger in polemic than in analysis. It is but one possible element in an overall scheme for strategic reorientation and no panacea. This chapter examines some of the issues that would be raised by such a reorientation.

NATO's Nuclear Doctrine and Force Posture

NATO's doctrine for the possible employment of nuclear weapons, as embodied in the 1967 NATO document MC-14/3, is based on the strategy of flexible response, which encompasses the triple function of direct defense, deliberate escalation, and general nuclear response. Employment is constrained by agreed political guidelines, beginning with the 1962 Athens guidelines and including the 1969 guidelines concerning consultation procedures, the 1970 guidelines for initial tactical use, the 1970 guidelines for atomic demolition munitions, and the 1972 guidelines concerning the role of theater nuclear weapons.[2] The 1972 agreements are not really guidelines but rather concepts designed to produce a set of options that might or might not be used. Nuclear release must be authorized by the American president in consultation with the allies in the North Atlantic Council in accordance with agreed procedures. The release procedures apply to all nuclear weapons that are deployed to Europe under agreements establishing programs of cooperation. Once a "package" of battlefield nuclear weapons has been released, its tactical use is controlled by the corps commander; subpackage employment can be delegated to the division level, but generally not below.[3] A corps package could but need not consist of a hundred or more weapons to be used over a period lasting from several hours to a day.[4] According to American doctrine, five general categories of constrained theater nuclear employment may be distinguished: (1) demonstration, (2) limited defensive use, (3) restricted battle area use, (4) extended battle area use, and (5) theater-wide use.[5]

SACEUR's nuclear operations plan includes prepared selective employment plans, as well as a general strike plan coordinated with the American single integrated operations plan (SIOP). Battlefield weapons reportedly are not included in the prepared attack options.

Current NATO doctrine holds open the option of first use of nuclear weapons but does not prescribe it for all circumstances. It is a doctrine for first use if necessary, but not necessarily first use. In this respect MC-14/3 represents a considerable departure from the early and extensive nuclear retaliation emphasis of MC-14/2, drawn up thirteen years earlier. The question now, sixteen years after the adoption of flexible response, is whether NATO should consider further adjustments in the announced and planned role of nuclear weapons in its overall defense posture. Answering that question requires examining the premises of the current doctrine and posture as well as their validity and implications under the politico-military conditions of the 1980s.

A key premise of the present strategy is that a potential aggressor should be left uncertain about the nature and scope of NATO's response in the event of an attack. While that is unquestionably a valid consideration, it is not the only one. Another is whether the uncertainties are balanced in a way that benefits NATO. A third is that war can never be made wholly predictable and that residual uncertainties about the unfolding of events will always remain. The choices are not between calculability and uncertainty, but rather among largely incalculable risks. Nations may stumble into war, as they did in August 1914. Final decisions may be driven as much by plans, doctrine, and deployments as by calculations of risk. NATO's strategy must be designed with respect to the limits of deterrence. It must be designed also to cope with contingencies other than a deliberate and massive attack aimed at the establishment of military mastery in Europe. The political realities of Europe in the 1980s include the possibility of conflicts escalating as spillovers from turmoil in Eastern Europe and tensions rising in Europe because of direct East-West confrontations in other areas. These possibilities warrant consideration as well.

Another premise that should be examined is the assumption that NATO will be politically able to make a deliberate decision to initiate the use of nuclear weapons, breaking the tradition of nonuse in effect since Hiroshima and Nagasaki. This assumption in turn is predicated on NATO's ability to decide quickly and to prevent its force posture from driving the decision. NATO's consulting procedures on the release and use of nuclear weapons are necessarily cumbersome and, in the view of many observers and practitioners alike, rather unlikely to function rapidly and smoothly in the fog of war. A military posture that is designed around the presumption of early use of nuclear weapons is not readily compatible with the political emphasis on caution and prudence that is likely to dominate in the decisionmaking councils of the Alliance on the threshold of war or during its early and ambiguous phases. NATO's dependence on early use could indeed produce the "deepening trap" foreseen by the current American under secretary of defense, Fred C. Iklé.[6]

The days when NATO enjoyed a near-monopoly in theater nuclear weapons are irretrievably lost. NATO has yet to develop a doctrine and posture that are designed to cope with the condition of bilateral theater nuclear deterrence and that can be sustained through the decisionmaking procedures of a coalition of states that may have differing perceptions of the stakes involved in a crisis or war. Indeed, it is arguable that dependence on early resort to nuclear weapons is likely to accentuate differences in the perceived stakes and reduce cohesion, particularly during the early phases of an intense crisis or war. Deterrence depends to a large extent on a high likelihood of carrying out the threatened response. The threat of early use of nuclear weapons is deficient in credibility because it seems unlikely that NATO governments will in fact consent to carry it out in the maelstrom of war.

The likelihood of consent is even lower because of the widely shared belief that initiating the use of nuclear weapons would lead inexorably to widespread use. Recurrent suggestions that it might be possible to limit nuclear war have consistently failed to command political credibility. Governments have supported measures and plans designed to apply brakes to nuclear war should it start, but they have never had confidence in the reliability of the brakes. Hence, any decision about first use is bound to be viewed as a decision to go to nuclear war in a massive way. Only if the alternatives were unprecedentedly catastrophic could NATO agree on such a decision.

Three possible consequences are worrisome. The immobilizing impact of a first-use policy might invite brinkmanship from an adversary during a crisis. Alternatively, even if an adversary were to believe that NATO would use nuclear weapons first, that perception could drive him toward large-scale preemption; in the context of ambiguous conflict, political miscalculation could become an engine of tragedy. Finally, a defense posture and doctrine predicated on the possible first use of nuclear weapons could produce strong pressures and incentives for appeasement during crises. The result could be self-deterrence rather than deterrence of the adversary.

Beyond the doctrinal premises, NATO's present posture for theater nuclear warfare is highly vulnerable. Nuclear munitions are concentrated in a rather small number of storage sites that are physically vulnerable to preemptive attack. Launchers in forward positions are especially so: according to table 3-1, 2,250 are artillery shells that can strike targets at ranges of fifteen kilometers or less. Western artillery is becoming increasingly overmatched by long-range Warsaw Pact artillery. The present posture may exert considerable pressure for early release and use of nuclear weapons in order to avoid being overrun by attacking forces; a use-them-or-lose-them syndrome may weigh on the decision-making authorities. Similar pressures could arise from nuclear air defenses and atomic demolition munitions, which must be used early in order to maximize their effectiveness. NATO has 300 atomic demolition munitions (ADMs), which can be installed in a few hours in previously dug sites, tunnels, mountain passes, and similar locations in order to stop or retard the advance of tanks and other vehicles. Seven hundred nuclear munitions are kept for the Nike-Hercules surface-to-air missiles, which in due course will be replaced by the conventional Patriot system.

The present doctrine and its associated posture seem particularly mismatched. The doctrine of first demonstrative use, combined with the large-scale forward emplacement of nuclear munitions in vulnerable storage sites, to be distributed to vulnerable launcher positions and fired from launchers that are outdistanced by the ranges of comparable systems on the other side, may indeed produce a trap to be avoided. Demonstrative use could invite Soviet preemption by conveying the impression that a large-scale battlefield nuclear war was about to begin in Europe, leaving the guidelines for follow-on use to be defined in practice by the Warsaw Pact. This combination of doctrine and posture is hardly likely to reassure restive societies in Western Europe.

There is no escape from the dilemmas posed by nuclear weapons, but NATO's present doctrine and posture seem to exacerbate those dilemmas. Though not designed that way originally, NATO's force posture has been overtaken by events and changed circumstances. NATO has failed to produce a convincing strategy encompassing the use of battlefield nuclear weapons in a condition of bilateral nuclear deterrence, at the level of strategic forces as well as on the ground in Europe. The posture survives from a period when conditions were different. There is a need for realignment in order to provide for a credible doctrine and force posture in the 1980s.

Reconciling the Competing Roles of Nuclear Weapons in Europe

Six different, sometimes conflicting purposes underlie the role of nuclear weapons in NATO's strategy for the defense of Europe: (1) deterring attack, (2) ensuring political control, (3) defending Europe if deterrence fails, (4) extending American protection, (5) structuring Alliance political relationships, and (6) reassuring societies. These purposes may impose competing requirements, and a credible policy must reconcile them.

In principle, deterrence could be maximized by a tripwire arrangement to automate the nuclear response to an attack. In practice, such an arrangement could be vulnerable to accidents and malfunctions as well as to the uncontrollable unfolding of events, leading to a sequence of trapped decisions. Governments cannot in fact abdicate responsibility for assessment and decision and would jeopardize public confidence if they did.

In this connection it seems useful to distinguish among three aspects of deterrence: deterrence of war, deterrence of certain actions in a war, and deterrence of certain deployments and postures in peacetime. On balance it seems rather unlikely that a move away from a first-use-if-necessary policy to a no-first-use policy would degrade NATO's capacity to deter war. On the contrary, to the extent that NFU is associated with improvements in the capacity of the Alliance to contain a conventional attack with conventional means and to reduce the pressures for rapid and widespread nuclear preemption, deterrence would improve. The deterrence of first use of nuclear weapons by the adversary and of his pushing for military victory could be accomplished with a much smaller nuclear arsenal than the one NATO has deployed in Europe at present.

The argument that nuclear weapons are needed to compel the adversary to disperse his forces and thus degrade his capacity for conventional attack cannot be readily dismissed. Yet the extent to which conventional armaments such as multiple-launch rocket systems can force similar dispersal is worth examination. Furthermore, nuclear weapons are needed to deter first use by the adversary. For this purpose, care should be taken not to provoke or invite first use by the adversary, which the current posture tends to do. This is not an argument for the denuclearization of Europe, but rather for selective withdrawal of those kinds of nuclear weapons that appear to endanger rather than enhance NATO security at the point of crisis or war. The requirements for dispersal and the deterrence of first use of nuclear weapons by the adversary hardly require 6,000 nuclear munitions predominantly for battlefield use.

Finally, and in many ways most important, it must be considered whether an NFU policy would stimulate nuclear intimidation by the adversary. The Soviet Union has already given an NFU pledge. It is very hard to see how NATO's adoption of an NFU policy in such circumstances could enhance Soviet options for nuclear blackmail unless Moscow changed its declaratory policy. Nuclear initiation should be deterred by a credible second-strike option.

A policy of NFU would not mean the renunciation of a nuclear option. No adversary could have confidence that it could push NATO to the wall without risking nuclear escalation, even if the Alliance were to adopt NFU. Nuclear weapons would still exist, and there is no physical way in which they could be rendered incapable of first use. The uncertainties would be compounded by the existence of British and French nuclear forces, which have the capability to initiate nuclear attacks against conventional as well as nuclear targets. It seems rather unlikely that deterrence would be adversely affected in a measurable way, especially given the serious defects of the present policy with respect to deterrence.

A strategy must also provide for defense in the event that deterrence should fail. At that point, two objectives would become salient: stopping the war and preventing defeat. Here we must consider postures for conventional defense and the impact of a strategy and posture for early use of nuclear weapons on the course of events in wartime. The velocity of military operations has increased in quantum jumps during the twentieth century. The velocity of decisionmaking cannot keep pace with the rapid and extensive escalation resulting from the use of nuclear weapons. One purpose of military planning is to space out and slow down military operations in order to create time for reflection and bargaining. The role of nuclear weapons should be viewed from that perspective as well.

History is replete with instances in which nations have been surprised by the arrival of war. Most often surprise was not due to an absence of warning signals but rather to an inability of governments to read the signals correctly, to piece together the right picture amid large quantities of confusing noise, and to act on it. Warning signals are seldom clear and unambiguous. The complexity of modern warfare will multiply the signals from military activities as well as the opportunities for differing interpretations. NATO therefore must have a capacity for responding to ambiguous warning. High dependence on early use of nuclear weapons will limit the availability of repeatable responses to ambiguous warning and raise the threshold against implementation. If a doctrine of early use is coupled with a posture of vulnerability, NATO's responses could invite preemption rather than convey determination. The commingling of nuclear and conventional forces in the NATO armory of dual-capable systems further complicates alert procedures in the Alliance. Immobility rather than responsiveness could come to characterize NATO's performance in a crisis.

NATO provides a framework for extending an American security guarantee to the states of Western Europe. The treaty does not specify how the American commitment to Europe should be carried out. The structure and size of the military forces in the Alliance must be shaped to accommodate changing circumstances. The American guarantee includes a nuclear guarantee. The credibility and management of extended deterrence rested for a long time on the existence of a substantial American margin in strategic nuclear forces. As Soviet strategic forces grew, questions arose concerning the continued reliability of the American guarantee under conditions of bilateral deterrence and later approximate parity. Would the American president risk New York or San Francisco in order to defend Frankfurt, Amsterdam, or Berlin? Nobody knows, since much would depend on circumstances and on the president and his advisers. A potential adversary does not know the answer either, and must take into account the possibility that announced commitments may be honored. Furthermore, any challenge is unlikely to be clear cut.

Ambiguity and incremental moves would probably predominate. Residual uncertainties would be enormous and contribute to deterrence.

Yet it seems unwise to compound doubts about extended deterrence. A posture for first use of battlefield nuclear weapons in Europe is likely to put American cities more irrevocably on the nuclear hook than would be sustainable in American domestic politics, particularly during a period of recurrent differences in political assessments between Europe and the United States. Postwar history suggests that the capacity of the American nuclear guarantee to reassure European societies depends less on the structure and size of the American nuclear deterrent than on confidence in American political judgment and in Washington's ability to combine firmness, flexibility, and prudence in the conduct of East-West relations. The salience of a policy of reliance on early and first use of nuclear weapons may produce European fears of American adventurism during periods when the United States pursues more assertive policies toward the East than does Europe. Divergent emphases are likely to occur in the future, sometimes with Europeans and sometimes with Americans at the "softer" end of the scale. It seems prudent to design a military doctrine and posture for the Alliance that does not amplify and aggravate such transatlantic differences through public fears of nuclear war. Intra-Alliance diplomacy therefore would seem to benefit from a doctrine and posture that do not put the issue of nuclear response up front. The increasing complexity and fluidity of the international situation, and the issues they give rise to, suggest the need for NATO to adopt a policy of reduced reliance on nuclear weapons.

It is arguable, of course, that any departure from the present reliance on first use of nuclear weapons could be seen as a sign of American disengagement. Yet the conclusion to be drawn would depend very largely on the way in which a shift in emphasis was presented. There is no need for a formal change in the present overall strategy as embodied in MC-14/3; a presumption of no first use could be accommodated within the existing framework of strategic principles. A plan for a plausible conventional defense combined, perhaps, with a formal commitment to maintain American troops in Europe could very largely allay fears of decoupling.

It has been argued that adoption of the principle of no first use would endanger the strategic unity of the Alliance, rendering Europe more exposed than the United States.[7] It should be recalled, however, that the United States is vulnerable to direct nuclear attack by the strategic forces of the Soviet Union. The security of the United States cannot be based on a first-strike option. Indeed, American concerns about the vulnerability of land-based missile forces and the rejection of launch-on-warning options indicate a second-strike orientation. The strategic unity of the Alliance can hardly be maintained if Europeans insist on being able to ignite the strategic forces of the United States through first use of nuclear weapons in Europe. Indeed, a second-strike strategic posture combined with the adoption of NFU could establish a strategic unity around principles that could significantly enhance public reassurance while hardly degrading deterrence of the Warsaw Pact. The primary task of an Eastern policy for the West is to gain acceptance and observance of the principle of mutual restraint. This requires shaping the West's military posture in a manner consistent with that principle.

A nuclear shadow would pervade any war in Europe. The possibility of escalation beyond the nuclear threshold would be omnipresent and deterring. But a policy of giving substance to the shadow through early and first use could cause allies to abandon unity precipitously at the point of maximum danger.

The essential requirement for preserving the strategic unity of NATO is the presence of American troops in Europe, promising a would-be aggressor that an attack on Western Europe will result in a war also with the United States. Western Europe shares a continent with the Soviet Union and could be attacked by conventional and theater nuclear forces. The United States is not directly vulnerable to that threat, but the presence of American troops in Europe amounts to a sharing of the threat, including the inescapable and implicit risk of escalation across the nuclear threshold. Consequently, a shift toward a policy of NFU by NATO should be accompanied by a renewed commitment to mustering a credible conventional defense, and by a contractual commitment by the United States and the United Kingdom to maintain troops on the central front in Europe. Deterrence and reassurance could thereby be enhanced.

The present unease in Western Europe is related not only to the presence of large arsenals of nuclear weapons and to the prospect of additional deployments, but also to an American policy toward the Soviet Union that is at best unclear and inconsistent and, in the perception of many, based on the assumption of an unmitigated conflict leading to the eventual collapse of the Soviet system. The prospect of war looms larger in that context, and sharing a continent with the Soviet Union compels most Western Europeans to conclude that a modus vivendi must be found. Publics in Western Europe expect their governments to ensure adequate protection, but they also expect them to pursue peace and an easing of conflict. The twin objectives of deterrence and détente that were canonized in the Harmel report of 1967 still constitute the only basis on which Alliance consensus may be maintained. The defense policy and posture of NATO should be arranged in consonance with both goals.

Paradoxically, a reason for the current tensions within the Alliance is that peace has come to be taken for granted by people who have enjoyed it, along with unprecedented prosperity, for more than three decades. The current troubles are in part a by-product of NATO's success. Prosperity and peace now appear to be threatened at the same time. The West's own military instruments rather than the Russians' appear to many to be the primary threat to peace. A serious effort to create a plausible conventional military posture is needed in order to reforge the identification between Western European societies and the defense of Western Europe.[8] Relying on first use of nuclear weapons has the opposite effect: it transfers to the United States the primary responsibility for the defense of Europe. The American presence in Europe, however, is a necessary condition for a conventional defense to seem feasible in European eyes. Plausible conventional defense is attainable, provided governments give priority to its creation. The adoption of NFU arguably would make it harder for governments to escape the challenge, and military authorities would be forced to set conventional priorities and abandon laundry list approaches to force improvements.

The requirements of deterrence and reassurance may not coincide completely. Yet, other things being equal, the probability that a given response would be carried out would seem to rise if the nature of the response were such as to command broad public support. It is clearly desirable as well as feasible for NATO to muster a credible posture for conventional defense in Europe, thereby transferring to a would-be adversary the onus of nuclear initiation.

Existing ambiguities in the relationship between the deployment of nuclear weapons in Europe and NATO's actual employment doctrine may have served to diffuse potential disagreements in the past. Now they have become a source of public restiveness. Ambiguity in the 1980s could create a crisis of confidence between state and society about security policy in general and coalition defense in particular.

Europeans are concerned above all with the prevention of war. They have resisted American proposals for conventional defense in the past in part for economic reasons, but in part also for fear of making Europe "safe for conventional war." In recent years that fear has been overtaken by another, that the superpowers were making Europe "safe for limited nuclear war." Such fears are not immutable or beyond influence. They are, in fact, largely a product of the rhetoric in which defense options are wrapped for public presentation. The mood in Europe is neither pacifist or neutralist, but care must be taken lest present fears of an uncontrollable arms race and the absence of a coherent policy toward the East lead to a de facto movement in that direction. Public attention must be drawn to the feasibility of preventing war through acceptable means, rather than numbed by the unacceptable consequences of implementing official strategy. Nuclear weapons inspire awe rather than trust; they may cause governments to deter their own people more than their adversaries, and inspire the latter to play on the fears of nuclear war in order to dissipate NATO's spirit of resistance. For the sake of reassurance, nuclear weapons should be a means of last and not of first resort.

NFU and Arms Control

NATO's policy on nuclear weapons may have effects on nuclear proliferation outside Europe. The decisions of would-be nuclear weapon states have complex origins and in many important ways are determined by local factors. However, the major nuclear weapon states influence the general climate in which those decisions are made. Developing countries, sensitive to problems of distribution and equity in a world in which maldistribution and inequity prevail, are unlikely to accept the proposition that nuclear weapons are a privileged option for the industrial states of the North and must be eschewed by those in the South. A change of emphasis away from reliance on early resort to nuclear weapons and adoption of the principle of NFU could strengthen the case for nuclear abstention by would-be nuclear weapon states in the South. Care must be taken, of course, lest changes of emphasis in NATO's military doctrine and posture stimulate proliferation in the North by suggesting that allies cannot be entrusted with the task of nuclear deterrence—that an NFU policy is incompatible with extended deterrence. NFU need not carry such disruptive connotations, but much would depend on the manner in which the shift is implemented and presented.

Arms control is usually viewed as a means of reducing the risk of war, the destruction if war should occur, and the burden of maintaining arms. Hence it is worthwhile to consider whether changes in the NATO defense posture and in the deliberations of a potential adversary that could result from NATO's adoption of a no-first-use policy are consistent with arms control objectives.

Issues related to the deterrence of war have already been addressed. But war may also result from events that are beyond deterrence or tend to undermine it, creating pressures for preemption that may overpower interests in prudence and moderation. Such pressures are influenced by the deployment and configuration of the military forces on both sides.

The burdens of the arms race cannot be measured only in terms of financial outlays; they also involve the social costs of maintaining arms. A posture of heavy reliance on nuclear weapons is likely to constitute an increasing burden on social consensus and cohesion, even if the alternative of a larger conventional effort were to cost more money.

Arms control encompasses explicit or tacit measures to constrain the use or accumulation of military force, and includes negotiated as well as unilateral measures. The two approaches may be mutually reinforcing, and their orchestration requires attention. The institutionalization of arms control that took place during the 1960s and 1970s tended to obscure the purposes of arms control and the obstacles to its achievement—most notably the interrelationships among political order, the military balance, and stability in its various dimensions and contexts. Arms control became linked to defense policy and international behavior, and came to be viewed as a tactical lever. From the linkage a "dual hostage" relationship has emerged: defense policy has tended to become hostage to the uncertain fortunes of negotiated arms control in order to broaden its social acceptability, while arms control has become hostage to world insecurity and to tensions arising outside Europe from East-West competition. The linkage to defense policy has tended to increase conflicts over NATO's strategy and defense policy because the latter appear to present obstacles to arms control. Similarly, linkage to the foreign policy behavior of the Soviet Union tends to widen differences in the assessment of non-European crises. Double linkage creates double hostage situations that make it difficult to pursue arms control by other means, or indeed to pursue shared interests through arms control. Arms control should be viewed neither as a reward for good behavior nor as a sweetener for unpopular decisions on defense.

Two distinct approaches to the regulation of nuclear weapons in Europe have been suggested, the geographical and the functional. The geographical approach has focused on the establishment of nuclear weapon free zones (the Rapacki plan)[9] or nuclear freeze zones (the Gomulka plan)[10] in central Europe. They have come to naught because their political implications seemed to preempt defense decisions in NATO or to prejudice the political role of West Germany in the security order in Europe. France's withdrawal from the integrated defense organization in NATO increased the asymmetrical impacts of such zones on the strategic positions of the two alliances, putting NATO in the disadvantageous position of lacking space for defense in depth and depending on transatlantic reinforcement. Subregional nuclear weapon free zones in Nordic Europe or in the Balkans could be integrated into broader schemes involving the reduction and regulation of nuclear weapons. In central Europe, however, nuclear weapon free zones that included West Germany would raise major issues of political balance and equality of status in addition to posing intractable problems of military strategy. Hence a functional approach seems to offer more promising solutions.

Functional arms control arrangements should be examined for their impact on stability, especially crisis stability and political stability. Measures designed to enhance crisis stability must also be assessed with a view to their possible impact on strategic stability and arms race stability (see chapter 6). Preemptive instabilities associated with NATO's present nuclear posture in Europe arise from the disproportionate number of short-range weapons in NATO's nuclear arsenal; from the physical location of nuclear munition storage sites and the difficulty of dispersal; and from the commingling of nuclear and conventional forces.

Almost 60 percent of NATO's nuclear munitions are associated with short-range delivery systems (artillery, short-range missiles, ADMs). All of the artillery tubes that can fire nuclear munitions are dual capable. Thirty percent of NATO's nuclear arsenal in Europe consists of gravity bombs for tactical aircraft of medium range. All of the tactical aircraft also contribute to the conventional fighting power of the Alliance.[11]

NATO's options are severely constrained by the existing deployment and configuration of the nuclear posture. The bulk of NATO's nuclear munitions are stored in a rather small number of identifiable sites.[12] Nuclear artillery shells are stationed a few hours' march from the intra-German frontier. Dispersal of the munitions to reduce their vulnerability could increase popular opposition to the presence of nuclear weapons in addition to requiring larger numbers of custodial personnel; dispersal during crises or war would increase the risk that the weapons might be preempted, overrun, or used prematurely and precipitously.

Crisis stability could be enhanced by withdrawing nuclear munitions from forward positions, by reducing the number of battlefield nuclear systems, and by separating nuclear from conventional weapons and deployments. A posture of reduced emphasis on battlefield nuclear weapons and of enhanced stability during crises would facilitate a shift in NATO policy toward NFU.

At the same time, a move toward NFU could create incentives and opportunities to pursue arms control arrangements that could strengthen the security order in Europe and alleviate the destabilizing pressures that arise from public dissatisfaction with the current posture in peacetime and from incentives to preemption in a crisis. Restructuring, withdrawal, and reduction could result in greater stability at significantly lower levels of nuclear deployment in Europe.[13] It is important, however, to avoid the trap of making desirable changes in the NATO posture hostage to Soviet reciprocation in arms control agreements. Arms control negotiations cannot substitute for prudent and consistent defense policies, but they can be complementary. NATO could seek agreement on certain broad measures of reciprocal restraint, such as a ban on the deployment of nuclear munitions in forward areas where the two alliances come into direct geographical contact. This could be done unilaterally as a confidence-building measure while challenging the Soviet Union to reciprocate. Such an initiative would not reduce the ability of either side to initiate the use of nuclear weapons, but it could reduce pressures and fears of wide and precipitous use.

In addition, the concept of dual-capable aircraft should be thoroughly reexamined. It introduces ambiguities and pressures for large-scale preemption against NATO airfields in Europe and complicates alert procedures. For NATO, a quick deterioration of the air power ratio in a war is a more disturbing aspect of the balance of forces in central Europe than the ground force ratio. Relieving tactical aircraft of the burden of nuclear missions and transferring the latter to a small number of dedicated missiles would improve NATO's flexibility and staying power. Since NATO's arsenal in Europe includes some 1,850 nuclear gravity bombs, NATO could offer a substantial reduction in the number of nuclear warheads in Europe in return for Soviet reciprocation or a preferential withdrawal of offensive force components such as main battle tanks. Furthermore, NATO could propose prohibiting the collocation of nuclear storage sites and military airfields as a means of demonstrating the conventional role of tactical air power units and the abandonment of dual-capable forces.

Verification of compliance could be sought through on-site inspection, possibly on the challenge principle. Similar arrangements could be envisaged for the denuclearization of air defenses and the prohibition of collocating nuclear storage sites and surface-to-air missile sites. Such arrangements could constitute important confidence-building measures. Inspection could be designed to verify adherence to other constraints as well, such as a prohibition of storage facilities for chemical weapons and of training troops in clothing that protects against chemical and nuclear weapons.

Confidence-building measures could be construed as undertakings that link defense postures and agreements on arms control. The adoption of NFU could usefully be thought of as a confidence-building measure in this context.

Battlefield nuclear weapons as well as medium-range nuclear weapons could become subjects for negotiation in the Vienna negotiations on mutual and balanced force reductions (MBFR), possibly as part of a comprehensive agreement involving preferential reductions of offensive force elements such as tanks. The MBFR context has the advantage of relating theater nuclear forces to the conventional force balance in Europe, thereby permitting a comprehensive assessment. Earlier attempts to trade off Western nuclear weapons for Soviet tanks suggest that such arrangements are not easy to negotiate. However, as an element in a broader scheme designed to break the stalemate, the prospect could be brighter. Another alternative would be a follow-on phase of the negotiations on intermediate-range nuclear forces (INF). However, such a phase is likely to merge negotiations on strategic arms reductions (START) and INF, and theater weapons are likely to be viewed as a potential means of circumvention that should be constrained through collateral measures. Such measures could, however, have a stabilizing effect on the military situation in central Europe.

What Is to Be Changed?

In moving toward NFU, it is necessary to distinguish between its adoption as a *principle,* a general rule or guide to action, and as a *policy,* a formal course of action adopted by the relevant authorities and then implemented through changes in military forces, posture, and operational plans. It is possible to envisage NATO embracing the principle of NFU and changing its forces, posture, and plans in accord with that principle without formally changing the doctrine of flexible response embodied in MC-14/3.

The changes in NATO's posture that should be considered in order to make it consistent with an NFU principle include (1) withdrawal of battlefield nuclear weapons from forward areas in Europe, (2) substantial reductions (several thousand) in the number of battlefield weapons in Europe, (3) conventionalization of NATO's air defense systems, (4) withdrawal of atomic demolition munitions (ADMs), (5) stand-down of quick reaction alert (QRA) forces, and (6) abandonment of dual-capable systems, leaving a small force of dedicated systems for the medium-range delivery of nuclear munitions. The purpose of such a reconfiguration would be to reduce both the pressures on NATO's decisionmaking authorities for early use and a would-be aggressor's incentives for preemption. The posture would be designed to deter first use by the adversary and to impose operational constraints on him by holding his forces at risk.

A policy of NFU does not imply a policy of nuclear disengagement from Europe. However, the nuclear posture in Europe would have to be changed in order to lend credibility to the principle of NFU. Most of the nuclear munitions for short-range battlefield artillery could be withdrawn from Europe, as well as ADMs and nuclear air defense munitions. Nuclear munition sites could be moved back from forward areas. With respect to medium-range (150–1,500km) nuclear systems, NFU could be strengthened by the abrogation of present arrangements for dual-capable systems, including aircraft.

Counter-air operations would constitute time-urgent missions in the early phases of a war and be directed principally but not exclusively against the adversary's major operating bases. Strong expectations that NATO would use nuclear-armed tactical aircraft for such missions could elicit nuclear preemptive strikes to destroy the aircraft in their shelters before takeoff. It follows that stability might be improved by a stand-down of QRA aircraft and possibly by moving toward "conventionalizing" NATO's tactical aircraft. QRA procedures involve only 10 percent of NATO's fighter aircraft in peacetime, but at higher levels of alert (DEFCONs) increasingly large portions of the force are drawn into the nuclear mission. Dual-capable systems create ambiguity with respect to the nuclear threshold, and the commingling of nuclear and conventional systems is likely to complicate alert procedures within the Alliance, exacerbating the problem of preemption. Removing tactical aircraft from nuclear strike roles could improve conventional defense capabilities, particularly upon the procurement of modern area-effect weapons for dispensing submunitions. A residual nuclear role could be assigned to dedicated and distinguishable missile systems. Great care should be taken to ensure a high degree of survivability for them. If the force is small and vulnerable, it might be seen as lending itself to total destruction and hence offer incentives for preemption.

The problem of denuclearizing larger portions of NATO's defense posture will require careful political assessment and management. The approach should be incremental in nature. It should not be designed solely around high technologies that are then inserted as magical fixes, with the attendant danger that they come to be viewed as an another expression of American love for gimmickry or simply as a high-powered sales campaign. Furthermore, the political climate in Europe in the current controversy over intermediate-range nuclear forces is such that schemes for the deployment of substantial numbers of intermediate-range missiles for delivery of conventional munitions would not be acceptable to large parts of the public. Fears of subsequent nuclearization would abound. An announced policy of no first use might be an important political precondition for gaining acceptance of new delivery systems for Assault Breaker and Airfield Breaker munition packages.

Particular attention must be paid to the impact of new weapon technologies on the velocity and scale of military operations. High reliance on a dense delivery of advanced conventional munitions in large quantities could affect the tempo of war and the scale of destruction in a manner that would reduce the chance of stopping the violence and preventing explosive escalation across the nuclear threshold. Some high technology approaches to conventional defense could lead to an acceleration of the tempo and an intensification of the scale of operations that could impose the same strains on the decisionmaking system and the momentum of war that are characteristic of nuclear weapons, and hence reduce the chance of avoiding escalation across the nuclear threshold. The threshold may be blurred from the conventional as well as the nuclear end of the spectrum of violence in war.

The role of intermediate-range nuclear forces (INF) requires special assessment. NATO's dual-track decision of December 1979 was basically concerned with the long-term political balance in Europe in the context of nuclear parity between the Soviet Union and the United States. A "zero option" that involves substantial Soviet reductions in return for NATO's abstaining from the deployment of intermediate-range missiles in Europe makes little sense if the forces are needed for military missions, such as deep-strike interdiction of the Warsaw Pact's second- and third-echelon forces. This is not the place to examine alternative outcomes of the negotiations. The overriding objective seems to be a significant drawdown of Soviet deployments and the imposition of a ceiling to prevent future deployments. The agreement should not concede to Moscow a *droit de regard,* much less a *droit de contrôle* over British and French decisions in the future, which does not mean that the existence of British and French nuclear forces cannot be taken into account in a Soviet-American agreement linking reductions in and limitations on INF and intercontinental-range nuclear forces, as was envisaged in the NATO communiqué of December 12, 1979.[14]

The question of NFU is intimately linked with the manner in which INF are handled in the negotiations. The broad political issues are much more important than operational considerations. The most important objective would seem to be linking INF negotiations to START and aiming for a comprehensive agreement that encompasses reductions in and limitations on intermediate-range and intercontinental systems. The treaty should impose a common ceiling, principally on warheads, with freedom to mix forces in chosen proportions under the common ceiling. In this manner the existence of British and French forces could be taken into account without Moscow's gaining a supervisory role. Equally important, the distribution of assets under the ceiling would remain a Western decision. Moscow would have to trade off SS-20 warheads against its ICBM warheads. The original issue of a separate intermediate-range missile threat against Western Europe outside the boundaries of a SALT agreement codifying strategic parity would no longer pertain.

It is possible to envisage a comprehensive agreement containing specific provisions limiting or banning the deployment of destabilizing systems *by both sides* according to agreed criteria. It is important to avoid another "singularity" issue by defining Germany as a no-deployment zone for intermediate-range nuclear forces. A separate agreement on such forces that equated Soviet SS-20 deployments with British and French forces while banning other deployments of intermediate-range systems in Europe could exacerbate such political concerns. Under these conditions an NFU policy could add to perceived pressures on West Germany, which would have a politically destabilizing effect on German alignment and the real options for credible defense in Western Europe. A formula that would induce NATO to make an independent decision on the relative distribution of warheads among intercontinental systems, submarine-launched systems, and INF could have the effect of recoupling the American nuclear guarantee to the defense of Europe. An interim agreement on INF is needed for political reasons and as a bridge to a comprehensive agreement. It should include a commitment by the United States and the Soviet Union to merge the negotiations about intermediate-range and strategic nuclear weapons as well as an agreement to reduce SS-20 deployments in return for a scaling down of the prospective NATO deployment, including a preferential reduction and even elimination of the deployment of Pershing II. (Pershing II's threat to the Soviet command and control system has been exaggerated, given the small number of missiles involved and their limited range.) Provided the number of SS-20 missiles capable of reaching targets in central Europe were reduced to a level below that which existed in December 1979, NATO should be able to accept a mutual freeze on the deployment of intermediate-range nuclear forces pending the outcome of negotiations for a comprehensive agreement, since the ground rules would have been changed.[15]

If new intermediate-range missiles are to be deployed in Europe, great care must be taken to ensure a highly survivable configuration. Public acceptance of the West's position in the negotiations and beyond might be broadened if NATO were to move in the direction of NFU.

A policy of no early use of nuclear weapons requires a capability for initial conventional defense. A policy of NFU would seem to require a capacity for sustained conventional defense. Much of the discussion concerning reduced dependence on early or first use of nuclear weapons has understandably focused on the feasibility of NATO's establishing stronger conventional defenses. Beyond consideration of the opportunities and costs associated with substitution, it is necessary to question the implied assumption that nuclear weapons can substitute for conventional inferiority.

That assumption appears to take two forms. One postulates that the use of nuclear weapons would compensate for inadequate conventional forces and thus turn defeat into victory. Since the Soviet Union has caught up with NATO in theater nuclear weapons, thus promising to turn nuclear warfare in Europe into bilateral nuclear warfare, the validity of this assumption is highly questionable. Indeed, it seems more likely that the enormous casualties that would result from theater nuclear warfare in Europe would accentuate the advantages of the party with superior conventional forces.

The second, more subtle variant of the substitution assumption recognizes that nuclear weapons are generically different from other weapons and that using them first is an act of political signaling, a warning of the dangers—indeed, the shared dangers—of pushing conventional advantage to the limit, a threat to lose control. The aim is to induce a political reappraisal, not to pursue the mirage of military victory by the use of nuclear weapons. But several questions arise: what signal would be conveyed by demonstrative shots of nuclear weapons across the bow? Would NATO be demonstrating resolve or desperation? NATO has been unable thus far to agree on the political guidelines for follow-on use of nuclear weapons, even if contingency plans for follow-on use do exist. That failure may signify the inadequacy of a gesture that the adversary may choose to ignore, respond to in kind, or seize upon as justification for large-scale preemption or retaliation. What would NATO do if the signal were ignored? Would the pressures move in the direction of preemptive surrender or deliberate escalation? Is it not possible that the chosen policy would foster immobilism and vacillation rather than perseverance and tenacity?

The game of chicken may provide an interesting metaphor for analyzing interpersonal competition, but it seems far removed from the political behavior of a multinational alliance, particularly an alliance of democratic polities. The measure of a successful defense policy is its ability to deter would-be adversaries and to reassure societies in need of protection. The doctrine of first demonstrative use of nuclear weapons is seriously flawed from the standpoint of deterrence, and it seems particularly unsuitable as a basis for reassuring societies in which fears of nuclear war and its disastrous consequences are increasing. Such a doctrine seems likely to deepen the estrangement and exacerbate the tensions between society and the state, especially in the Europe of the 1980s.

If changing the policy and not just the principle is to be considered, it is necessary to distinguish between "early use" and "first use" of nuclear weapons. Both relate to the timing of nuclear use, but the former is a time-dependent prescription, the latter an actor-dependent one. It is possible to envisage a posture and doctrine of "no early use" that nevertheless includes the option of "first use," as well as a doctrine of NFU that does not exclude early use in retaliation. A gradual revision of NATO strategy, moving from "first use if necessary, but not necessarily first use" to NFU, could be achieved through the intermediate step of "no early first use." It is preferable to concentrate on constraining first use rather than early use for reasons of deterrence and morality. The overriding purpose should be to prevent the use of nuclear weapons. A first-use policy is highly questionable for that purpose. If deterrence should fail, governments must have the option of considering their response, including withholding nuclear retaliation. This requires a survivable force posture that permits time for reflection. It implies, of course, a willingness to risk nuclear retaliation as the price of deterring first use by the adversary.[16]

Adoption of the principle of NFU would enhance deterrence by paving the way for programs that could actually be processed through NATO's decisionmaking machinery and implemented during a crisis. It would also reassure societies in which the threat of nuclear war has very largely replaced the fear of Soviet military power and possible ambitions as the principal source of anxiety. The principle would tend to raise the nuclear threshold, although residual uncertainty about the triggering of nuclear weapons would overhang any crisis or armed conflict in Europe.

The final issue is the declaratory policy NATO should adopt. It is possible in theory for the Alliance to adopt the principle of NFU and put it into practice without making a public announcement. The shift would require a change in NATO's posture, both nuclear and conventional, in order to influence the expectations and incentives of a potential adversary. It is questionable whether changes of such a fundamental nature could, let alone should, be kept secret in an alliance of open, pluralistic societies. Moreover, the absence of a public announcement would greatly lessen the reassuring impact of the policy change on Western societies. Conversely, a public declaration that was not accompanied by concrete changes in the present military posture, particularly in the nuclear part of the posture, would lack credibility and promote public questioning and controversy rather than reassurance.

An NFU declaration might be made into a legal contractual arrangement with the Warsaw Pact, but the costs of such a formality appear to outweigh the possible benefits. Since NFU is self-enforcing, a formal agreement would convey no advantage over a unilateral statement of intent, but it could raise serious problems for Alliance confidence in that it would cut to the very core of extended deterrence and Alliance guarantees. A negotiated agreement would also be open to contentious claims of *droits de regard* (and *droits de contrôle*) for arrangements on both sides that would contribute to East-West tension as well as to public unrest. NATO's adoption of a sensible and viable defense policy and posture should not be made dependent on Soviet acceptance of the same principle. It happens that the Soviet Union made a unilateral NFU pledge in the United Nations General Assembly in the fall of 1982. Parallel unilateral declarations appear preferable to a joint one.

Declarations may be empty gestures unless they are accompanied by actual changes in strategy and deployments. An NFU pledge could contribute to stability provided both sides take steps to reduce the vulnerability of their nuclear postures in Europe and to withdraw weapons that are likely to exert pressures for early and massive use. The credibility of the pledge would depend in large measure on the physical changes undertaken to make NFU into an operational as distinguished from a declaratory concept. Unless such changes are made, dangerous tensions could arise between the declaratory policy and the actual posture of the Alliance. Declarations about military policy acquire their substance from actual military dispositions. Declarations about NFU that are explicitly related to concrete changes could indeed contribute to building confidence in East-West as well as West-West relations.

Notes

1. See Richard H. Ullman, "No First Use of Nuclear Weapons," *Foreign Affairs,* vol. 50 (July 1972), pp. 669–83; McGeorge Bundy and others, "Nuclear Weapons and the Atlantic Alliance," *Foreign Affairs,* vol. 60 (Spring 1982), pp. 753–68; and Karl Kaiser and others, "Nuclear Weapons and the Preservation of Peace: A German View,"

Foreign Affairs, vol. 60 (Summer 1982), pp. 1157–70. See also various correspondence in "The Debate over No First Use," *Foreign Affairs,* vol. 60 (Summer 1982), pp. 1171–80; McGeorge Bundy, " 'No First Use' Needs Careful Study," *Bulletin of the Atomic Scientists,* vol. 38 (June 1982), pp. 6–8; and John Kristen Skogan, "NATO's Forste-bruksdoktrine: Bakgrunn, Innvendinger og Ettertanke," *Internasjonal Politikk,* 1B (1982), pp. 141–72. A particularly incisive analysis is found in Fred Charles Iklé, "NATO's 'First Nuclear Use': A Deepening Trap?" *Strategic Review,* vol. 8 (Winter 1980), pp. 18–23. Early advocacy of NFU is found in Morton H. Halperin, "A Proposal for a Ban on the First Use of Nuclear Weapons," Institute for Defense Analyses, Special Studies Group, Study Memorandum 4, Washington, D.C., October 6, 1961. A more recent example is *No First Use,* A Report by the Union of Concerned Scientists (Cambridge, 1983). Counterarguments appear in Theodore Draper, "How Not to Think About Nuclear War," *New York Review of Books,* vol. 29, July 15, 1982, pp. 35–43; and Maxwell D. Taylor, "The Trouble with 'No First Use,' " *Washington Post,* April 18, 1982.

2. See North Atlantic Treaty Organization, *Facts and Figures,* 10th ed. (Brussels: NATO Information Service, 1981), pp. 152–54.

3. John P. Rose, *The Evolution of U.S. Army Nuclear Doctrine, 1945–1980* (Boulder, Colo.: Westview Press, 1980), p. 175. See also U.S. Department of the Army, *Operations: FM100-5* (Dept. of the Army, 1982), p. 7-12.

4. Rose, *The Evolution of U.S. Army Nuclear Doctrine,* p. 172.

5. Ibid., p. 170.

6. Iklé, "NATO's 'First Nuclear Use,' " p. 20.

7. Kaiser and others, "Nuclear Weapons and the Preservation of Peace," p. 1162.

8. See the brilliant exposition of the dual tasks by Michael Howard, "Reassurance and Deterrence: Western Defense in the 1980's," *Foreign Affairs,* vol. 61 (Winter 1982–83), pp. 309–24.

9. The "first" Rapacki plan was presented to the UN General Assembly on October 2, 1957. See U.S. Department of State, *Documents on Disarmament, 1945–1959,* vol. 2: *1957–1959,* Dept. of State pub. 7008 (Government Printing Office, 1960), pp. 889–92, 944–48. The "second" Rapacki plan was outlined on November 4, 1958. Ibid., pp. 1217–19. The "third" Rapacki plan was presented to the Eighteen Nation Disarmament Committee on March 28, 1962 (ENDC/C.1/1). U.S. Arms Control and Disarmament Agency, *Documents on Disarmament, 1962,* vol. 1: *January–June,* USACDA pub. 19 (GPO, 1963), pp. 201–05.

10. The Gomulka plan was presented in a memorandum by the Polish government, February 24, 1964. See U.S. Arms Control and Disarmament Agency, *Documents on Disarmament, 1964,* USACDA pub. 27 (GPO, 1965), pp. 53–55.

11. See table 3-1, chapter 3 above, and appendix B, table B-1, in Donald R. Cotter, James H. Hansen, and Kirk McConnell, *The Nuclear "Balance" in Europe: Status, Trends, Implications,* USSI Report 83-1 (Cambridge, Mass.: United States Strategic Institute, 1983), p. 41.

12. Jeffrey Record, "Theater Nuclear Weapons: Begging the Soviet Union to Pre-empt," *Survival,* vol. 19 (September–October 1977), p. 208.

13. See Independent Commission on Disarmament and Security Issues, *Common Security: A Blueprint for Survival* (Simon and Schuster, 1982), pp. 146–50; Cyrus R. Vance and Robert E. Hunter, "The Centrality of Arms Control" and "Arms-Control Steps," *New York Times,* December 26 and 27, 1982; Sam Nunn, *NATO: Can the Alliance Be Saved?* Report to the Senate Committee on Armed Services, 97 Cong. 2 sess. (GPO, 1982); Johan Jørgen Holst, "Arms Control in Europe: Towards a New Political Order," *Bulletin of Peace Proposals,* vol. 13, no. 2 (1982), pp. 81–89; and

Johan Jørgen Holst, "Domestic Concerns and Nuclear Doctrine: How Should the Nuclear Posture Be Shaped?" *Adelphi Papers* (forthcoming).

14. It states explicitly: "Limitations on United States and Soviet long-range theater nuclear systems should be negotiated bilaterally in the SALT III framework in a step-by-step approach." "Special Meeting of Foreign and Defence Ministers: Communiqué," *NATO Review,* vol. 28 (February 1980), p. 26.

15. See Johan Jørgen Holst, *Kjernevapen og forhandlinger: Hva ma gjöes?* (Oslo, Den norske atlanterhavskomité, 1983), and The *"Dual-Track" Decision Revisited,* NUPI/N 267 April 1983, Oslo, Norsk utenrikspolitisk institutt (to be published in Hans-Henrik Holm and Nikolaj Petersen, eds., *Nuclear Modernization in Europe*).

16. For a challenging investigation into some of the ethical dimensions of nuclear deterrence, see Gregory S. Kavka, "Some Paradoxes of Deterrence," *Journal of Philosophy,* vol. 75 (June 1978), pp. 285–302. The author's view is outlined in Johan Jørgen Holst, "Strategiog etikk," *Kirke og Kultur,* vol. 88, no. 3 (1983), pp. 177–81.

CHAPTER TEN

ALLIANCE SECURITY

John D. Steinbruner

As is apparent from the preceding discussion, the policy issues involved in the no-first-use idea have had long gestation, are affected by differences in judgment that flourish in an alliance of democratic governments, and have not yet found decisive resolution. The changes in NATO's defense posture that a complete no-first-use (NFU) policy would require do not appear to be imminent, but established NATO policy is not irrevocably anchored against major evolution. The arguments for altering NATO's reliance on nuclear weapons are too powerful to be dismissed with no effect whatsoever, though the necessary changes are too fundamental for all of them to be implemented immediately.

It is useful to distinguish those criticisms of NATO security policy that appear to enjoy substantial consensus, serious points of disagreement about the problem and its solution, and options for adjusting the NATO position. Broad consensus is the most reliable guide to what can be done. Disagreements are a major source of uncertainty about what will be done. Options define the practical choices that might be made.

Priorities for Change

There is agreement among the collaborating authors, reflected in the broader professional community, that the current nuclear posture of NATO has defects too serious to be tolerated indefinitely. Major segments of the NATO forces cannot accomplish their assigned missions and risk provoking Soviet attack. In particular the short-range nuclear weapons deployed in Western Europe for battlefield use, some 3,000 in number, are highly vulnerable to preemptive destruction, certainly by Soviet nuclear forces, probably even by Soviet conventional aviation.

In order to assure peacetime control, the weapons are stored and guarded at known locations. Given the strict procedures that necessarily accompany the handling of nuclear weapons and given the intersecting decisions of numerous governments, the process of dispersing these weapons to forward commanders, assigning their targets, and authorizing their use would in all probability be impractically slow in comparison to the Soviet threat. As the conditions of war are imagined, Soviet forces are usually conceded the initiative and at any rate would be in a position to seize it.

Systematic preemption against the infrastructure that supports NATO's nuclear operations is both the highest priority mission of Soviet Frontal Aviation and apparently the current limit of its capacity for conventional operations.[1] With full commitment of its tactical air resources, the Soviet Union with timely preemption could reasonably expect to prevent any coordinated use of NATO's battlefield weapons and would surely preclude achievement of even the most rudimentary Western military objectives. Although there is some military utility in forcing Soviet commanders to contemplate this diversion of resources, it is almost certainly outweighed at a moment of intense crisis by the risk of triggering Soviet offensive air operations that might otherwise be avoided. Moreover, the Soviets could accomplish major disruption even with limited actions designed to preserve their tactical air resources. NATO's nuclear forces depend upon critical communication facilities that could be destroyed without a full-scale air campaign, and organized sabotage with deep raiding parties and covert agents could be highly effective.

The burden of operating NATO's forces under the pressure of threatened preemption creates major conflicts between nuclear and conventional operations. Details of tactical management differ markedly, depending upon which type of warfare is contemplated. At the moment, nuclear weapons are so fully integrated into NATO ground forces and tactical air units that NATO commanders are poorly prepared to fight without them.

This situation violates one of the cardinal principles of strategic planning. Forces designed to deter war, whether by threat of unacceptably damaging retaliation or by promise of effective defense, must be substantially invulnerable to preemptive attack. Otherwise, in the midst of crisis they serve more to provoke attack than to deter it.

Vulnerable nuclear forces, moreover, are not an acceptable means of coupling the larger and inherently more protected strategic forces of the

United States to the security of Western Europe. That link is indeed vital and must be materially represented, but its embodiment must be compatible with the U.S. deterrent policy that emphasizes the capability for second-strike retaliation. Force elements that cannot support retaliation and can be used *only* to initiate a nuclear attack do not meet the test of compatibility.

In particular the link between U.S. strategic forces and Western Europe cannot be established by deployments that are plausibly subject to effective conventional interdiction by Soviet Frontal Aviation without the use of nuclear weapons and perhaps even without Soviet ground force penetration of Western Europe. Responsible military management of U.S. nuclear forces for the purposes of preventing war requires a disassociation from weapons that are so highly vulnerable. Declarations of an inexorable link issued for political purposes and designed to deter conventional attack cannot be rendered credible in the face of that military reality.

This analysis suggests strong priorities for the evolution of NATO's defense posture. Whatever else is done, battlefield nuclear weapons should be removed from forward positions and provided a degree of protection that is at least proof against conventional attack. Moreover, combat management of these weapons should be strictly separated from conventional operations, not only to allow greater protection but also to make possible the optimum use of conventional forces.

A second element of emerging consensus is that NATO defense planning should be based on assessments of relative conventional force capabilities that are more detailed and militarily more precise than the simple comparisons of division strength and categories of equipment that have dominated prevailing conceptions throughout the history of the Alliance. The often rehearsed numerical advantages of the Warsaw Pact in organized divisions and in inventories of tanks and tactical aircraft do not translate into a decisive capability to invade Western Europe. The levels of manpower and financial investment are not nearly so disparate as they once seemed, and at any rate a great many determinants would intervene between these basic inputs and the outcome of an actual war. The central fact is that neither side can anticipate with confidence what the outcome of conventional war in Europe would be—a condition that generally serves to deter attack in the absence of powerful motives compelling it.

While acknowledging an inability to make clear predictions of victory or defeat, both Soviet and American military professionals have developed similar methods of assessing the relative capabilities of conventional forces based on those factors that can be plausibly quantified and calibrated against combat experience in the battles of World War II. These methods offer as precise and comprehensive a definition of relative position as broadly established judgment is likely to allow. When applied to current NATO and Warsaw Pact forces, as presented in chapter 4, these calculations suggest an uncomfortable possibility of Soviet penetration into Western Europe but hardly the decisive triumphal sweep to the Rhine or the Channel that might tempt ruthless ambitions. NATO would be at risk in conventional war, but not outclassed and not compelled by necessity to rely on the early use of nuclear weapons.

These assessments indicate that the deterrence of conventional attack by conventional means alone is feasible in principle. Options for improving NATO's relative conventional force capability for the purpose of clarifying and enhancing conventional deterrence emerge as the most effective military measures available for increasing the security of the Alliance.

Matters of Disagreement

The vulnerability of battlefield weapons, the disruption they cause to conventional operations, and the inherent feasibility of conventional deterrence are all conditions that motivate changes in NATO's defense posture in the direction of an NFU policy. Conclusions about the desirability of those changes, however, are affected by continuing disagreements within the Alliance, the most important of which concern the relative weights to be given to different aspects of Alliance security.

There is a body of opinion prominent in European defense ministries and in the security establishments of NATO governments for which the dominant concern remains that of securely attaching apocalyptic consequences to any act of war in Europe. If massive destruction is clearly seen to be the likely—or better, unavoidable—result of any serious aggression against Western Europe, then Soviet leaders will avoid such an act and war of any kind will be prevented. From this perspective the principal problem is the link to U.S. strategic forces, which hold the capacity for truly massive retaliatory destruction. If that link is secure, then deterrence is likely to be secure and war will probably be prevented. All else is secondary.

Among those who hold this position in some form there are differences as to what threatens the link and what must be done to strengthen it. For some it is largely a matter of political resolve in the United States. Holders of this view are primarily concerned to preserve the historical symbols of the American nuclear force commitment to the Alliance and to reaffirm them whenever evolving circumstances seem to require it. For others it is largely a matter of establishing specific military operations that would credibly serve as a bridge between limited actions in Europe and full-scale global war. If that is done, they believe, then political constancy will follow. Both variants share a reluctance to alter the policy or defense posture of the Alliance in any significant way. Their adherents do not foresee a need to fight in Europe but only to preserve the deterrent effect. Though it is impolite to state the point too bluntly, they see considerable convenience in the vulnerability of NATO's nuclear forces: the very fact of it serves to elicit supplementary support from the American nuclear forces and to trigger the momentous act of retaliation with sufficient probability in the minds of Soviet leaders to maintain deterrence. By contrast the availability of a robust conventional defense is distinctly inconvenient, for it appears to diminish the link and to introduce a calculus of destruction that is limited to Europe and potentially exempt from the dramatic effects of nuclear weapons.

Few people hold these judgments with such categorical certainty that they would deny any adjustment in NATO's security arrangements. Many hold them to the extent that they contemplate suggested changes with great reluctance and impose a heavy burden of proof on the advocates of change.

A second set of judgments questions on several grounds the degree of reliance to be placed on military preparations in providing for the overall security of the Alliance.

Some are simply reluctant to increase the economic burdens of defense in a period when sluggish economic performance imposes severe pressures on state budgets that are heavily committed to social welfare programs. The conflicting demands of defense, economic policy, and domestic services erode the ability of Western governments to maintain political support for Alliance commitments. Political cohesion is seen as an asset of greater importance than any marginal adjustment in military capability. Others directly doubt the efficacy of preventing war by threatening nuclear retaliation and fear that weapons deployed in the name of deterrence will themselves be the cause of war. Though they would welcome any reduction in the role of nuclear weapons, they would not support a limited reconfiguration designed to preserve a strong unilateral deterrent policy. Their principal commitment is to mutual arms reduction. Finally, there is a particular concern in West Germany about the effects that conventional military preparations have on civilian society and on the symbolism of national division.

At the moment, prevailing opinion in Europe does not perceive a threat of Soviet invasion that is sufficiently likely or imminent to override these sources of doubt and make it possible to repair the defects in NATO security on an urgent basis. The difficult effort required to change well-established policies in the manner that the NFU idea requires labors against substantial political inertia.

Options

Nevertheless, a number of adjustments in current NATO security policy could realistically be made. They do not require such extensive changes as to exceed the political capacity of the member governments to undertake them. They do represent departures that are significant enough to require deliberate decisions and systematic efforts to implement them. These are the practical options upon which NATO's evolution will turn. Depending upon how many of these options are adopted, NATO policy could evolve substantially toward the reduced reliance on nuclear weapons that is the essence of the NFU idea. If none of the options is pursued, NATO's defense posture will predictably drift in the opposite direction—toward increased dependence on nuclear weapons to prevent war.

Reconfiguration

A reconfiguration of NATO's short-range nuclear weapons, designed to reduce their current vulnerability and to remove the interference they cause to conventional operations, could be accomplished by adjustments within the theater force modernization program of the United States and would not require changes in the basic NATO policy embodied in MC-14/3. Redeployment of weapons into more secure rearward locations, the establishment of a separate nuclear command, and the provision of helicopters both for protective dispersal and for mobile combat use would cost between $2 billion and $2.5 billion over five years. Compensating economies could be achieved within the $13.7 billion allocated to theater nuclear forces and their modernization in the current five-year defense plan of the United States.[2] These adjustments are desirable as unilateral measures whatever the Soviet reaction to them might be. Because their implementation would not be encumbered by the inevitable uncertainties of a formal negotiation, there is a presumption that they should be undertaken unilaterally.

Withdrawal

A complete withdrawal of U.S. battlefield nuclear weapons from the European continent would offer a more decisive resolution of the problems of vulnerability and interference with conventional defense. Except for troop concentrations of a transient nature, there are few if any serious military targets that cannot be covered by better protected, more controllable weapons of longer range. A complete withdrawal of U.S. weapons thus would render attacks on some targets more difficult, but it would leave the allied forces better able to withstand the pressures that Soviet forces might bring to bear and hence better able to manage a crisis while preserving a deterrent threat. Over the history of the Alliance, however, the deployment of battlefield weapons in Europe has been such a strong symbol of the American nuclear commitment that a complete unilateral withdrawal probably could not be accomplished as a matter of general agreement. A partial reduction taking into account the prospect of more effective conventional weapon technologies and the increased emphasis within the Alliance on longer-range nuclear weapons does appear to have substantial support.

There is a presumption that complete withdrawal of short-range nuclear weapons from Europe would depend upon reciprocity by the Soviet Union, occurring either through independent Soviet decisions or by means of formal negotiation. Serious Soviet interest is implied by Moscow's own NFU declaration and the endorsement by Soviet spokesmen of privately advanced proposals for limited nuclear free zones in Europe. NATO reductions would test that interest. Because formal negotiations have usually served to lock in commitments to current weapon programs even when their independent military rationale could not justify them, there is a strong argument for proceeding with partial reductions in existing stockpiles through independent allied decisions before considering an attempt to institute formal negotiations.

Arms Control for Intermediate-Range Weapons

Beyond the particular question of battlefield weapons, the posture of the Alliance depends critically on the outcome of the formal arms control negotiations on intermediate-range nuclear forces that are under way in Geneva. A compromise that reduced both the existing Soviet forces of intermediate range and the planned deployment of U.S. missiles in Western Europe would make a direct contribution to the underlying purpose of limiting the role of nuclear weapons strictly to that of deterring nuclear attack by a credible threat of retaliation. Such an agreement would not have a decisive effect on actual capabilities; a large Soviet capacity to attack Western Europe would remain that, as now, could be balanced only by U.S. nuclear forces. Nonetheless, an agreement would help to reestablish the sense of mutual restraint that has been damaged as U.S.-Soviet relations have deteriorated in recent years and would inevitably reaffirm basic deterrence as the only military mission each side is willing to concede to the other.

The more important potential contribution of an arms control agreement on intermediate-range weapons, however, is indirect; it would divert from NATO's nuclear posture serious military and political pressures that will predictably occur in the absence of an agreement. Soviet leaders have repeatedly asserted that they will respond to the actual deployment of U.S. intermediate-range missiles in Europe with new Soviet weapon deployments that are similar in character. Given their undoubted capacity to do so, it is unlikely that these assertions are a diplomatic bluff. New Soviet deployments would increase and make more apparent the vulnerability to preemptive attack of even the most protected nuclear weapon deployments in Western Europe. Moreover, if Soviet diplomacy is even moderately skillful, the controversy in Western Europe that has plagued the scheduled emplacement of new U.S. missiles would probably intensify and leave an enduring political division. A substantial portion of those who supported the original NATO deployment decision in 1979 did so in the belief that it would ultimately produce an arms control agreement. If it produces an intensifying arms competition instead, broad political support for NATO policy will be undermined.

Improvements in Conventional Defense

The major defect in NATO's conventional forces is their questionable ability to withstand a full-scale, highly deliberate mobilization of the Warsaw Pact. An attempt by the Soviet Union to mount a surprise attack of sufficient size to attain meaningful objectives is sufficiently uncertain of success that its deterrence appears reasonably assured. An extended Warsaw Pact mobilization lasting 90 to 120 days, however, could create sufficient probability of success to burden deterrence and plausibly support political coercion. Such a mobilization could be undertaken only at substantial cost and risk to the Soviet Union, and the likelihood of its occurrence appears to be low in foreseeable circumstances. It nonetheless represents the most clearly defined threat to NATO and the most demanding contingency. If political judgments are made that the overall security of the Alliance is sufficiently precarious to require investment in additional military capacity, then conventional force improvements designed to counter an extended Warsaw Pact mobilization should have top priority.

Chapter 4 outlines a set of conventional force improvements that would effectively remove the imbalance that full Warsaw Pact mobilization could presently create. Five levels of investment are defined involving the preparation of defensive positions, additions to existing stocks of munitions, the creation and equipping of additional reserve divisions and reserve tactical air wings, and additional sealift required to move reserve forces from the United States. Five year costs for these efforts range from $36 billion to $267 billion. An intermediate level of effort costing $128 billion would entail increases in NATO government defense budgets no greater than 3 percent a year (in real terms), which remains the officially adopted Alliance guideline. That level of effort would be sufficient to reduce the calculated probability of success for a Warsaw Pact invasion of Western Europe to less than 10 percent even after full mobilization. Though such calculations cannot predict the actual outcome of a war, they do state the best odds that can be assessed in advance on the basis of basic military capacity. With a chance of successful invasion assessed at less than 10 percent, conventional deterrence would be strong enough to allow reliance on nuclear weapons to be reduced to a minimum.

The NATO governments can reasonably choose to forgo this investment on the ground that the economic burden would be greater than the resulting increase in security would warrant—an implicit judgment that the current degree of risk is acceptable. They can also reasonably choose to focus their efforts to improve security more on diplomatic measures than on additional military capacity. The only argument is that if military improvements are judged necessary, then these are the improvements that should be made. The essential programs would require either a reallocation of effort within current allied defense budgets or the addition of new resources. Either way, they would probably encounter significant political resistance.

Conventional Arms Control

It would be possible in principle to achieve a stable balance of fully mobilized conventional force potential through arms control measures rather than unilateral Western force increases. This would require disproportionate reductions in Warsaw Pact forces, and for that reason the prospects for a successful negotiation are quite uncertain. Even the most optimistic assessment would have to concede a substantial period of time to accomplish such a result, the likelihood that it would have to be related to benefits to the Soviet Union outside the context of conventional force balances, and significant improvement in the state of East-West political relations as a precondition. The diplomatic history of conventional arms control discussions does not encourage optimism.

A fruitful approach to conventional arms control might be developed by focusing on the principle of establishing high-confidence conventional defensive positions for both NATO and the Warsaw Pact, a result that would not necessarily require an exact equalization of force balances. Since the U.S. Army and the Soviet Army use similar methods to calculate the combat potential of conventional forces, as summarized in the appendix, a basis for eventual agreement appears to exist and should be explored. Within the general framework of these calculations, a variety of specific measures could be examined for enhancing conventional defense and constraining conventional offense.

Doctrinal Innovations

All of the preceding options are consistent with existing NATO policy and would not require altering the basic document MC-14/3. Given the procedural difficulties associated with changes in that document and the strong political sensitivities aroused by the suggestion of a formal NFU declaration, there is a strong presumption that at least some of these options would have to be developed separately as a precondition for any generalized statement of policy. Even at that point there are alternative ways of articulating the basic principle in question. Limiting reliance on nuclear weapons for purposes other than the deterrence of nuclear attack and an emphasis on conventional deterrence of conventional threats can be introduced as explicit guiding principles of NATO defense planning without formal comment on the question of initiating the use of nuclear weapons. Beyond that, the separation of the nuclear and nonnuclear forces and their commands would do more for NATO defense planning than an official diplomatic declaration proscribing the initial use of nuclear weapons.

For a serious opponent such as the Soviet Union, the constructive deterrent effect of nuclear weapons is achieved almost entirely by the *capacity* to initiate their use in a credible and controlled fashion, a capacity the Alliance now possesses and would retain under any of the options posed. Declarations of intent that could readily be changed in crisis circumstances will have little effect on such an opponent's calculus of the relative attractiveness of war, even though they could have a substantial effect on the prevailing political atmosphere. Though that latter consideration should not be entirely neglected, judgments of the desirability of an official NFU policy in any of its alternative forms are reasonably made primarily in terms of their effects on the allied governments. If in context NFU promotes any of the options identified above, the declaration would be helpful. If it serves to retard those options by increasing political resistance, it can readily be forgone.

Notes

1. See Joshua M. Epstein, *Measuring Military Power* (Princeton University Press, forthcoming).

2. William W. Kaufmann, "The Defense Budget," in Joseph A. Pechman, ed., *Setting National Priorities: The 1984 Budget* (Brookings Institution, 1983), pp. 62–63.

The Arithmetic of Force Planning

William W. Kaufmann

A DYNAMIC analysis of ground and tactical air forces focuses on the outcome of a conflict and relates changes in that outcome to time. In addition to time, it requires a number of other inputs and the use of several models, usually in the form of equations. How the conclusions were reached in chapter 4 can best be explained by applying the analysis to a hypothetical case.

Suppose that Red, the attacker, has a force of ninety divisions at his disposal. Blue, the defender, is able to deploy a total of forty divisions. Red and Blue divisions differ considerably in size and composition. To complicate matters further, Red will have the advantage of the initiative and of picking the time, place, and scale of his attack. But Blue will be able to occupy prepared positions and establish a defense in depth. The terrain may also be favorable to Blue.

Red and Blue are separated by a frontier 700 kilometers in length. Since Blue is uncertain where Red might attack, he must plan to man the entire frontier with covering forces. Red, for his part, must plan to do likewise in order to pin down Blue's forces and guard against the eventuality that Blue at some point might launch a counterattack.

On the assumption that Red will attack after fourteen days of preparation and that Blue will be fully deployed to meet the attack, who can be expected to win this fight? Where will the two forces stand after seven days of combat? And what will Blue need to stalemate Red?

Answers to these questions can be obtained by taking a series of analytical steps.

1. *Making the opposing forces comparable through a common measure of their combat power.*

Various methods exist by which to compare opposing forces on a common scale. All of them are based on assigning numerical values to the weapons contained in combat units.[1] Thus a standard rifle might be worth one firepower unit (FPU) and a tank 100 FPUs. Numerical weights for armor and mobility can also be included. A Red division by these measures might be valued at 40,000 FPUs and a Blue division at 50,000 FPUs.

Given these values, the ninety Red divisions have a combat power of 3.6 million FPUs, while the forty Blue divisions are worth 2 million FPUs. Note that Red has an advantage in divisions of 2.25:1, but a superiority in combat power of only 1.8:1. Note also that if after only fourteen days, Blue's forces are fully manned, equipped, and maintained, while Red's units are still short of their potential by 10 percent, it becomes possible to discount their combat power accordingly.

2. *Determining the effectiveness of the two forces.*

A modern ground combat division can deliver more than a kiloton of firepower during a day of intense fighting. But how effective will that firepower be? With these, as with other forces, a probability of damage can be assigned based on historical experience (see table 4-9 in the text) and on a number of variables such as target acquisition, the probability of firing a weapon (which reflects training and morale), accuracy, and reliability. The combat power of 40,000 FPUs assigned to a Red division thus might have a daily effectiveness (stated probabilistically) of only 0.02 when used in an attack against hastily prepared defenses, while the 50,000 FPUs of the Blue division might have as much as a 0.04 probability of damaging the more exposed, attacking Red forces.

This would mean that, on the average, the Red division (at full combat power and effectiveness) could be expected to kill, wound, or capture 800 Blue FPUs. The Blue division similarly could inflict losses on the Red force of 2,000 FPUs during a day of intense combat. By this measure and with these assumptions, the Blue division would be 2.5 times more effective than the Red division. The full Red force of 3.6 million FPUs would have an initial damage potential of 72,000 Blue FPUs, while the full Blue force of 2 million FPUs could cause the loss of 80,000 Red FPUs in the first day of a campaign.

Should units be deemed low in training or motivation, as might be the case with Polish forces, the effectiveness of these units can be reduced. The existence of major defensive belts would also result in a lower effectiveness for the attacking force, since targets would be more difficult to destroy.

3. *Deciding on division frontages, the commitment of forces to the front, and establishment of reserves.*

Each side can be expected to man the entire front with a fairly continuous and solid barrier of combat forces based on the nature of the terrain and the amount of frontage that an organization such as a division can cover without being infiltrated or quickly overrun.[2] Assuming that such a barrier requires 1,500 FPUs per kilometer of front, each side must commit 1.05 million FPUs to cover the 700 kilometer front. This leaves Red with reserves of 2.55 million FPUs, while Blue's reserves consist of 950,000 FPUs. Thus, Red can gain an even more favorable force ratio than 1.8:1 if he concentrates his reserves on a particular sector of the front. And he may be able to improve that ratio still further by means of feints and secondary attacks that cause Blue to delay his reponse or misallocate his reserves.

4. *Estimating the results of a ground campaign.*

The expected results of a Red attack on Blue can be estimated by the use of several equations derived from the pioneering work of Frederick William Lanchester, an English engineer.[3] These equations and the problems they attempt to solve are listed below.

Assuming a fight to the finish, and the problem is to determine (a) which side totally destroys the other, (b) the residual forces of the winner, and (c) the time (in days) it takes to complete the process, the following equations apply.[4]

The winner (estimating Red as the winner) and his residual forces will be

$$n_{end} = R \sqrt{1 - \frac{B^2 b}{R^2 r}} ,$$

where

R = Red's combat power (in FPUs)
B = Blue's combat power (in FPUs)
r = Red's probability of damage per day against Blue
b = Blue's probability of damage per day against Red.

The time, in days, to the end of the fight, again assuming Red is the winner, will be

$$t_{end} = \frac{1}{\sqrt{rb}} \ln \left(\frac{\sqrt{R^2 r} + \sqrt{B^2 b}}{\sqrt{R^2 r} - \sqrt{B^2 b}} \right)^{\frac{1}{2}} .$$

Estimating the winner, it should be noted, is a straightforward task. The measure of a force's performance, as can be seen, is ($FPU^2 \cdot$ effectiveness). Thus, if $R^2 r$ is greater than $B^2 b$, Red will be the winner.

Since, in the example being used here, $R^2 r$ equals 2.592×10^{11}, while $B^2 b$ equals only 1.6×10^{11}, Red is predicted to defeat Blue—all other things being equal.

Assuming that the fight proceeds in daily cycles, and the problem is to determine the combat power of Red and Blue (in FPUs) at the end of a given day, the following equations apply.[5]

The combat power of Red (in FPUs) at time t will be

$$Rn_t = \frac{\left(R_o - \frac{\sqrt{b}}{\sqrt{r}} B_o\right)e^{\sqrt{rb} \cdot t} + \left(R_o + \frac{\sqrt{b}}{\sqrt{r}} B_o\right)e^{-\sqrt{rb} \cdot t}}{2},$$

and the combat power of Blue (in FPUs) at time t will be

$$Bn_t = \frac{\left(B_o - \frac{\sqrt{r}}{\sqrt{b}} R_o\right)e^{\sqrt{br} \cdot t} + \left(B_o + \frac{\sqrt{r}}{\sqrt{b}} R_o\right)e^{-\sqrt{br} \cdot t}}{2},$$

where

t = time, in days, since beginning of fight

Rn_t = Red's combat power (in FPUs) at time t

Bn_t = Blue's combat power (in FPUs) at time t

R_o = Red's combat power (in FPUs) at outset of fight

B_o = Blue's combat power (in FPUs) at outset of fight

r = Red's probability of damage per day against Blue

b = Blue's probability of damage per day against Red.

Using these equations, one can now find out: (a) what residual forces Red would have after a fight to the finish, and how long such a fight would take; (b) where Red and Blue would stand after seven days of combat; (c) what additional forces Blue would need to stalemate the fight; and (d) how many more units Blue would need in order to attack Red successfully. The results are:

$$n_{end} = 3,600,000 \sqrt{1 - \frac{2,000,000^2 \cdot 0.04}{3,600,000^2 \cdot 0.02}}$$

$$= 2,227,106 \text{ Red FPUs (or 55.7 divisions) and 0 Blue;}$$

$$t_{end} = \frac{1}{\sqrt{0.02 \cdot 0.04}} \ln \left(\frac{\sqrt{3,600,000^2 \cdot 0.02} + \sqrt{2,000,000^2 \cdot 0.04}}{\sqrt{3,600,000^2 \cdot 0.02} - \sqrt{2,000,000^2 \cdot 0.04}}\right)^{\frac{1}{2}}$$

$$= 37.5 \text{ days;}$$

$$Rn_7 = \frac{1}{2}\left[\left(3,600,000 - \frac{\sqrt{0.04}}{\sqrt{0.02}} \cdot 2,000,000\right)e^{\sqrt{0.02 \cdot 0.04} \cdot 7}\right.$$
$$\left. + \left(3,600,000 + \frac{\sqrt{0.04}}{\sqrt{0.02}} \cdot 2,000,000\right)e^{\sqrt{0.02 \cdot 0.04} \cdot 7}\right]$$

$$= 3,107,125 \text{ FPUs (or 77.7 divisions);}$$

$$Bn_7 = \frac{1}{2}\left[\left(2,000,000 - \frac{\sqrt{0.02}}{\sqrt{0.04}} \cdot 3,600,000\right)e^{\sqrt{0.04 \cdot 0.02} \cdot 7}\right.$$
$$\left. + \left(2,000,000 + \frac{\sqrt{0.02}}{\sqrt{0.04}} \cdot 3,600,000\right)e^{\sqrt{0.04 \cdot 0.02} \cdot 7}\right]$$

$$= 1,532,029 \text{ FPUs (or 30.6 divisions).}$$

Note that, by t_7, the FPU ratio favoring Red has gone from 1.8:1 to 2:1. Note also that, in order to stalemate Red at the outset of the fight, Blue would have needed

$$Bn_{\text{stalemate}} = \sqrt{\frac{3,600,000^2 \cdot 0.02}{0.04}} = 2,545,584 \text{ FPUs.}$$

Since Blue started with 2 million FPUs, he would have needed

$$Bn_{\text{stalemate}} = \frac{2,545,584 - 2,000,000}{50,000} = 11 \text{ more Blue divisions,}$$

or a total of 51 rather than 40 divisions.

In order to take the offensive against Red at the outset of the fight, and assuming the attacker's effectiveness is 0.02 and the defender's effectiveness 0.04, Blue would need more than

$$Bn_{\text{offensive}} = \sqrt{\frac{3,600,000^2 \cdot 0.04}{0.02}} = 5,091,169 \text{ FPUs}$$

$$= 102 \text{ Blue divisions.}$$

Indeed, to have as much as a 70 percent chance of defeating Red in an offensive fight, Blue would need:

$$Bn_{\text{offensive}} = \sqrt{\frac{3,600,000^2 \cdot 0.04}{0.51 \cdot 0.02}} = 142.6 \text{ divisions.}$$

These calculations assume that the attack and the defense occur uniformly along the front. Suppose, however, that Red concentrates his reserves of 2.55 million FPUs in a sector of the front covering 200 kilometers. This will give him a total attack force of 2.55 million FPUs plus (200 · 1,500 FPUs), which equals 2.85 million FPUs. If Blue makes the right decision and concentrates all his reserves in the same sector, he will have available a total of 950,000 FPUs plus (200 · 1,500 FPUs), which equals 1,250,000 FPUs. But if Blue has only a 70 percent chance on the average of making the correct decision, the commitment will consist of

$$(950,000 \cdot 0.7) + (200 \cdot 1,500) = 965,000 \text{ FPUs.}$$

In other words, 285,000 FPUs will be misallocated or will not be committed at all.

The main fight will now occur in the area of concentration, and the same equations used earlier can be applied to estimate both the outcome of the engagement and what Blue would need to create a stalemate. Thus, if Red attacks with 2.85 million FPUs, Blue would have to have

$$Bn_{\text{stalemate}} = \sqrt{\frac{2,850,000^2 \cdot 0.02}{0.04}} = 2,015,254 \text{ FPUs.}$$

In addition, he would need another 750,000 FPUs to cover the rest of the front. In total, then, his force would have to come to 2,765,254 FPUs, or 55.3 divisions. And if Blue wanted to hedge against a misallocation of his reserves, the requirement could go as high as 3,050,254 FPUs, or 61 divisions.

Whether Red's attack is concentrated or occurs uniformly along the front, Blue faces the danger of breakthroughs and encirclements. Should they occur, their consequences are relatively easy to estimate. However, the necessary calculations are long and tedious. It is customary, therefore, to assume that Blue will retreat and reform his line before Red completes a breakthrough or creates a deep salient. The U.S. Army uses tables that relate the distance retreated to the ratio of the opposing forces.

A somewhat more systematic way of determining Blue's retreat (or Red's advance) is to establish Red's movement potential—let us say twenty kilometers a day over relatively easy terrain, if unopposed—and then find the actual movement as a percent of the movement potential, using the equation[6]

$$y = \frac{1}{\sqrt{e^{(4/x)^2}}},$$

where

y = percent of daily movement potential

x = ratio of the opposing forces after a given day of fighting.

Thus, if Red concentrated 2.85 million FPUs against Blue's 1.25 million FPUs, the following results could be expected:

Day	Red	Blue	Ratio	Advance (km)	Cumulative advance (km)
t_0	2,850,000	1,250,000	2.28	. . .	. . .
t_1	2,801,000	1,193,000	2.35	4.7	4.7
t_2	2,755,000	1,138,000	2.42	5.1	9.8
t_3	2,710,000	1,083,000	2.50	5.6	15.4
t_4	2,668,000	1,030,000	2.59	6.1	21.5
t_5	2,628,000	977,000	2.69	6.6	28.1
t_6	2,590,000	924,000	2.80	7.2	35.3
t_7	2,554,000	873,000	2.93	7.9	43.2

Note, incidentally, that by t_7 Blue has lost more than 30 percent of his forces (measured in FPUs) and would be in danger of disintegrating.

5. *Substituting close air support aircraft for ground forces.*

As has been seen, Blue would need at least 15.3 more divisions to have high confidence of halting a concentrated Red attack. Conceivably he could not acquire the manpower for an increment of this size, but could deploy close air support aircraft as a substitute for the more manpower-intensive ground forces. How many aircraft would he need to replace the 15.3 divisions, assuming that such a substitution is even possible?

Fortunately for the analysis, the U.S. Army treats close air support aircraft as highly mobile firepower and values their sorties highly. Suppose that each aircraft generates 200 FPUs a day and has an effectiveness of 0.3. But suppose also that Red's ground forces contain air defense units that, against close air support aircraft, can deliver 427,500 FPUs with a daily effectiveness of 0.04. In these circumstances,

Blue must be able not only to stalemate Red's ground combat units but also to destroy the air defenses organic to them.

To solve this problem, Blue must first find out how many of Red's ground forces he can stalemate with 1.25 million FPUs in his own ground forces. To obtain that answer, he has only to calculate the following:

$$\sqrt{\frac{B^2 b}{r}} = R; \text{ or}$$

$$\sqrt{\frac{1,250,000^2 \cdot 0.04}{0.02}} = 1,767,767 \text{ Red FPUs.}$$

Since Red's total ground combat power equals 2.85 million, Blue's close air support, in order to create the stalemate, will have to deal with another 1,082,233 ground FPUs plus the 427,500 air defense FPUs, each force with a different effectiveness.

Where such heterogeneous capabilities are deployed, Lanchester argues that "the measure of the total fighting strength of a force will be *the square of the sum of the square roots of the strengths of its individual units.*"[7] With this approach, Red's total force can be seen as consisting of

$$\left(\sqrt{1,767,767^2 \cdot 0.02} + \sqrt{1,082,233^2 \cdot 0.02} + \sqrt{427,500^2 \cdot 0.04} \right)^2 .$$

Therefore, to a first approximation, a heterogeneous Blue stalemating force must consist of

$$\sqrt{\frac{1,767,767^2 \cdot 0.02}{0.04}} + \sqrt{\frac{1,082,233^2 \cdot 0.02}{0.3}} + \sqrt{\frac{427,500^2 \cdot 0.04}{0.3}} .$$

Solving for each of these terms gives a Blue force of

$$1,250,000 + 279,431 + 156,101.$$

Blue already has the 1.25 million FPUs in his ground forces. Consequently, he must acquire the additional 435,532 FPUs in close air support aircraft. Since each aircraft generates 200 FPUs, Blue will need 435,532/200, or 2,178, close air support aircraft to ensure a stalemate. In sum, 2,178 aircraft (or 30¼ wings) can, on these assumptions, substitute for 15.3 Blue divisions.

Notes

1. For examples of numerical force evaluations, see Congressional Budget Office, *Army Ground Combat Modernization for the 1980s: Potential Costs and Effects for NATO,* prepared by Nora Slatkin (Government Printing Office, 1982), pp. xv, 32, 61–67; Colonel T. N. Dupuy, *Numbers, Predictions and War: Using History to Evaluate Combat Factors and Predict the Outcome of Battles* (Bobbs-Merrill, 1979), pp. 188–89; and William P. Mako, *U.S. Ground Forces and the Defense of Central Europe* (Brookings Institution, 1983), pp. 105–13.

2. The evolution of division frontages is discussed in B. H. Liddell Hart, *Deterrent or Defense: A Fresh Look at the West's Military Position* (Praeger, 1960), pp. 97–109.

3. See Frederick William Lanchester, "Mathematics in Warfare," in James R. Newman, ed., *The World of Mathematics,* vol. 4 (Simon and Schuster, 1956), pp. 2138–57.

4. These equations are taken from Yu. V. Chuyev and Yu. B. Mikhaylov, *Forecasting in Military Affairs: A Soviet View* (GPO, 1980), p. 182.

5. Ibid., p. 181. The equation is incorrectly written in the text.

6. Derived from the equation for the standard normal curve, in Frederick Mosteller, Robert E. K. Rourke, and George B. Thomas, Jr., *Probability and Statistics* (Reading, Mass.: Addison-Wesley, 1961), p. 233.

7. Quoted from Lanchester, "Mathematics in Warfare," p. 2149. The italics are in the original text.

Index

Acheson, Dean, 6
Adenauer, Konrad, 153, 155
Afghanistan, 51, 70, 129–30, 139
Afheldt, Horst, 160
Aircraft: bombers, 28–29, 111, 116, 125; British, 124; commingling and, 116; costs, 105; dual-capable, 94, 186–87; helicopters, 41, 78, 82, 97, 105, 203; land-based, 38; Soviet, 45; Soviet Frontal Aviation, 198, 199; Soviet naval, 47, 100, 102; as substitute for missiles, 41–42; tactical, 75–79, 185, 189; tactical and ground forces and, 3; West German, 160
Airpower: NATO and Warsaw Pact tactical, 75–79; Soviet and U.S. tactical, 45; tactical, 84, 85, 89
Allied defense plan for 1970 (ADP-70), 83
Antinuclear movement, 134–35, 141–42
Antisatellite weapons, 109
Antitank mines, 159
Antitank missiles, 164
Apel, Hans, 2, 149, 163
Arms control: conventional, 206; for intermediate-range weapons, 204–05; NFU and, 183–88; West Germany and, 155, 156, 157, 166, 168, 169
Army: manpower added to U.S., 17–18; NFU and U.S., 143; Soviet conventional forces and U.S., 55; U.S. attack helicopters and, 78. See also Manpower; Reserve forces
Artillery, 3, 7, 32, 94, 118, 176; binary chemical shells and, 130; dual-capable (British), 124; howitzers, 116 nuclear shells and, 112
Atomic demolition munitions (ADMₒ), 32, 38, 118, 176, 188; location and relocation issue and, 112–13; number, 111; warheads for, 40

Bahr, Egon, 148, 151, 152, 154, 156, 157, 168

Barriers, 65–68, 69, 71, 72, 84, 89, 108
Battlefield nuclear systems, 7, 94, 118, 136, 177, 180, 187, 188, 200; British, 124; commingling and, 116–18; deterrence and, 107, 110; forward positions and, 199; limited war and, 115–16; "package" of, 173–74; West Germany and, 158; withdrawal of, 203
Beaufre, André, 123
Belgium, 134, 135, 142
Berlin. See West Berlin
Berlin blockade (1948), 74
Berlin crisis (1961), 11–12
Biedenkopf, Kurt, 147
Blockade, 47, 100–02. See also Sea lane defense
Bombs, 32; chemical binary, 130; gravity, 7, 125, 185, 187; neutron, 17, 34, 134
Border fortifications, 159
Bourges, Yvon, 120, 122
Brezhnev, Leonid, 100
Britain, 28, 30, 152, 178, 190, 191; antinuclear movement, 134–35; deterrence and, 31, 107, 108; independent nuclear deterrents and, 10, 23; nuclear forces, 122–27; retaliation and, 32; second-center argument and, 123–24; second-strike capabilities, 80; SLBMs and, 39; troops on central front and, 181
Brown, Harold, 18, 44
Bundy, McGeorge, 1

Carte Blanche (air exercise), 34, 150
Carter, Jimmy, 134
Chemical weapons, 73, 127–31, 158, 187
Chirac, Jacques, 120
Clifford, Clark, 14
Command, control, and communications (C³), 109, 125
Communications: emergency and U.S., 72; improving, 84; NATO's nuclear forces and, 198

217